CW00494026

STREET~~~~~S

Inverness and Moray

First published 2004 by

Philip's, a division of
Octopus Publishing Group Ltd
2-4 Heron Quays, London E14 4JP

First edition 2004
First impression 2004

ISBN-10   0-540-08651-7 (spiral)
ISBN-13   978-0-540-08651-1 (spiral)

© Philip's 2004

Ordnance Survey®

This product includes mapping data licensed
from Ordnance Survey® with the permission of
the Controller of Her Majesty's Stationery Office.
© Crown copyright 2004. All rights reserved.
Licence number 100011710.

Ordnance Survey and the OS Symbol are
registered trademarks of Ordnance Survey, the
national mapping agency of Great Britain

Post Office is a trade mark of Post Office Ltd
in the UK and other countries.

Printed and bound in Italy by Rotolito

Contents

Digital Data

The exceptionally high-quality mapping found in this atlas is available as digital data in TIFF format, which is easily convertible to other bitmapped (raster) image formats.

The index is also available in digital form as a standard database table. It contains all the details found in the printed index together with the National Grid reference for the map square in which each entry is named.

For further information and to discuss your requirements, please contact Philip's on 020 7644 6932 or james.mann@philips-maps.co.uk

PHILIP'S MAPS

the Gold Standard for serious driving

- Philip's street atlases cover every county in England, plus much of Wales and Scotland.

- All our atlases use the same style of mapping, with the same colours and symbols, so you can move with confidence from one atlas to the next

- Widely used by the emergency services, transport companies and local authorities.

- Created from the most up-to-date and detailed information available from Ordnance Survey

- Based on the National Grid

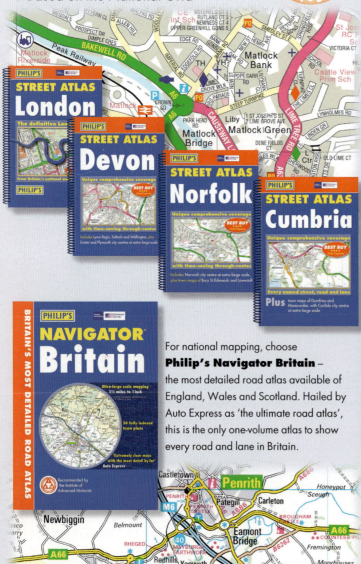

For national mapping, choose **Philip's Navigator Britain** – the most detailed road atlas available of England, Wales and Scotland. Hailed by Auto Express as 'the ultimate road atlas', this is the only one-volume atlas to show every road and lane in Britain.

England

Bedfordshire
Berkshire
Birmingham and West Midlands
Bristol and Bath
Buckinghamshire
Cambridgeshire
Cheshire
Cornwall
Cumbria
Derbyshire
Devon
Dorset
County Durham and Teesside
Essex
North Essex
South Essex
Gloucestershire
North Hampshire
South Hampshire
Herefordshire Monmouthshire
Hertfordshire
Isle of Wight
East Kent
West Kent
Lancashire
Leicestershire and Rutland
Lincolnshire
London
Greater Manchester
Merseyside
Norfolk
Northamptonshire
Nottinghamshire
Oxfordshire
Shropshire
Somerset

All-England coverage

Staffordshire
Suffolk
Surrey
East Sussex
West Sussex
Tyne and Wear Northumberland
Warwickshire
Birmingham and West Midlands
Wiltshire and Swindon
Worcestershire
East Yorkshire Northern Lincolnshire
North Yorkshire
South Yorkshire
West Yorkshire

Wales

Anglesey, Conwy and Gwynedd
Cardiff, Swansea and The Valleys
Denbighshire, Flintshire, Wrexham
Herefordshire Monmouthshire

Scotland

Aberdeenshire
Edinburgh and East Central Scotland
Fife and Tayside
Glasgow and West Central Scotland
Inverness and Moray

How to order

Philip's maps and atlases are available from bookshops, motorway services and petrol stations. You can order direct from the publisher by phoning **01903 828503** or online at **www.philips-maps.co.uk** For bulk orders only, phone 020 7644 6940

Motorway with junction number	
Primary route – dual/single carriageway	
A road – dual/single carriageway	
B road – dual/single carriageway	
Minor road – dual/single carriageway	
Other minor road – dual/single carriageway	
Road under construction	
Tunnel, covered road	
Rural track, private road or narrow road in urban area	
Gate or obstruction to traffic (restrictions may not apply at all times or to all vehicles)	
Path, bridleway, byway open to all traffic, road used as a public path	
Pedestrianised area	
Postcode boundaries	
County and unitary authority boundaries	
Railway, tunnel, railway under construction	
Tramway, tramway under construction	
Miniature railway	
Railway station	
Private railway station	
Metro station	
Tram stop, tram stop under construction	
Bus, coach station	

Ambulance station	
Coastguard station	
Fire station	
Police station	
Accident and Emergency entrance to hospital	
Hospital	
Place of worship	
Information Centre (open all year)	
Parking	
Park and Ride	
Post Office	
Camping site	
Caravan site	
Golf course	
Picnic site	
Important buildings, schools, colleges, universities and hospitals	
Built up area	
Woods	
Tidal water, water name	
Non-tidal water – lake, river, canal or stream	
Lock, weir, tunnel	
Non-Roman antiquity	
Roman antiquity	
Adjoining page indicators and overlap bands	

The colour of the arrow and the band indicates the scale of the adjoining or overlapping page (see scales below)

Acad	Academy	Inst	Institute	Recn Gd	Recreation Ground
Allot Gdns	Allotments	Ct	Law Court		
Cemy	Cemetery	L Ctr	Leisure Centre	Resr	Reservoir
C Ctr	Civic Centre	LC	Level Crossing	Ret Pk	Retail Park
CH	Club House	Liby	Library	Sch	School
Coll	College	Mkt	Market	Sh Ctr	Shopping Centre
Crem	Crematorium	Meml	Memorial	TH	Town Hall/House
Ent	Enterprise	Mon	Monument	Trad Est	Trading Estate
Ex H	Exhibition Hall	Mus	Museum	Univ	University
Ind Est	Industrial Estate	Obsy	Observatory	W Twr	Water Tower
IRB Sta	Inshore Rescue Boat Station	Pal	Royal Palace	Wks	Works
		PH	Public House	YH	Youth Hostel

■ The small numbers around the edges of the maps identify the 1 kilometre National Grid lines

■ The dark grey border on the inside edge of some pages indicates that the mapping does not continue onto the adjacent page

The scale of the maps on the pages numbered in blue is 5.52 cm to 1 km • 3½ inches to 1 mile • 1: 18103

0	¼	½	¾	1 mile
0	250m	500m	750m	1 kilometre

The scale of the maps on pages numbered in green is 2.76 cm to 1 km • 1¾ inches to 1 mile • 1: 36206

0	¼	½	¾	1 mile
0	250m	500m	750m	1 kilometre

IV

Key to map pages

Little Creich **1**
Clashmore
Dornoch
A949
A836
2 **3** **4**
Edderton
148
Tain
Loandhu
7 **8** **9** **10**
Fearn
Stittenham
Dorrachan
Milton
A9
Boath **12** **13** **14**
Kilmuir
Nigg
Nonikiln
Mossfield
15
16
149 **150** **151**
Balnapaling
Alness **Invergordon**
Evanton
Balblair
Cromarty
A835
A9
26 **27**
Jemimaville
Gorstan
Mountgerald
28 **29** **30**
23 **24** **25**
Garve
Culbokie
Raddery
Fodderty
Killen
A832
A832
Strathpeffer
Dingwall
A834
152
A890
Craigdarroch
Maryburgh
Fortrose
Contin
Conon Bridge
Avoch
Ardersier
A835
42 **43** **44** **45** **46** **47** **48** **49**
Marybank
A862
Tore
Munlochy
A832
A835
A9
Inverness
153
Croy
Muir of Ord
Charlestown
Culloden
A96
162 **163**
62 **63** **64** **65** **66** **67** **68**
Beauly
Kirkhill
Newlands
Drumindorsair
A862
Inverness
Kilmorack
Leachkin
164 **165**
Struy
Eskadale
Kiltarlity
Dochgarroch
Daviot
A831
82 **83** **84** **85** **86** **87** **88** **89**
A833
Balchraggan
Dores
Tombreck
Moy
Farr
A9
100 **101** **102** **103**
Milton
104 **105** **106** **107** **108** **109**
Cannich
A831
Balnain
Tomatin
Shenval
Drumnadrochit
East Croachy
Clune
Slochd
Inverfarigaig
120 **121** **122** **123** **124** **125** **126**
A82
Errogie
Dalmigavie
Foyers
Invermoriston
Whitebridge
137 **138** **139**
Portclair
A87
A887
172
Fort Augustus
A87
A82
142 **143**
Kincraig
A82
Balavil
A9
Kingussie
170
Newtonmore
Drumguish
171
A86
146 **147**
A889
A9
A82
A86
A830
Lochyside
173
A861
Fort William
A9

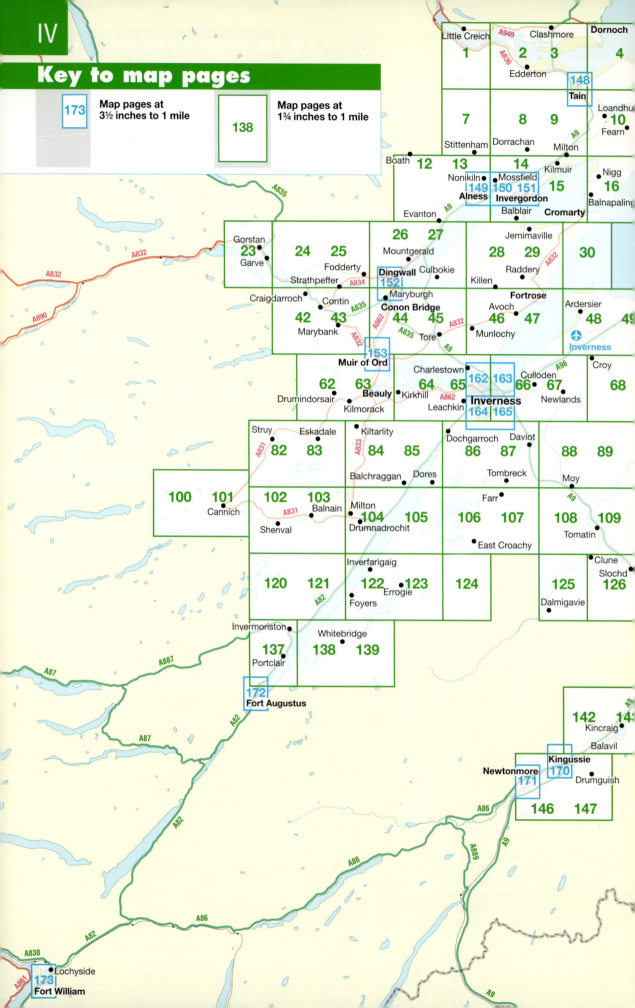

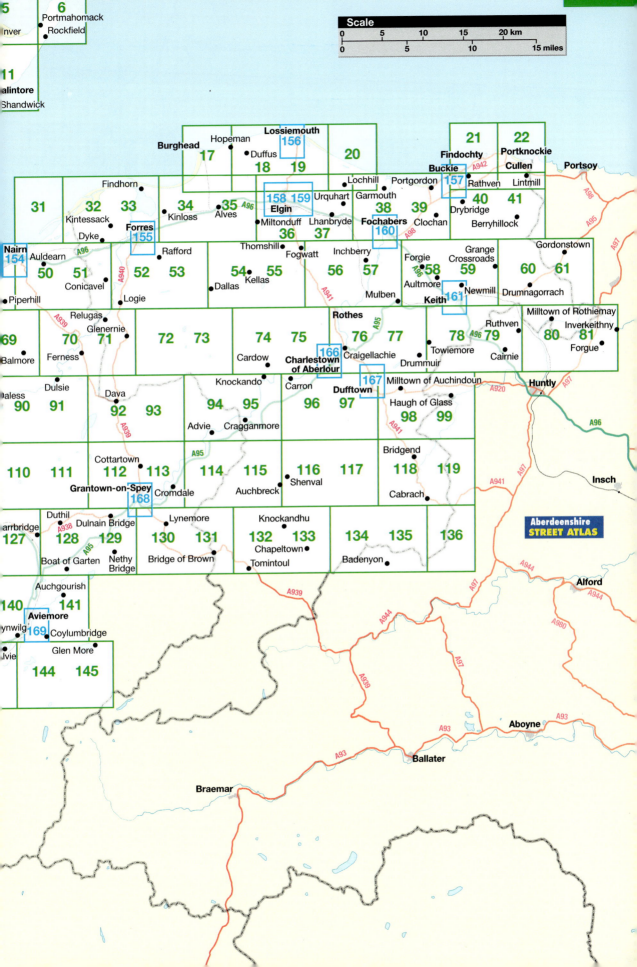

Scale

0   5   10   15   20 km

0   5   10   15 miles

5
Inver

6
Portmahomack
Rockfield

11
alintore
Shandwick

Burghead
17

Hopeman
Duffus
18   19

Lossiemouth
156

20

21

22
Portknockie
Cullen

Findochty
Buckie
157

Portsoy

Findhorn

31   32   33   34   35
Kintessack   Kinloss   Alves
Dyke
Forres
155

Elgin
158 159
Miltonduff
36

Urquhart   Garmouth
Lhanbryde
37

Lochhill   Portgordon
38
Fochabers
160

39
Clochan

40
Drybridge

41
Lintmill
Berryhillock

Rathven

Nairn
154

Auldearn
50   51   52   53
Conicavel
Piperhill

Rafford

Thomshill
Fogwatt
54   55
Kellas
Dallas

Inchberry
56   57

Mulben

Forgie
58   59
Crossroads
Aultmore

Grange

Newmill
Keith
161

60   61
Gordonstown
Drumnagorrach

69   70   71
Relugas
Glenernie
Balmore   Ferness

72   73

74   75
Cardow
Charlestown
of Aberlour
166

Rothes

76   77
Craigellachie
Drummuir

78   79
Towiemore   Ruthven
Cairnie

Milltown of Rothiemay
80   81
Inverkeithny
Forgue

Daless   Dulsie
90   91
Dava
92   93

Knockando
94   95
Advie   Cragganmore

Carron
96   97
Dufftown
167

Milltown of Auchindoun

98   99
Haugh of Glass

Huntly

Insch

110   111
Grantown-on-Spey
168

Cottartown
112   113
Cromdale

A95
114   115
Auchbreck   Shenval

116   117

Bridgend
118   119
Cabrach

Alford

arrbridge
127

Duthil
128   129
Boat of Garten   Nethy Bridge
Dulnain Bridge

Lynemore
130   131
Bridge of Brown

Knockandhu
132   133
Chapeltown
Tomintoul

134   135
Badenyon

136

Aberdeenshire
STREET ATLAS

140   141
Auchgourish

Aviemore
169
Coylumbridge
ynwilg
Ivie

Glen More
144   145

Aboyne

Ballater

Braemar

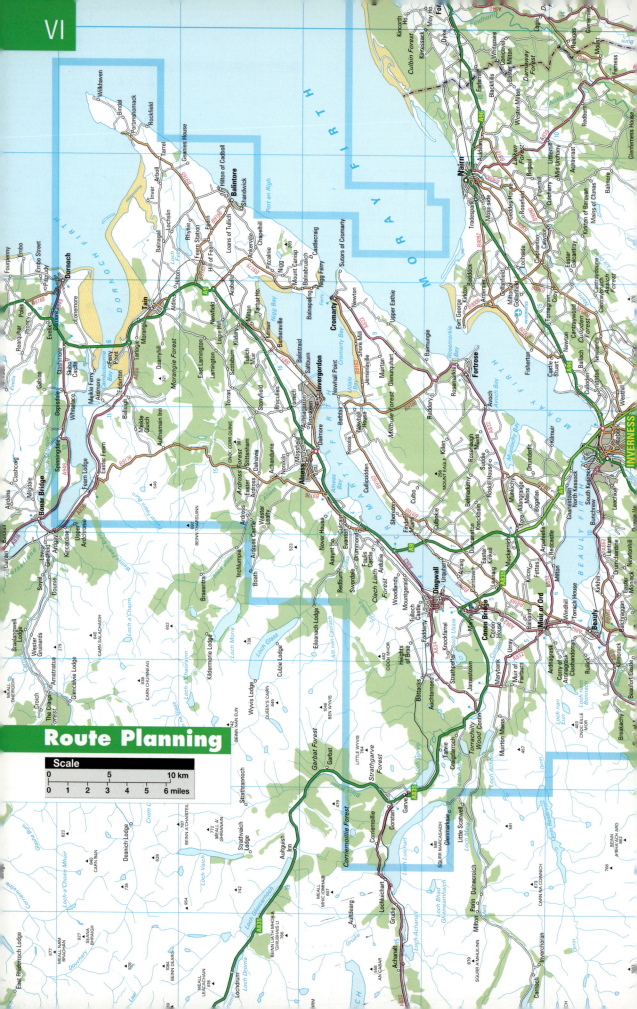

Route Planning

Scale

0   5   10 km

0   1   2   3   4   5   6 miles

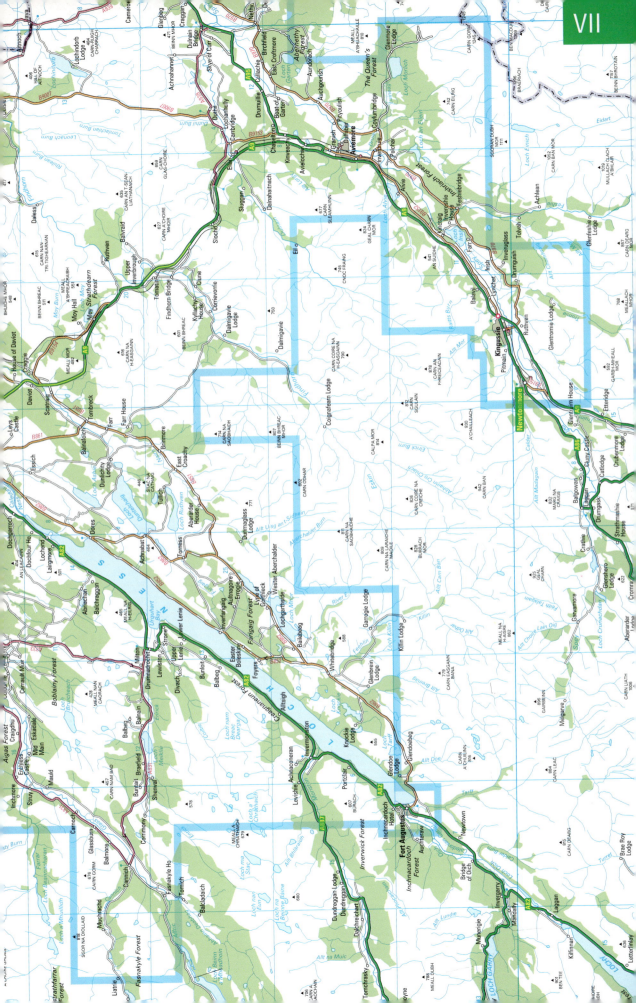

X

Administrative and Postcode boundaries

Legend:
- County and unitary authority boundaries
- Postcode boundaries
- Area covered by this atlas

Scale
0 5 10 15 20 25 30 km
0 5 10 15 20 miles

Aberdeenshire

Moray

Highland

NH NJ · NN NO · NH NN

Postcodes: AB45, AB56, AB55, AB54, AB33, AB36, AB37, AB38, IV32, IV31, IV30, IV36, PH26, PH25, PH24, PH23, PH22, PH21, PH20, IV12, IV13, IV11, IV10, IV9, IV8, IV7, IV1, IV2, IV5, IV3, IV63, IV4, IV6, IV14, IV15, IV16, IV17, IV23, IV24, IV25, IV19, IV18, IV20, PH32

Towns: Gordonstown, Marnoch, Milltown of Rothiemay, Cullen, Portknockie, Findochty, Buckie, Kirktown of Deskford, Drumnagorrach, Keith, Ruthven, Bridgend, Cabrach, Badenyon, Dufftown, Fochabers, Lossiemouth, Elgin, Mosstodloch, Miltonduff, Rothes, Charlestown of Aberlour, Tomnavoulin, Tomintoul, Burghead, Kinloss, Dallas, Upper Knockando, Marypark, Findhorn, Forres, Logie, Dava, Dellifure, Grantown-on-Spey, Nethy Bridge, Dyke, Reluggas, Auldearn, Dulnain Bridge, Boat of Garten, Aviemore, Inverdruie, Nairn, Cawdor, Daless, Carrbridge, Kingussie, Dornoch, Portmahomack, Balintore, Hill of Fearn, Cromarty, Tomatin, Moy, Milton of Farr, Newtonmore, Spinningdale, Edderton, Tain, Invergordon, Fortrose, Avoch, Culloden, East Croachy, Barbaraville, Balblair, Munlochy, Inverness, Strathpeffer, Alness, Evanton, Dingwall, Conon Bridge, Muir of Ord, Beauly, Easter Moniack, Strone, Inverfarigaig, Wester Aberchalder, Maryburgh, Kilmorack, Kiltarlity, Balchraggan, Drumnadrochit, Bunloit, Whitebridge, Garve, Tarvie, Cannich, Carnoch, Invermoriston, Fort Augustus

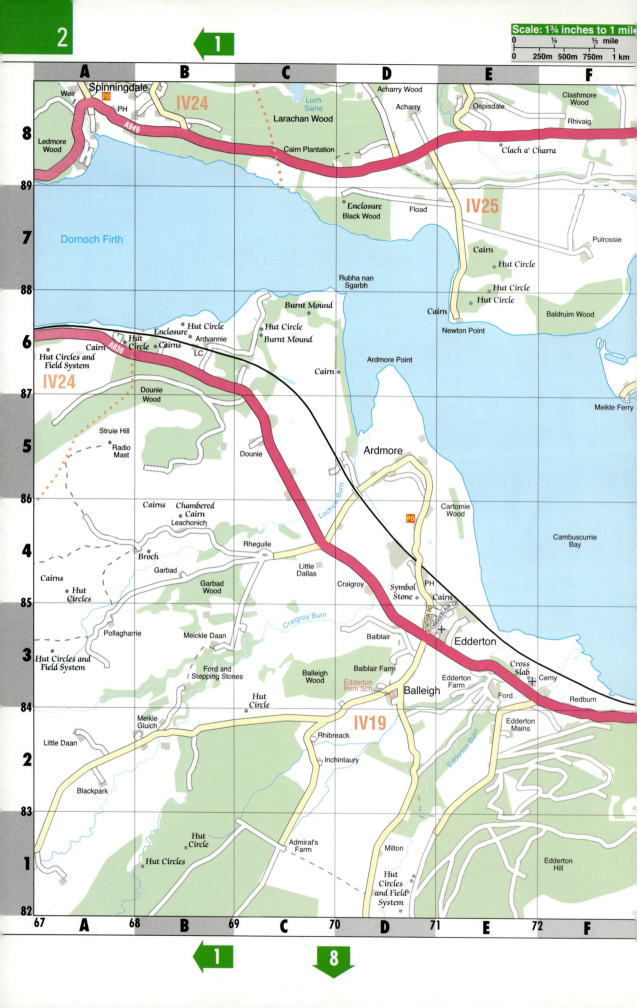

A   B   C   D   E   F

Clashmugach
Overskibo
Chambered Cairn
A949
Clashmore

Clashmore Wood
A9 Thurso, Wick (A99)
A9
Lower Clashmore Plantation
Ford and Stepping Stones
Enclosure

Chambered Cairn
Loch-an-treel
Drumdivan
Standing Stone
EVELIX RD
A949

Camore Wood
Hut Circles and Field System

8

Chy
Bishop's Well
Skibo Castle (Hotel)

Ford
IV25

Sydera Wood
Hut Circles and Field System
Davochfin
Quarry

89

L Ospisdale

Cyderhall Farm
Pit (dis)
PO
Eaglefield

Dornoch Links

7

Lonemore

Lake Louise

88

CH
L Evelix
Carnegie Golf Course
Cuthill Links

Dornoch Sands

6

Cuthill Sands

Dornoch Firth

87

Ard na Callc

5

Dornoch Firth Bridge

86

Ferry Point

4

Tarlogie Scalps
Ardjachie Point

85

Ness of Portnaculter
A9

Edderton Sands
Ardjachie

3

148

A836
Meikle Ferry Inn

84

Chy
Glenmorangie Distillery
Visitor Centre
Cambuscurrie Wood
Tarlogie
Morangie

IV19
Long Cairn
Cairn
St Mary's Well

2

148

Tarlogie Wood

83

Sewage Works
B9174
MORANGIE RD
Ind Est
Sch
TAIN

Fuaran Baite (Well)
Hotel
A9
Tain
Mus

1

Loch Lapagial

82

73   A   74   B   75   C   76   D   77   E   78   F   82

9

4

For full street detail of the highlighted area see page 148.

Scale: 1¾ inches to 1 mile

¼   ½   mile
0   250m   500m   750m   1 km

A   B   C   D   E   F

8

89

7

88

6

87

5

86

4

85

3

Balnabruach

84

Dornoch Firth

DANGER AREA

Innis Mhòr

Paterson Island

Lower Seafield

IV19

DANGER AREA

Inver Bay

2

83

Skinnerton

SHORE ST
MAIN ST
ROSS ST
NEW ST
PIL
HILL ST

Inver

PH
SHOP ST

Arboll Links

Drumancroy Farm

B9165

Lower Arboll

IV20

Petley Farm

Rockfield House

1

Inver Prim Sch

SHORE ST

Gallow Hill

Mains of Arboll

Rockfield Mills

82

B1
1 FUARAN
2 FRONT ST

A   B   C   D   E   F

8

89

7

88

6

Dornoch Firth

Port Buckie

Tarbat Ness

Tarbatness Lighthouse

Port a' Chait

Wilkhaven Muir

Port Mòr   Castlehaven (rems of)

Blàr a' Chath   Wilkhaven   Wind Pump

5

Brucefield

86

Port Uilleim

Hilton Farm   Mast

IV20

4

Bindal Muir

Coastguard Lookout   Mast

85

Easter Bindal

CHAPEL ST

Portmahomack   Bindal

3

PH   PO

WELL ST

TIGH NA MARA   CH

Tarbat Old Prim Sch   Tarbat Golf Course

84

Cemy   Mast

B9165 MAIN STREET   Tarbat Discovery Centre   Ballone Castle (restored)

Fairfield

Moray Firth

Bankhead

Seafield

83

Rockfield

1

82

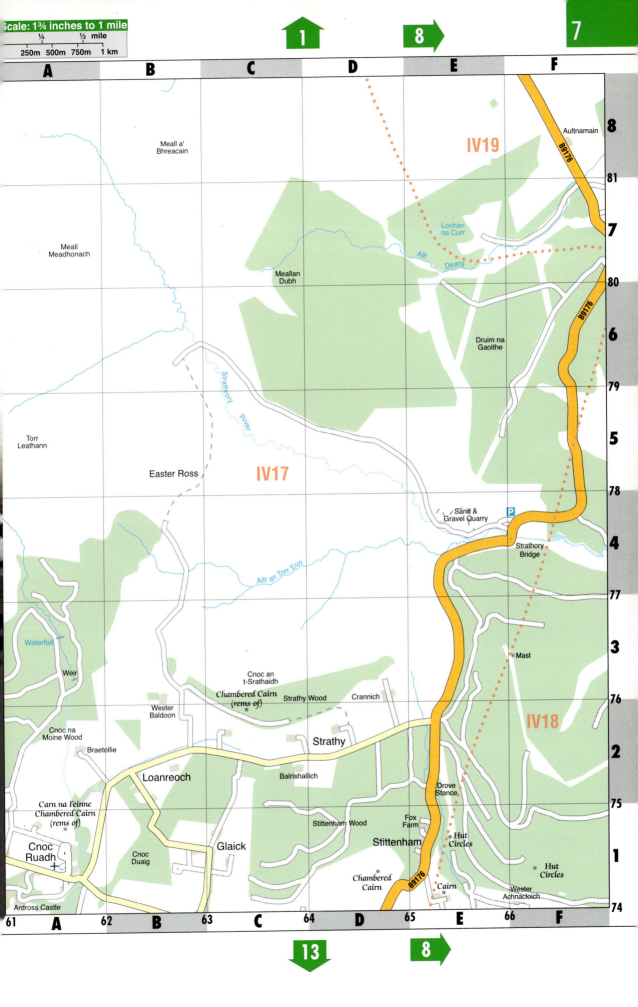

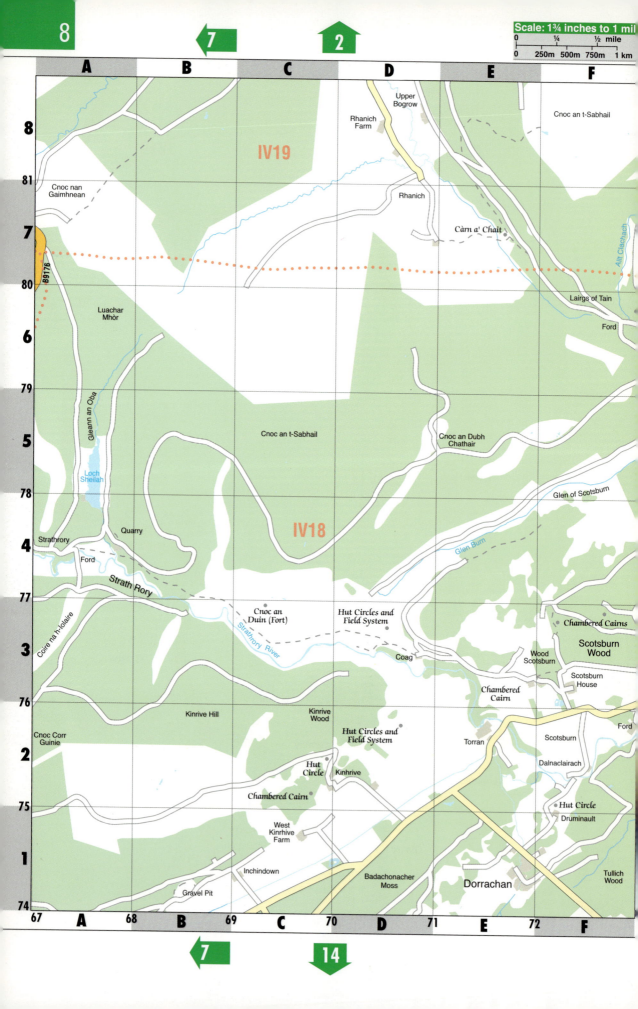

A B C D E F

8

81

7

80

6

79

5

78

4

77

3

76

2

75

1

74

Upper Bogrow

Rhanich Farm

Cnoc an t-Sabhail

IV19

Cnoc nan Gaimhnean

Rhanich

Càrn a' Chait

Allt Clachach

B9176

Luachar Mhòr

Lairgs of Tain

Ford

Gleann an Oba

Cnoc an t-Sabhail

Cnoc an Dubh Chathair

Loch Sheilah

Glen of Scotsburn

IV18

Quarry

Glen Burn

Strathrory

Ford

Strath Rory

Coire na h-Iolaire

Cnoc an Duin (Fort)

Hut Circles and Field System

Chambered Cairns

Scotsburn Wood

Coag

Wood Scotsburn

Scotsburn House

Chambered Cairn

Strathrory River

Kinrive Hill

Kinrive Wood

Hut Circles and Field System

Torran

Scotsburn

Ford

Cnoc Corr Guinie

Dalnaclairach

Hut Circle

Kinhrive

Hut Circle

Druminault

Chambered Cairn

West Kinrive Farm

Inchindown

Badachonacher Moss

Dorrachan

Tullich Wood

Gravel Pit

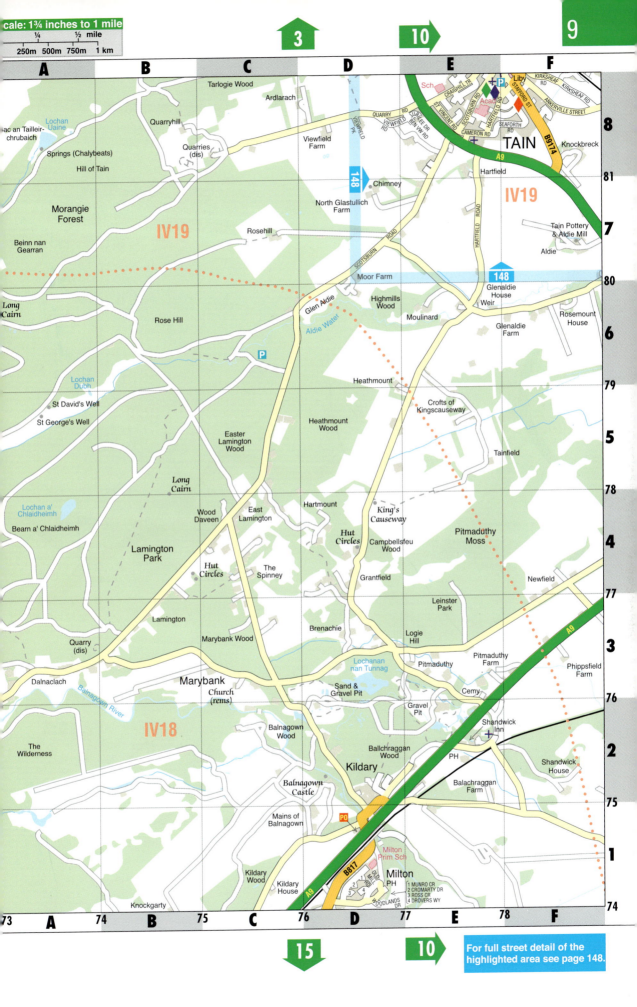

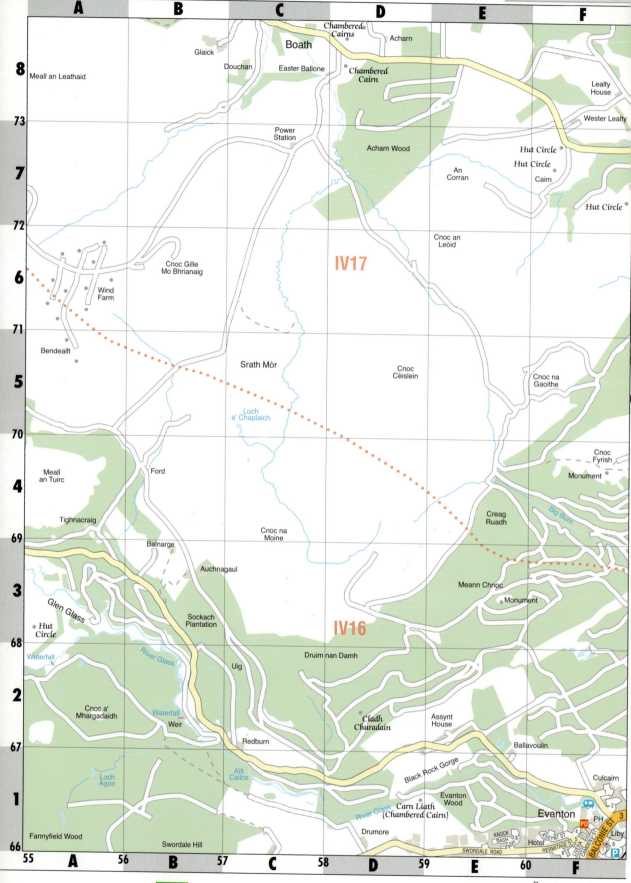

Scale: 1¾ inches to 1 mile

0	¼	½ mile
0	250m	500m	750m	1 km

A **B** **C** **D** **E** **F**

8 — Meall an Leathaid

Boath

Glaick

Douchan

Easter Ballone

Chambered Cairns

Acharn

Chambered Cairn

Lealty House

73 —

Power Station

Wester Lealty

Acharn Wood

Hut Circle

7 —

An Corran

Hut Circle

Cairn

72 —

Cnoc Gille Mo Bhrianaig

Cnoc an Leòid

Hut Circle

IV17

6 —

Wind Farm

71 —

Bendeallt

Srath Mòr

Cnoc Cèislein

Cnoc na Gaoithe

5 —

Loch a' Chaplaich

70 —

Meall an Tuirc

Ford

Cnoc Fyrish

Monument

4 —

Tighnacraig

Cnoc na Moine

Creag Ruadh

Big Burn

69 —

Balnarge

Auchnagaul

Meann Chnoc

3 —

Glen Glass

Sockach Plantation

Monument

IV16

Hut Circle

Druim nan Damh

68 —

Waterfall

River Glass

Uig

2 —

Cnoc a' Mhargadaidh

Waterfall

Weir

Cladh Churadain

Assynt House

Ballavoulin

Culcairn

67 —

Redburn

Black Rock Gorge

Evanton Wood

1 —

Loch Agoo

Allt Cailce

River Glass

Carn Liath (Chambered Cairn)

Evanton

PO PH Liby

3

Fannyfield Wood

Drumore

Knock Rash Ash Hk

Hotel

66 —

Swordale Hill

Swordale Road

A **B** **C** **D** **E** **F**

55 56 57 58 59 60

26

27

F1
1 CULCAIRN RD
2 GLENGLASS RD
3 STATION RD
4 HERMITAGE ST
5 CHAPEL RD
6 BALCONIE PK
7 FYRISH CT
8 TEANDALLON PL

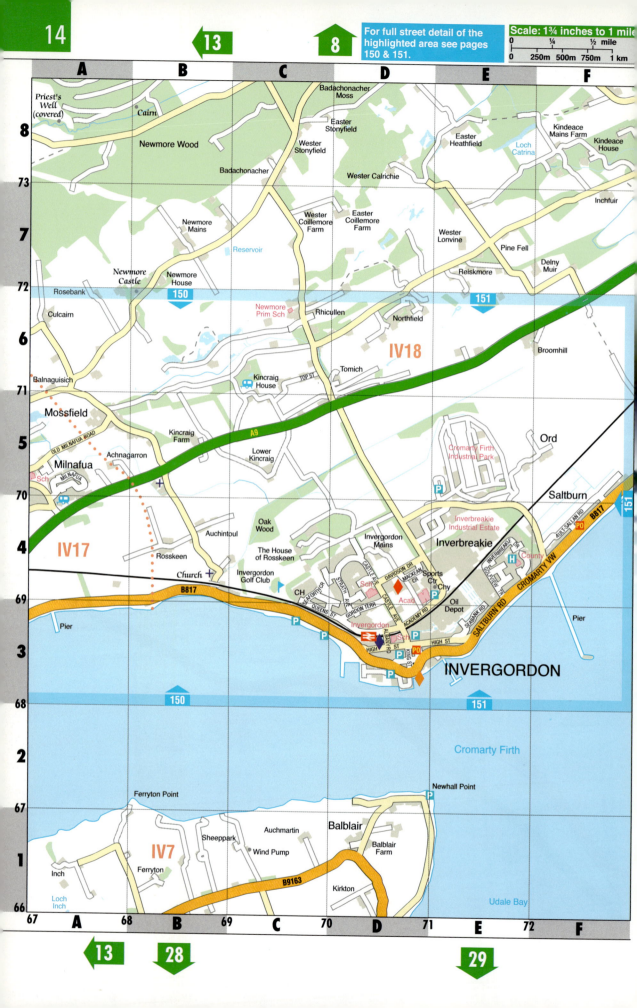

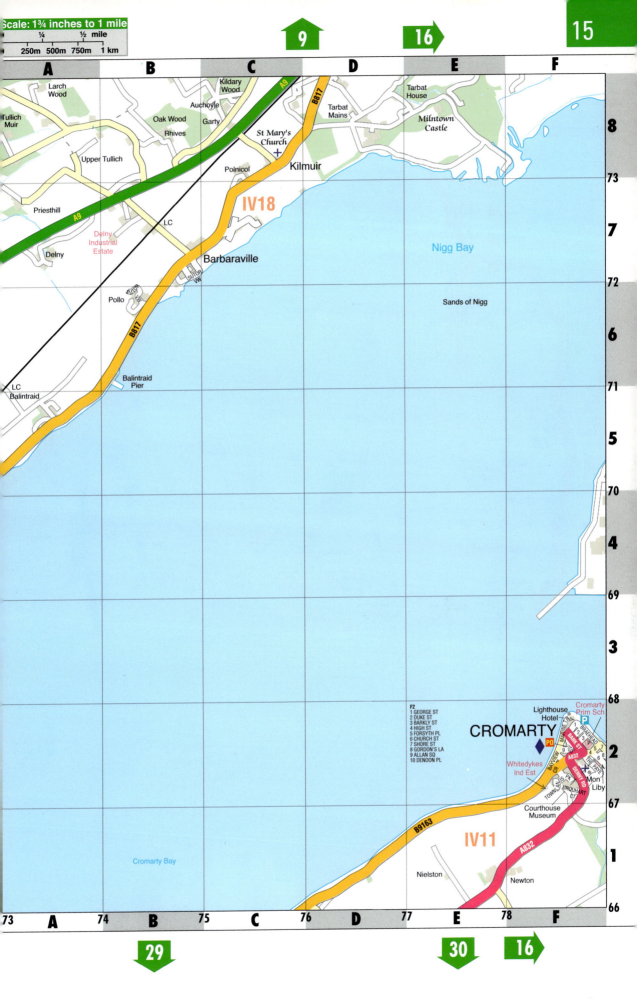

Scale: 1¾ inches to 1 mil•

0   ¼   ½   mile
0   250m 500m 750m 1 km

A   B   C   D   E   F

8

Carse of
Bayfield

Cemy
Chapelhill
Blackhill
Bayfield
Mains

Wester Rarichie
Farm

Dun

Fort &
Dun

73

Bayfield
House

Strath of
Pitcalnie

7

Quarry
(dis)

Culnaha

IV20

Pitcalnie

72

Cross
Slab

Dam

Bayfield
Loch

IV19

Pit
(dis)

Nigg
House

Nigg

6

Hill of
Nigg

King's
Cave

71

Gravel
Pit

5

Chy

Mount
Canisp

Pitcalzean
House

Waterfall

70

Helipad

Balnabruaich

Nigg
Oil
Terminal

4

Balnapaling

Castlecraig

Mast

Nigg
Ferry

69

B9175

PH

Dunskeath
Castle
(Earthwork)

Sandstone
Quarry

Cave

North Sutor

Caves

3

68

A2
1 BIG VENNEL
2 LITTLE VENNEL
3 CHURCH ST

2

Cross

Drooping
Cave

St Mary's
Well

Viewpoint

Sutors
Stacks

Colhegh
Well

P

P

Cromarty
House

IV11

Dowcale
Cave

1

Blue Head

Gallow
Hill

Cromarty
Mains Farm

Red Nose

66

79   A   80   B   81   C   82   D   83   E   84   F   85

Scale: 1¾ inches to 1 mile

¼   ½   mile

250m   500m   750m   1 km

A   B   C   D   E   F

8

71

7

70

6

69

5

68

4

67

3

66

2

65

1

64

F6
1 MORAY ST
2 FARQUHAR ST
3 GORDON ST
4 CLARK ST
5 HUTCHEON ST
6 INVERUGIE RD
7 MACPHERSON ST
8 SCHOOL RD
9 THOM ST
10 BAKERS LA
11 GOLF CR

Hopeman Prim Sch

Hopeman

SEA PK

DRUMMUIR ST
NEWS ST
COOPER
HANSE
CAMERON TR
FORSYTH ST EAST
Liby

Wedershill Farm

C6
1 PARK ST
2 DUNBAR LA
3 KING ST
4 YOUNG ST
5 CHURCH ST
6 BRANDER ST
7 GRANT LA

D5
1 SIGURD ST
2 BAYVIEW
3 TORRIDON
4 TORFNESS PL

B6
1 BATH ST

Well

Burgh Head
Fort

St Aethan's Well

St Aethans

Burghead Prim Sch

Quarries (dis)

Wells (dis)

Caves

BACK ST

SEAVIEW RD

B9040

Cummingston

FORTEATH ST

GRANARY ST

B9013

Liby & Mus

FRASER RD

KEITH RD

Hotel

Cemy

BURGHEAD

C5
1 SELLAR ST
2 GRANT LA
3 GRANARY LA
4 STATION RD
5 KINGLOSS ST
6 BRIDGE ST
7 FIRTH VW
8 BRUCE ST
9 STATION CT
10 FOREST RD
11 MCKENZIE PL
12 ST AETHANS AV
13 ST AETHANS CL
14 DAVIDSON PL

ST AETHANS

FOREST DR RD

PINEWOOD RD

FOREST RD

(dis)

West End

Masts

Clarkly Hill

Souterrain Cup and
Ring Marked Rocks

Football Gd

Bennet Hill

Roseisle Forest

B9089

IV30

Easter Oldtown Farm

Roseisle

Tappoch

Cairn

Charlestown

West Bank Farm

Mid Bank Farm

67

Millie Burn

Sewage Works

North Buthill Farm

College of Roseisle

Bridgend

Gravel Pit

Wester Buthill Farm

Mid Buthill Farm

Inchkeil

Chy

IV36

Easter Coltfield

Bruntlands Farm

Kirkhill Wood

Standingstones Farm

Longhillock Farm

Easterton Farm

B9013

White Cottage
Hatton Farm

B9089

(dis)

Scale: 1¾ inches to 1 mile

0   ¼   ½   mile
0   250m   500m   750m   1 km

A   B   C   D   E   F

8

71

Covesea Skerries Lighthouse

Natural Arch   Caves   CH   Easter Covesea Farm   Covesea Links

Balgreen

7

Sculptors Cave   Cave   Caves   North Covesea Farm   Covesea Hill   Wester Covesea Farm

B9040

North Greens

Covesea Quarry (dis)   Cave   WT Sta   Masts

Clashach Cove   Cave   Clashach Quarry   WT Sta

Caves

70

Braemou Well
The Home Farm
Hopeman
P
CH

East Rd

A6
1 GOLF CR
2 GOLF RD
3 MEADOW GDNS
4 GOLF VW
5 MEADOW VW
6 LODGE VW
7 MILLFIELD DR

Plewlands Farm

Windmill (remains)

Mountain Rescue Post

Sweethillock Farm

IV31

RAF Lossiemouth

6

Hopeman Golf Club
Burnside Farm

East Rd   B9040

Williamston

B9012

Duffus

B5
1 HALL PL
2 DUNBAR LA
3 ST PETER'S LA
4 CHURCH PL

NORTHFIELD   GORDONSTOUN RD
ST PETER'S BURN
MILL PL
CHURCH RD

St Peters Well

Dovecot

Cross

Gordonstoun Sch

Cross

69

Cairn
Inverugie

Begrow Farm

Hopeman Road

St Peter's Kirk (remains of)

Duffus House (Gordonstoun Sch)

DRAINIE ROAD

5

Camus's Stone

Hopeman Road

PH

St Lawrence's Well

Sewage Works

Cross

Shempston

Silverhills Farm

68

Keam Farm

Philixdale Farm
St Bennet's Well

Crosshill

Westerfolds Farm

4

Rothills

Old Duffus

Well

Duffus Castle (remains of)

Salterhill Farm

Well

Broomhill

Crosslots Farm

67

Mossyards

Unthank

IV30

Mid Mains

East Mains Farm

3

Crookies Moss

Gilston

Spindlemuir Wood   Easter Crookies

West Mains Farm

66

Orchardfield

Waterton Bridge

Waterton

Lower Mains Farm   Midtown Farm

Lochside Farm

2

Surradale Farm

Inchgarty

Kintrae Bridge

Easter Kintrae Farm

Dovecote

Findrassie

Westfield Farm

Inchbrock

Westerton

158

65

Spindle Muir

Terchick Burn

Wester Kintrae

Findrassie Wood

1

B9013

Rosehaugh Farm

Loanhead

158   B9012

DUFFUS ROAD

Spynie   H

Rosenewton

Rosebrae Sch   Rosebrae

Dovecote

Quarrywood

Woodpark Farm

64

15   A   16   B   17   C   18   D   19   E   20   F

17   35   For full street detail of the highlighted area see page 158.   36

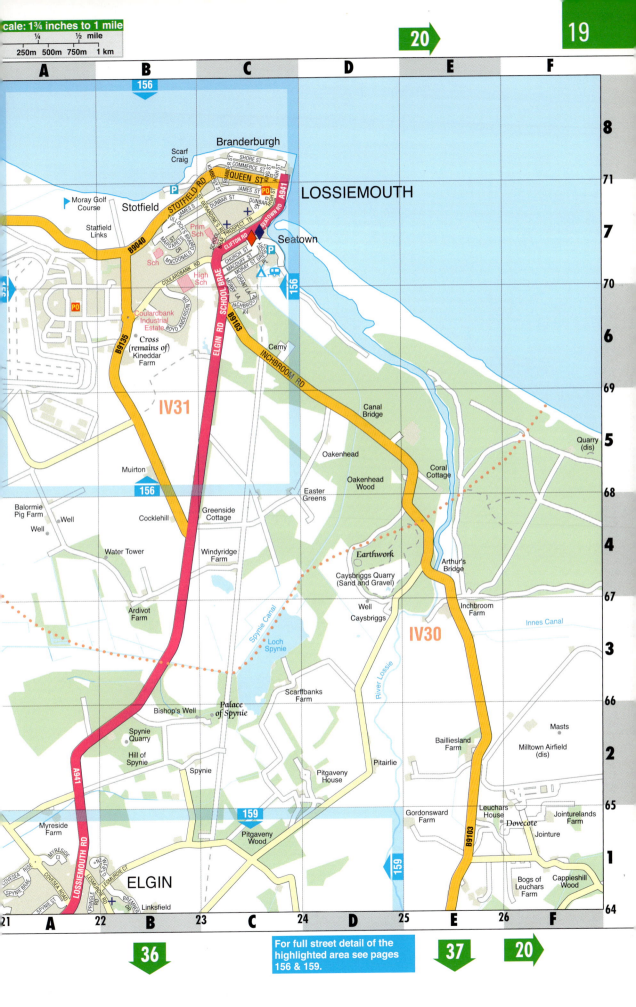

Scale: 1¾ inches to 1 mi

0   ¼   ½   mile
0   250m 500m 750m 1 km

A   B   C   D   E   F

8

71

7

70

6

69

5

Spey Bay

68

4

Innes Links

67

Cotts of Innes

Speyslaw Farm

3   Masts

Newton of Innes

Nether Unthank

DANGER AREA

66

IV30

Stonewells Farm

Broomhill Farm   Upper Unthank

Binn Hill

Corbiewell

Gladhill

2   Masts

Milltown Airfield (dis)

Branston Farm

Waterscot Farm

Wallfield Farm

65

Innes House

Motte

Lochhill Wood

Wallfield Wood

Fivefield

Binns

IV32

Corskie

1   Jointure Wood

Innes Home Farm

Lochhill

Lochill Farm

Slentack Wood

Fivefield

Binns

Tippertait

Viewfield Farm

Nether Meft Farm

Stone Circle (rems of)

Maverston Wood

64

27   A   28   B   29   C   30   D   31   E   32   F   3

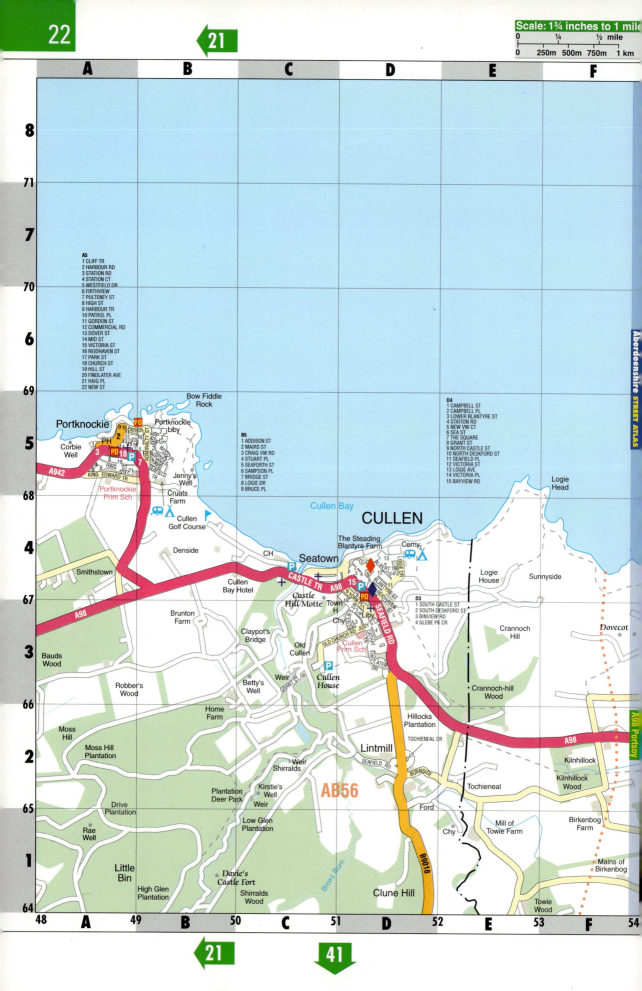

A   B   C   D   E   F

8
71
7
70
69

A5
1 CLIFF TR
2 HARBOUR RD
3 STATION RD
4 STATION CT
5 WESTFIELD DR
6 FIRTHVIEW
7 PULTENEY ST
8 HIGH ST
9 HARBOUR TR
10 PATROL PL
11 GORDON ST
12 COMMERCIAL RD
13 DOVER ST
14 MID ST
15 VICTORIA ST
16 REIDHAVEN ST
17 PARK ST
18 CHURCH ST
19 HILL ST
20 FINDLATER AVE
21 HAIG PL
22 NEW ST

B5
1 ADDISON ST
2 MAIRS ST
3 CRAIG VW RD
4 STUART PL
5 SEAFORTH ST
6 SAMPSON PL
7 BRIDGE ST
8 LOGIE DR
9 BRUCE PL

D4
1 CAMPBELL ST
2 CAMPBELL PL
3 LOWER BLANTYRE ST
4 STATION RD
5 NEW VW CT
6 SEA ST
7 THE SQUARE
8 GRANT ST
9 NORTH CASTLE ST
10 NORTH DESKFORD ST
11 SEAFIELD PL
12 VICTORIA ST
13 LOGIE AVE
14 VICTORIA PL
15 BAYVIEW RD

Aberdeenshire STREET ATLAS

6

Bow Fiddle Rock

Portknockie
Corbie Well
Portknockie Liby
PH
PO
3
A942
KING EDWARD TR
Portknockie Prim Sch

5

Jenny's Well
Cruats Farm
Cullen Golf Course

CULLEN
Cullen Bay
Logie Head

The Steading Blantyre Farm
Cemy

Denside
CH
Seatown
Logie House
Sunnyside

Smithstown

4

CASTLE TR
A98
Cullen Bay Hotel

Castle Hill Motte
Town H
Chy
Liby
SEAFIELD RD

Logie Head
Crannoch Hill
Dovecot

67

Brunton Farm
Cullen Prim Sch
D3
1 SOUTH CASTLE ST
2 SOUTH DESKFORD ST
3 BINVIEW RD
4 GLEBE PK CR

Claypot's Bridge
Old Cullen

Crannoch-hill Wood

3

Bauds Wood
Weir
GRANT ST
Cullen House

66

Robber's Wood
Betty's Well
Home Farm
Hillocks Plantation

Moss Hill
TOCHIENEAL CR

Lintmill
Crannoch Hill

2

Moss Hill Plantation
SEAFIELD RD
BURNSIDE
Tochieneal
Kilnhillock

Kilnhillock Wood

Drive Plantation
Plantation Deer Park
Kirstie's Well
Weir
AB56
Ford
Mill of Towie Farm
Birkenbog Farm

65

Rae Well
Low Glen Plantation
Chy

1

Little Bin
Davie's Castle Fort
Broxy Burn
B9018
Mains of Birkenbog

High Glen Plantation
Shirralds Wood
Clune Hill
Towie Wood

64

A   B   C   D   E   F
48   49   50   51   52   53   54

A98 Portsoy

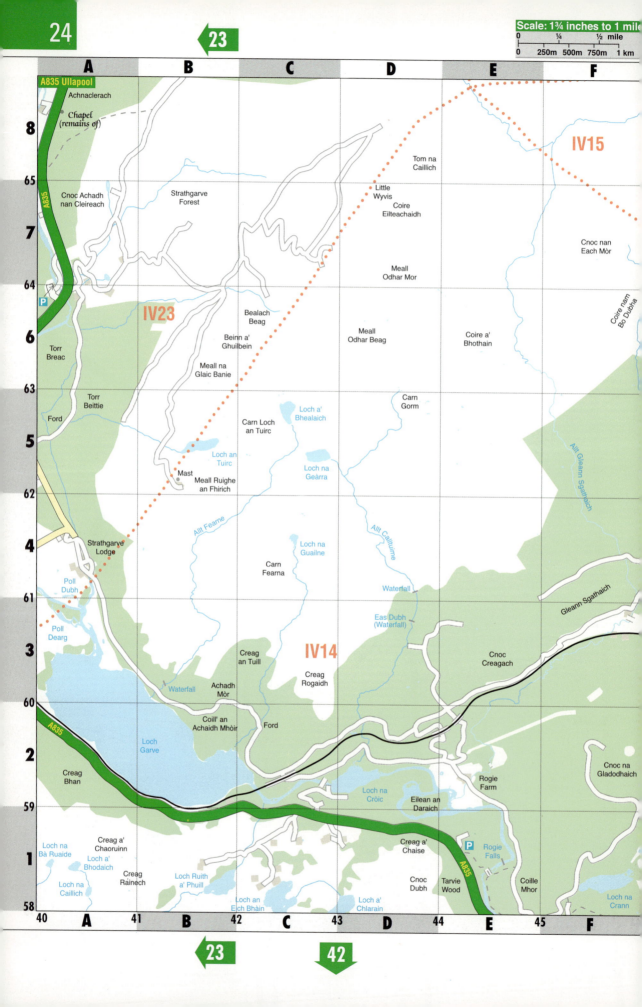

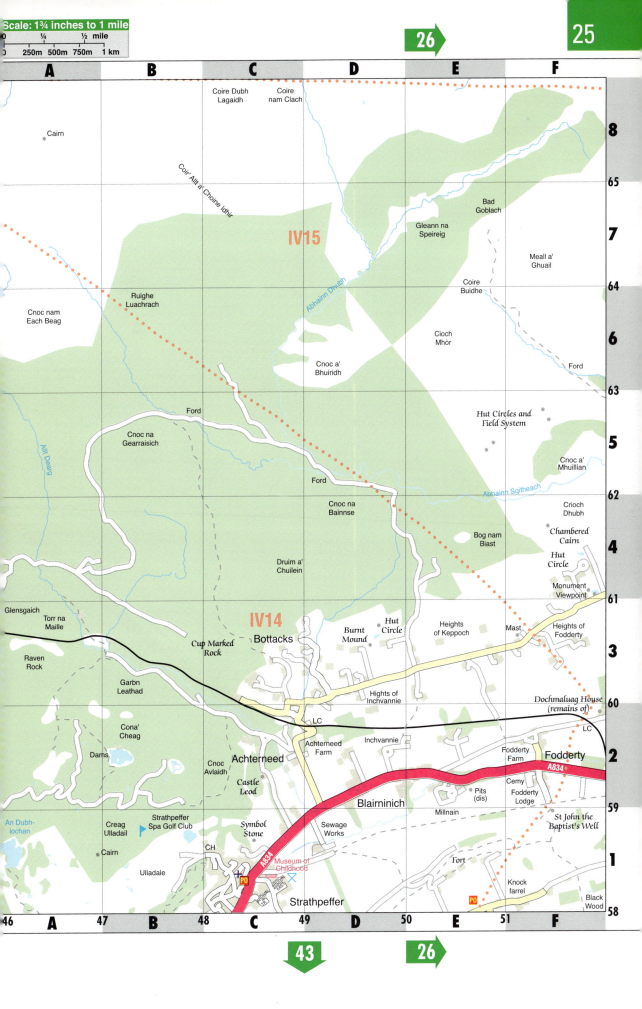

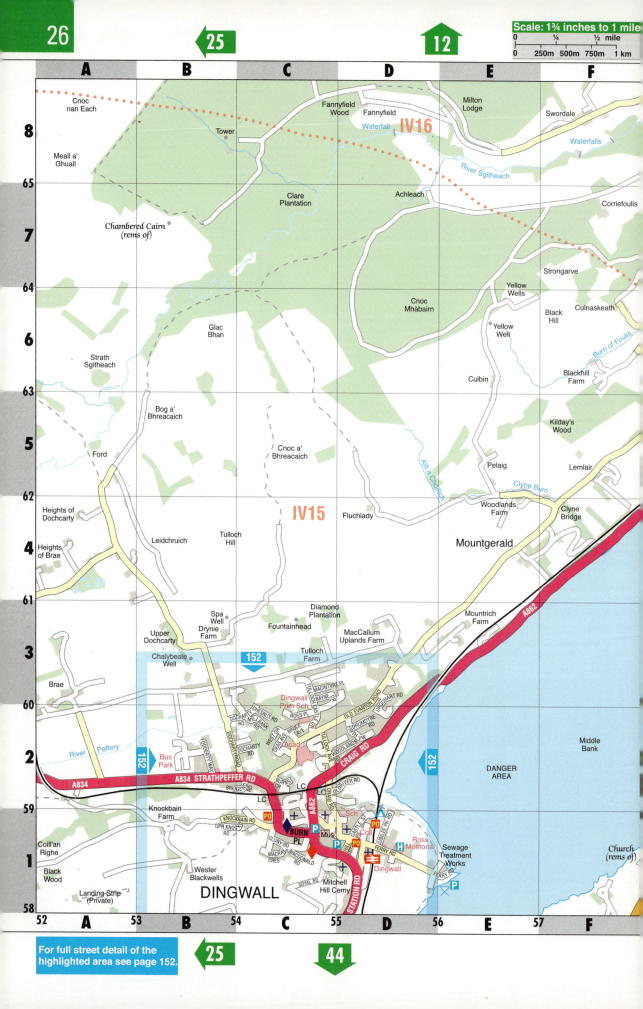

Scale: 1¾ inches to 1 mile

0 | ¼ | ½ | mile
0 | 250m | 500m | 750m | 1 km

Columns: A B C D E F

Rows: 8 65 7 64 6 63 5 62 4 61 3 60 2 59 1 58

Cnoc nan Each

Meall a' Ghuall

Tower

Fannyfield Wood

Fannyfield

Waterfall

IV16

Milton Lodge

Swordale

Waterfalls

River Sgitheach

Clare Plantation

Achleach

Corriefoulis

Chambered Cairn (rems of)

Cnoc Mhàbairn

Strongarve

Yellow Wells

Black Hill

Culnaskeath

Glac Bhan

Yellow Well

Burn of Foulis

Strath Sgitheach

Culbin

Blackhill Farm

Bog a' Bhreacaich

Kilday's Wood

Ford

Cnoc a' Bhreacaich

Allt a' Chaillich

Pelaig

Lemlair

Clyne Burn

Heights of Dochcarty

IV15

Fluchlady

Woodlands Farm

Clyne Bridge

Heights of Brae

Leidchruich

Tulloch Hill

Mountgerald

Mountrich Farm

A862

Brae

Spa Well

Drynie Farm

Diamond Plantation

Fountainhead

MacCallum Uplands Farm

Upper Dochcarty

Chalybeate Well

152

Tulloch Farm

River Peffery

Bus Park

152

DOCHARTY RD

FODDERTY WAY

CHESNUT RD

WEST DR

MILLBANK

DEAS AVE

BRUCE

TAVE

ROSS PL

MACINTYRE PL

BAYNE

Dingwall Prim Sch

TULLOCH RD

EAST LA

OLD EVANTON ROAD

URQUHART RD

DRUMDYRE RD

WOODLANDS RD

CRAIG RD

CRAIG RD

152

DANGER AREA

Middle Bank

A834

A834 STRATHPEFFER RD

BURNS

BRIDGE ST

LC

LC

Acad

LC

LC

A862

OLIVER RD

Sch

Coll

CASTLE ST

JUBILEE PK RD

PO

FERRY RD

Ross Memorial

H

Sewage Treatment Works

Church (rems of)

Knockbain Farm

KNOCKBAIN RD

UPR KNOCK RD

PO

CLUNY RD

MACRAE CRES

MACDONALD RD

BURN PL

P

Mus

PO

P

PO

Dingwall

FERRY RD

P

Coill'an Righe

Black Wood

Landing Strip (Private)

Wester Blackwells

GOYAL RD

STATION RD

Mitchell Hill Cemy

DINGWALL

For full street detail of the highlighted area see page 152.

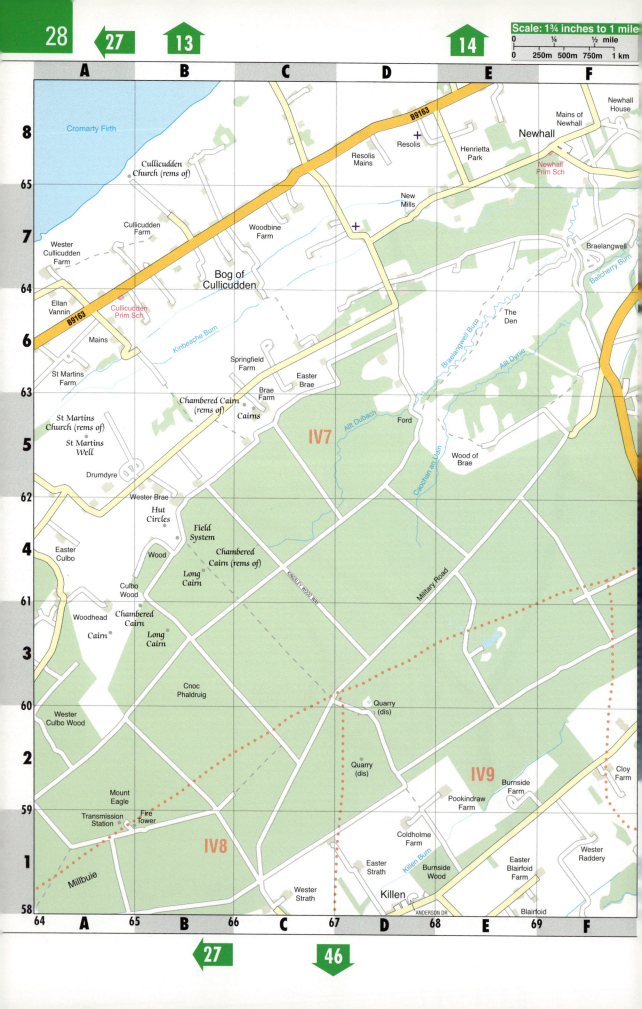

Scale: 1¾ inches to 1 mile

0   ¼   ½   mile
0   250m 500m 750m 1 km

A   B   C   D   E   F

Rosefarm

A832

Greenhill

IV11

Navity
Wood

McFarquhar's
Cave

Gipsies' Cave
Marquis's Cave

St Bennet's
Well

8

65

Navity
Farm

7

Kenny's
Plantation

Waterfall

Waterfalls

64

Castledownie
(rems of)

Eathie Mains
Farm

Bannans

Esthie Burn

6

Quarry
(dis)

63

Upper
Eathie

5

Masts

62

Moray
Firth

4

Cave

61

3

60

2

59

Whiteness
Head

1

DANGER
AREA

58

76   A   77   B   78   C   79   D   80   E   81   F   82

Scale: 1¾ inches to 1 mile

0   ¼   ½   mile

0   250m 500m 750m 1 km

A   B   C   D   E   F

8

65

7

64

6

63

5

62

4

Moray Firth

61

The Bar

3

60

2

59

Low Wood

Loch
Loy

IV12

1

Lochloy
Wood

58

88   A   89   B   90   C   91   D   92   E   93   F

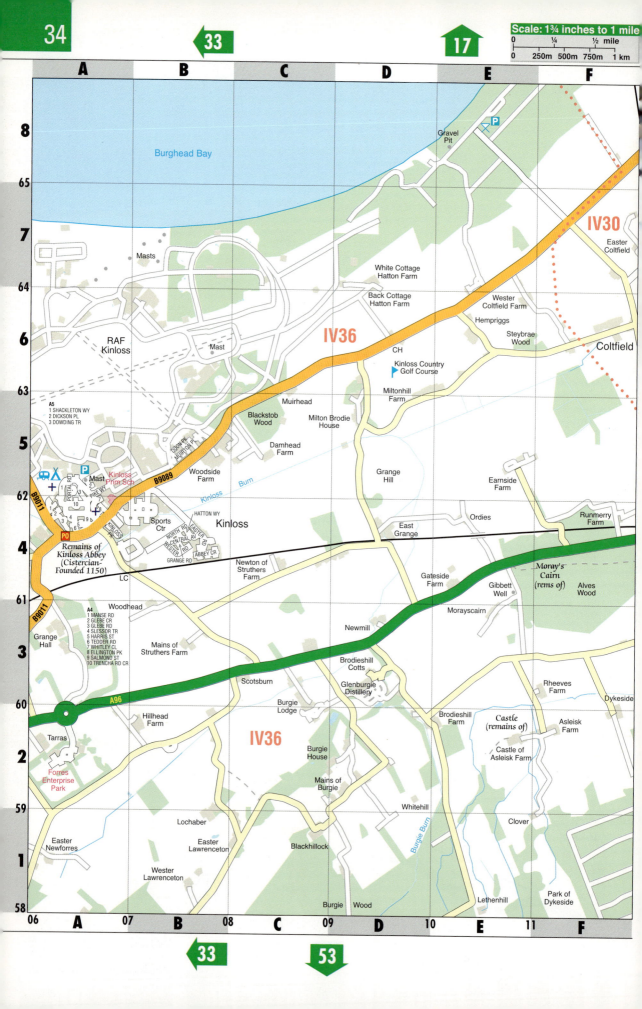

Scale: 1¾ inches to 1 mile

0   ¼   ½ mile
0   250m 500m 750m 1 km

A   B   C   D   E   F

8

Burghead Bay

65

Gravel Pit

P

7

IV30

Easter Coltfield

64

Masts

White Cottage Hatton Farm

Wester Coltfield Farm

Hempriggs

6

IV36

RAF Kinloss

Mast

Back Cottage Hatton Farm

Steybrae Wood

Coltfield

CH

Kinloss Country Golf Course

63

A5
1 SHACKLETON WY
2 DICKSON PL
3 DOWDING TR

Muirhead

Blackstob Wood

Milton Brodie House

Miltonhill Farm

5

DOON PK
MURTON PL

Woodside Farm

Damhead Farm

Grange Hill

Earnside Farm

PORTAL RD

PIKE WY

Mast

Kinloss Prim Sch

B9089

Kinloss Burn

62

B9011

Sports Ctr

Hatton WY

Kinloss

East Grange

Ordies

Runmerry Farm

NORTH RD
CENTRAL AV
WESTER RD
GRANGE RD
EASTER RD
ABBEY CR

P0

KINLOSS

4

Remains of Kinloss Abbey (Cistercian- Founded 1150)

Newton of Struthers Farm

Gateside Farm

Gibbett Well

Moray's Cairn (rems of)

Alves Wood

LC

61

B9011

Woodhead

Morayscairn

A4
1 MANSE RD
2 GLEBE CR
3 GLEBE RD
4 SLESSOR TR
5 HARRIS ST
6 TEDDER RD
7 WHITLEY CL
8 ELLINGTON PK
9 SALMOND ST
10 TRENCHA RD CR

Newmill

Grange Hall

Mains of Struthers Farm

Brodieshill Cotts

Rheeves Farm

Dykeside

3

Scotsburn

Glenburgie Distillery

Brodieshill Farm

Castle (remains of)

Asleisk Farm

A96

60

Tarras

Hillhead Farm

Burgie Lodge

IV36

Burgie House

Castle of Asleisk Farm

Clover

2

Forres Enterprise Park

Mains of Burgie

Whitehill

59

Lochaber

Burgie Burn

Easter Newforres

Easter Lawrenceton

Blackhillock

1

Wester Lawrenceton

Lethenhill

Park of Dykeside

58

Burgie Wood

06   A   07   B   08   C   09   D   10   E   11   F

A   B   C   D   E   F

8

B9012

Easter Kintrae Farm

Lower Mains Farm   Midtown Farm

Dovecote   Findrassie

Westerton

Lochside Farm

Bishop's Well
Palace of Spynie

A941

Spynie Quarry
Hill of Spynie

Spynie

65

Loanhead

Myreside Farm

158

159

Pitgaveny Wood

7

Dovecote   Quarrywood

B9012   DUFFUS ROAD

Woodpark Farm

Findrassie Wood

COVESEA RISE
SPYNIE ST
COVESEA BRAE

LOSSIEMOUTH RD

PRINGLE
RINGLE

LESMURDIE CT
BREMAR DR

64

Quarrywood Hill

Laverockloch

Spynie H

HAMILTON CR
DUNCAN DR

SMITH DRIVE

P

B BODIE DR
DEANSHAUGH

PO
Bishopmill

NORTH ST

DEANSHAUGH RD
LESMURDIE RD

CALCOTS RD

Bareflathills Farm

Woodside Farm

6

Quarry Wood

Oak Wood

BRUMLEY BRAE
MORRISTON RD
MITCHELL RD
DUFFS

Prim Sch

MITCHELL CR
HIGH ST

WOODSIDE TR
RIVERSIDE DR
Visitor Ctr

Ind Est

Sewage Works

Quarry

Moycroft

Henge

158

P

McINTOSH DR
MORRISTON RD

Elgin Academy
Oldmills Farm

HAUGH RD
BOROUGHBRIGG RD

Coll
Liby

Ind Est
Ind Est

Ind Est

63

Quarry (dis)

A96   WEST RD

SHERIFFMILL
JOCK INKSONS BRAE
OLD MILLS RD

Blackfriars

P P i
HIGH ST
GREYFRIARS

PANSPORT RD

GRAMPIAN RD

PO   A96   EAST RD

Waukmill

River Lossie

Aldroughty

Bruceland Farm

ELGIN

BRUCELAND RD
FLEURS PL
FLEURS DR

Bilbohall H

SOUTH ST

MAYNE RD
WITTET DR
FORTEATH ST

P
SOUTH ST
Prim Sch

HAY ST

Prim Sch

ACADEMY ST
DUKE ST

MAISONDIEU RD

SEAFIELD

VICTORIA RD

Bridge of Tyock

PINEFIELD CR

Ashgrove

REYNOLDS CR

62

Lochinver   Inverlochty Farm

Allarburn Farm   Palmerscross

PLUSCARDEN ROAD

IV30

WARDS RD

LC

H Day Centre

Elgin

Springfield

STATION RD

Cemy

MILLICENT DR
ASHGROVE RD

PO   Prim Sch

REIKIE LA

Wood Maggot
Linkwood Farm

4

B9010

Pittendreich Bridge
Pittendreich Mill
Easter Pittendreich Farm

Dovecot

Prim Sch

High Sch

Mayne Farm

EDGAR RD
GREEN
GLEN MORAY DR
SPRINGFIELD ROAD

BRINUTH

BAILIES DR

SMITH ST
BEZACK ST
ROBERTSON DR

MAIN ST

MURRAY RD
THORNHILL RD

Ret Pk

PO

New Elgin

Dunkinty Chimney

Linkwood Distillery

61

Muiryhall   Batchen

158

Mayne House

LAND ST
SANDY
BIRNIE RD
BIRNIE PL
SCHOOL DR

159

3

Black Burn

Miltonduff

Wester Manbeen Farm

Mayne Wood

Elgin Golf Club   CH

Glassgreen Farm

BURN OF LINKWOOD

Birkenhill Wood
Cemy

Dovecot   Distillery   Chy

60

Birkenhill Croft

2

Muir of Miltonduff

B9010

Pit (dis)

Duffushillock

Burnside of Birnie

59

Pit (dis)   Springburn

Easter Manbeen

Cloddach Quarry

Nether Birnie Farm

A941

1

Auchtertyre

Cloddach Farm

Hillhead

Paddockhaugh

Symbol Stone

Dykeside Farm

Pit (dis)

Wood of Level

Level Farm

Chy Distillery

Chy

Longmorn

58

18   A   19   B   20   C   21   D   22   E   23   F

For full street detail of the highlighted area see pages 158 and 159.

35   55

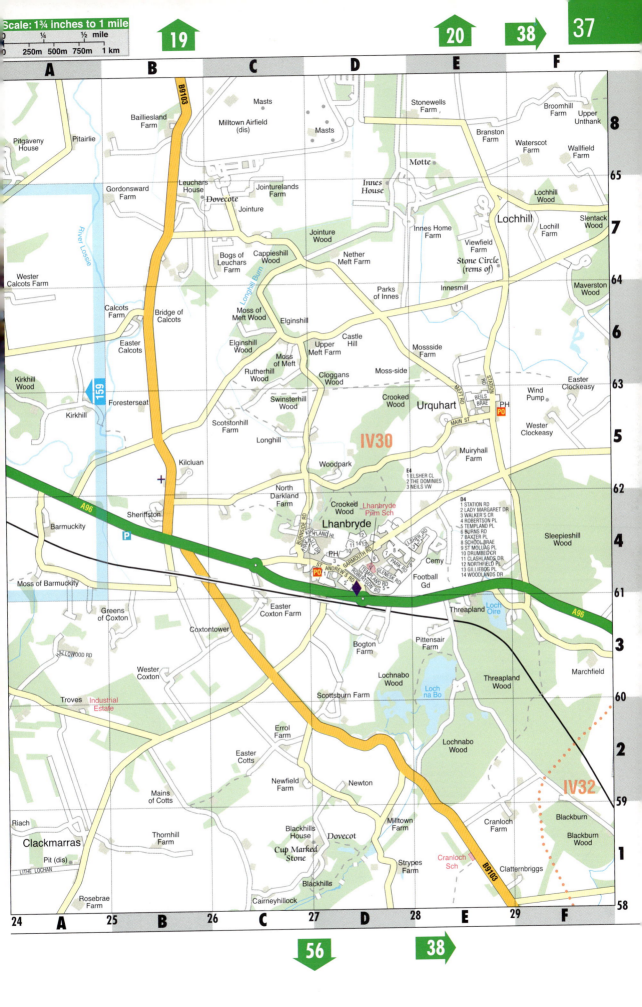

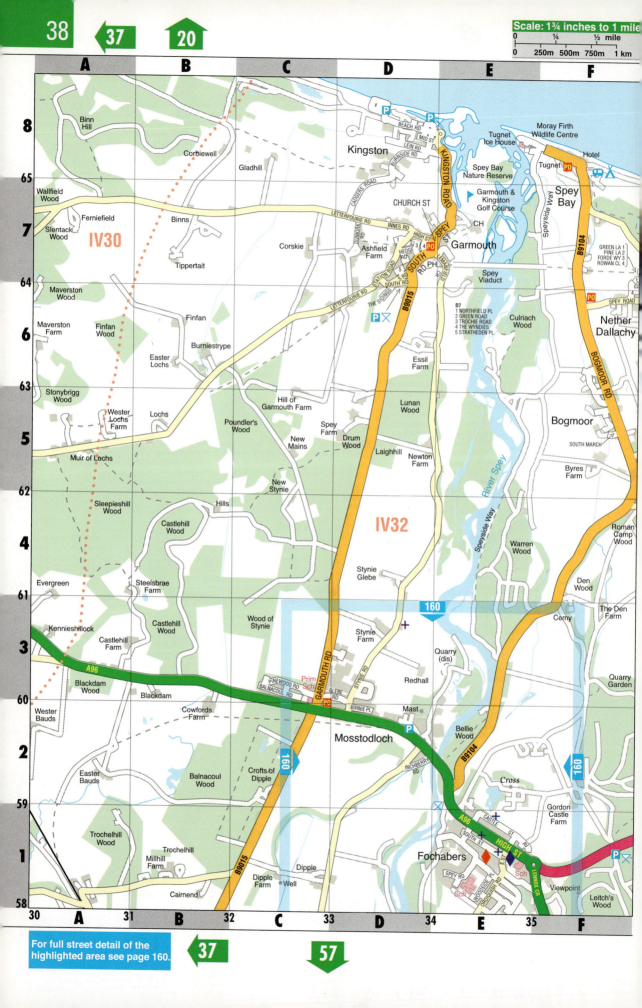

Scale: 1¾ inches to 1 mile

0 ¼ ½ mile
0 250m 500m 750m 1 km

A **B** **C** **D** **E** **F**

8

Binn Hill
Corbiewell
Gladhill
Kingston
BEACH RD
MID ST
LEIN RD
Moray Firth Wildlife Centre
Tugnet Ice House
Tugnet
Hotel
Spey Bay

65

Wallfield Wood
Ferniefield
Slentack Wood
IV30
Binns
BURNSIDE RD
CADGERS ROAD
LETTERFOURIE RD
INNES RD
CHURCH ST
KINGSTON ROAD
SPEY ST
HIGH ST
Spey Bay Nature Reserve
Garmouth & Kingston Golf Course
CH

7

Tippertait
Corskie
DUNKIRK RD
Ashfield Farm
HEDGE RD
SOUTH RD
Garmouth
PH
GREEN LA 1
PINE LA 2
FORDE WY 3
ROWAN CL 4
B9104

64

Maverston Wood
Finfan
STATION ROAD
THE SIDINGS
LETTERFOURIE RD
B9015
SOUTH RD
LEHANFIELD
Spey Viaduct
Spey Road
Nether Dallachy
PO

6

Maverston Farm
Finfan Wood
Burniestrype
Easter Lochs
D7
1 NORTHFIELD PL
2 GREEN ROAD
3 TROCHIE ROAD
4 THE WYNDIES
5 STRATHEDEN PL
Culriach Wood
Essil Farm

63

Stonybrigg Wood
Wester Lochs Farm
Lochs
Hill of Garmouth Farm
Poundler's Wood
New Mains
Spey Farm
Drum Wood
Lunan Wood
Laighhill
Newton Farm
Bogmoor
SOUTH MARCH
BOGMOOR RD

5

Muir of Lochs
New Stynie
IV32
Byres Farm

62

Sleepieshill Wood
Hills
Castlehill Wood
Warren Wood
Roman Camp Wood

4

Evergreen
Steelsbrae Farm
Castlehill Wood
Stynie Glebe
Den Wood
The Den Farm

61

Kennieshillock
Castlehill Farm
Wood of Stynie
160
Cemy
River Spey
Speyside Way

3

A96
Blackdam Wood
Castlehill Wood
GARMOUTH RD
Stynie Farm
STYNIE RD
Quarry (dis)
Redhall
Quarry Garden

Blackdam
Cowfords Farm
PINEWOOD RD
BALNACOUL RD
Prim Sch
GLEBE RD
BIRNIE PL
Mast
Bellie Wood

2

Wester Bauds
Balnacoul Wood
Crofts of Dipple
160
Mosstodloch
INCHBERRY RD
B9104
Cross
Gordon Castle Farm
160

59

Easter Bauds
Trochelhill Wood
Trochelhill
Millhill Farm
Dipple
Dipple Farm
Well
A96
HIGH ST
CASTLE ST
SOUTH ST
Fochabers
Sch
LENNOX CR
Viewpoint
Leitch's Wood

1

Cairnend
B9015
Spey Rd
WOODSIDE PL
ORCHARD RD
Sch
Sch

58

30 **A** 31 **B** 32 **C** 33 **D** 34 **E** 35 **F**

For full street detail of the highlighted area see page 160.
37
57

Scale: 1¾ inches to 1 mile

0   ¼   ½   mile
0   250m 500m 750m   1 km

A   B   C   D   E   F

8   65   7   64   6   63   5   62   4   61   3   60   2   59   1   58

Spey Bay Golf Course

The Links

Gravel Pit

Moor of Dallachy

Lower Auchenreath

Speyside Way

Airfield (dis)

Dryburn

Cowiemuir Farm

Cowiemuir Wood

Wood of Auchenreath

Upper Dallachy

IV32

Wood of Auchenhalrig

Auchinhalrig Farm

Upper Auchenwreath Farm

Moor of Auchenhalrig

Auchenhalrig

Romancamp Gate

The Moor

Newlands of Tynet

Deer Park

Tulloch Farm

Wellheads Farm

Redmoss Wood

Chapelford

Cemy

Whiteash Hill Wood

A98

Windsoer Farm

Howe of Enzie

Longhill Wood

Howcore

Hotel

Bridge of Tynet

Burnside of Tynet Farm

Burnside of Enzie

Braes of Enzie Farm

Ford

Chy

Core Farm

Broadley Wood

Cuffurach

Kirkland

Burn of Tynet

Braes Cairn

B9016

D7
1 HARBOUR HEAD
2 HOPE ST
3 MARCH ST
4 CATHCART ST
5 SHORE ST
6 CROSS ST
7 WEST HIGH ST
8 EAST HIGH ST

D6
1 REID TR
2 TANNACHY RD
3 TANNACHY TR

Craigan Roan

LETTERFOURIE RD   LENNOX PL
GARDEN LA
STATION RD
EARL ST
Porttannachy
Mains of Tannachy

GORDON ST
Liby
DUKE ST
RICHMOND TR
CROWN TR
CROWN STREET

PO
Gollachy

Portgordon Prim Sch

Portgordon

Slackend Farm

Glasterim

Broadley

Crem

Cuttlebrae Farm

Clochan

Newbigging

AB56

Mains of Oxhill Farm

Allaloth

Waterfall

Waterfalls

Waterfalls

B9016

Arthur's Point

Speyside Way

A990

Buckpool Golf Club

Mains of Gallachy

Auchintae

157

Buckpool

GT WESTERN RD   MAIN ST
SEAVIEW RD
GOLF VW DR
BARFIELD RD
ANTON ST
ST PETER'S RD
INWARD RD
NETHERHA RD
CH
Cemy
Seafield
Cemy
Prim Sch
H

A98

Arradoul

Smirack Farm

Slack Wood

Slackhead

Leitcheston Farm

Tarwathie

Easter Bogs

Cairnfield House

Oran

Holmie

Preshome

Muir of Holmie

Scabbed Hill Plantation

Waterfall

Weirs

157

Quarry (dis)

Corsekell Moss

For full street detail of the highlighted area see page 157.

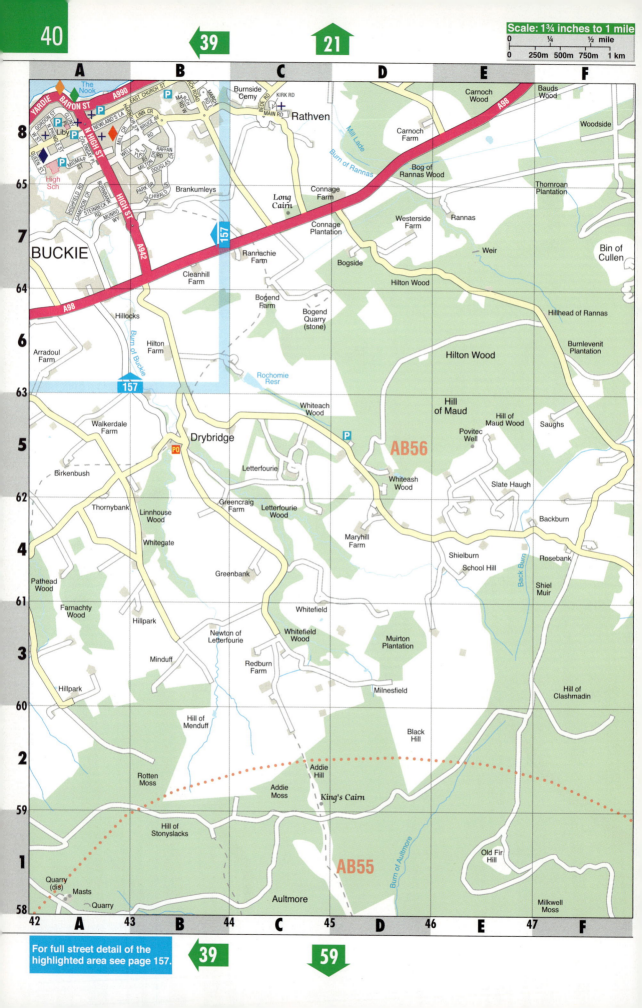

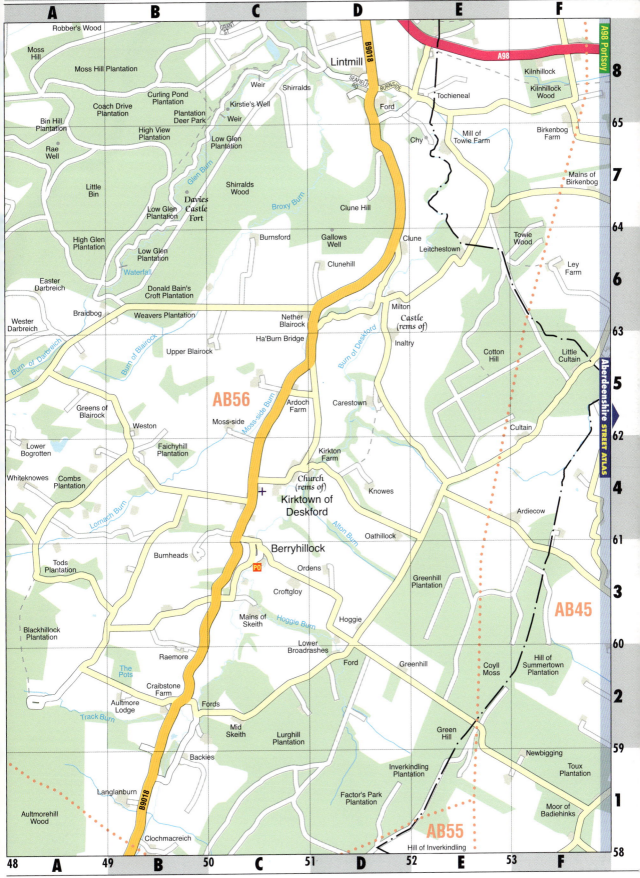

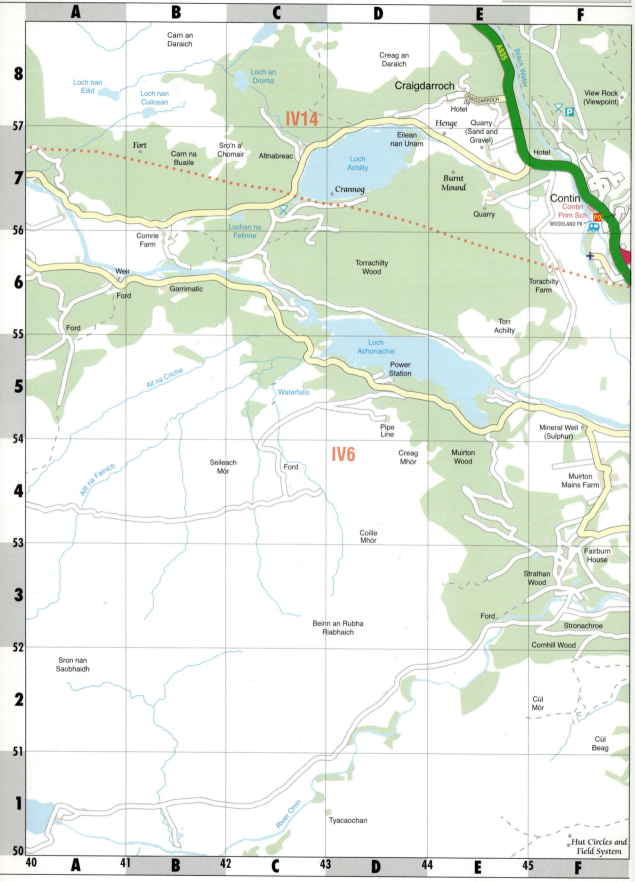

24

Scale: 1¾ inches to 1 mile
0   ¼   ½   mile
0   250m 500m 750m 1 km

A   **B**   **C**   **D**   **E**   **F**

8

Carn an
Daraich

Creag an
Daraich

Loch an
Droma

Loch nan
Eilid

Craigdarroch

57

Loch nan
Cuilcean

IV14

CRAIGDARROCH
DR

Hotel

View Rock
(Viewpoint)

Black Water

A835

P

Fort

Sro'n a'
Chomair

Altnabreac

Eilean
nan Unam

Henge

Quarry
(Sand and
Gravel)

7

Carn na
Buaile

Crannog

Loch
Achilty

Burnt
Mound

Hotel

Contin

Contin
Prim Sch

PO

56

Lochan na
Felinne

Quarry

WOODLAND PK

Comrie
Farm

Torrachilty
Wood

6

Weir

Garrimatic

Torrachilty
Farm

Ford

Torr
Achilty

55

Ford

Loch
Achonachie

Alt na Criche

5

Power
Station

Waterfalls

Mineral Well
(Sulphur)

54

Pipe
Line

Muirton
Mains Farm

IV6

Creag
Mhòr

Muirton
Wood

Seileach
Mòr

Ford

4

Alt na Fàinich

Fairburn
House

53

Coille
Mhòr

Strathan
Wood

3

Stronachroe

Beinn an Rubha
Riabhaich

Ford

Cornhill Wood

52

Sron nan
Saobhaidh

Cùl
Mòr

2

Cùl
Beag

51

River Orrin

1

Tyacaochan

Hut Circles and
Field System

50

40 **A** **41** **B** **42** **C** **43** **D** **44** **E** **45** **F**

62

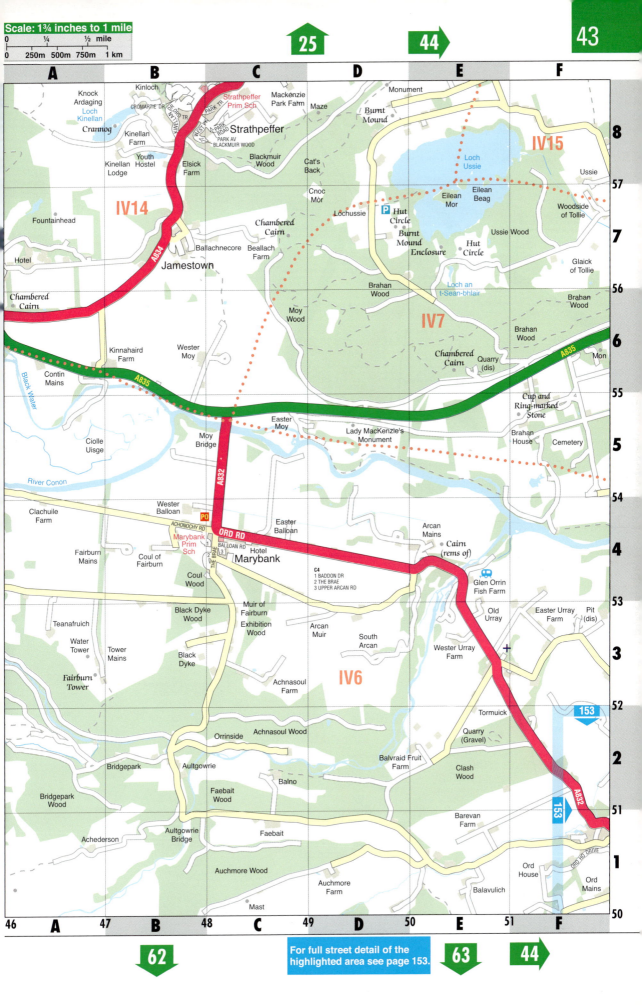

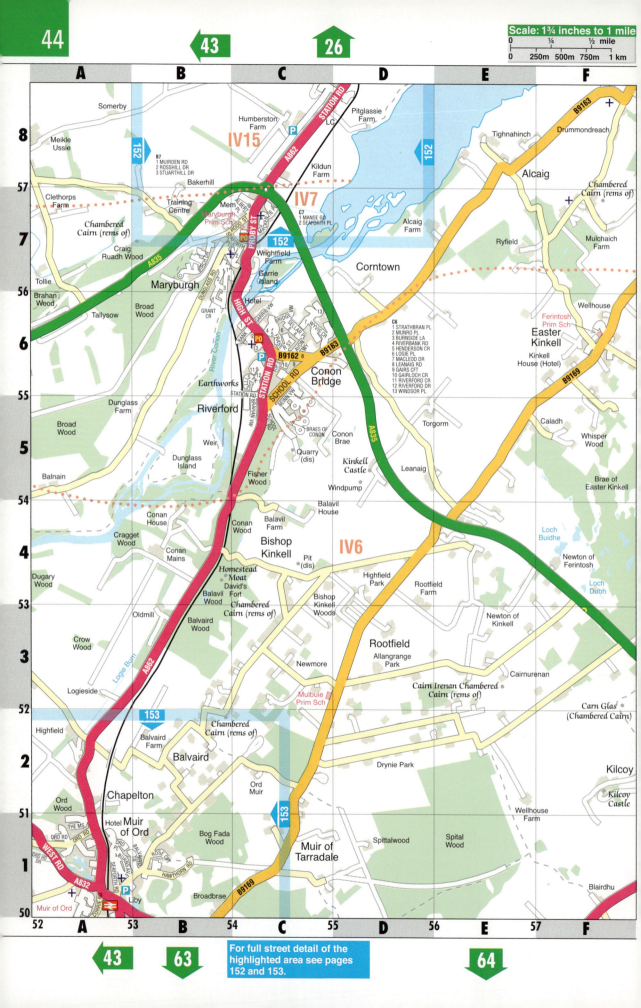

Scale: 1¾ inches to 1 mile

0 ¼ ½ mile
0 250m 500m 750m 1 km

8

Somerby

Humberston Farm

IV15

Pitglassie Farm

LC

Drummondreach

B9163

Meikle Ussie

B7
1 MUIRDEN RD
2 ROSSHILL DR
3 STUARTHILL DR

Tighnahinch

Kildun Farm

Alcaig

152

Chambered Cairn (rems of)

57

Clethorps Farm

Bakerhill

Training Centre

Mem

Maryburgh Prim Sch

IV7

C7
1 MANSE GD
2 SEAFORTH PL

Alcaig Farm

Ryfield

Mulchaich Farm

Chambered Cairn (rems of)

Craig Ruadh Wood

A835

152

Wrightfield Farm

Corntown

Wellhouse

7

Tollie

Brahan Wood

Maryburgh

Garrie Island

Ferintosh Prim Sch

56

Tallysow

Broad Wood

Hotel

GRANT CR

Easter Kinkell

Kinkell House (Hotel)

B9169

Broad Wood

C6
1 STRATHBRAN PL
2 MUNRO PL
3 BURNSIDE LA
4 RIVERBANK RD
5 HENDERSON CR
6 LOGIE PL
7 MACLEOD DR
8 LEANAIG RD
9 GAIRS CFT
10 GAIRLOCH CR
11 RIVERFORD CR
12 RIVERFORD DR
13 WINDSOR PL

6

PO

HIGH ST

STATION RD

B9162

B9163

Conon Bridge

Caladh

Whisper Wood

55

Dunglass Farm

Earthworks

STATION RD

SCHOOL RD

Riverford

Braes of Conon

Torgorm

Brae of Easter Kinkell

Broad Wood

Weir

Conon Brae

A835

Leanaig

Loch Buidhe

5

Balnain

Dunglass Island

Fisher Wood

Quarry (dis)

Kinkell Castle

Windpump

Newton of Ferintosh

Loch Dubh

54

Conan House

Conon Wood

Balavil Farm

Balavil House

IV6

4

Cragget Wood

Conan Mains

Bishop Kinkell

Pit (dis)

Highfield Park

Rootfield Farm

Dugary Wood

Homestead Moat

David's Fort

Chambered Cairn (rems of)

Newton of Kinkell

53

Oldmill

Balvaird Wood

Balavil Wood

A862

Bishop Kinkell Woods

Rootfield

Cairnurenan

Crow Wood

Logie Burn

Newmore

Allangrange Park

3

Logieside

Mulbuie Prim Sch

Cairn Irenan Chambered Cairn (rems of)

Carn Glas (Chambered Cairn)

52

Highfield

153

Balvaird Farm

Chambered Cairn (rems of)

Drynie Park

Kilcoy

2

Balvaird

Chapelton

Ord Muir

153

Muir of Tarradale

Spittalwood

Spital Wood

Wellhouse Farm

Kilcoy Castle

1

Ord Wood

THE MS

Hotel Muir of Ord

Bog Fada Wood

B9169

WEST RD

A832

Libry

A832

Broadbrae

Blairdhu

50

Muir of Ord

For full street detail of the highlighted area see pages 152 and 153.

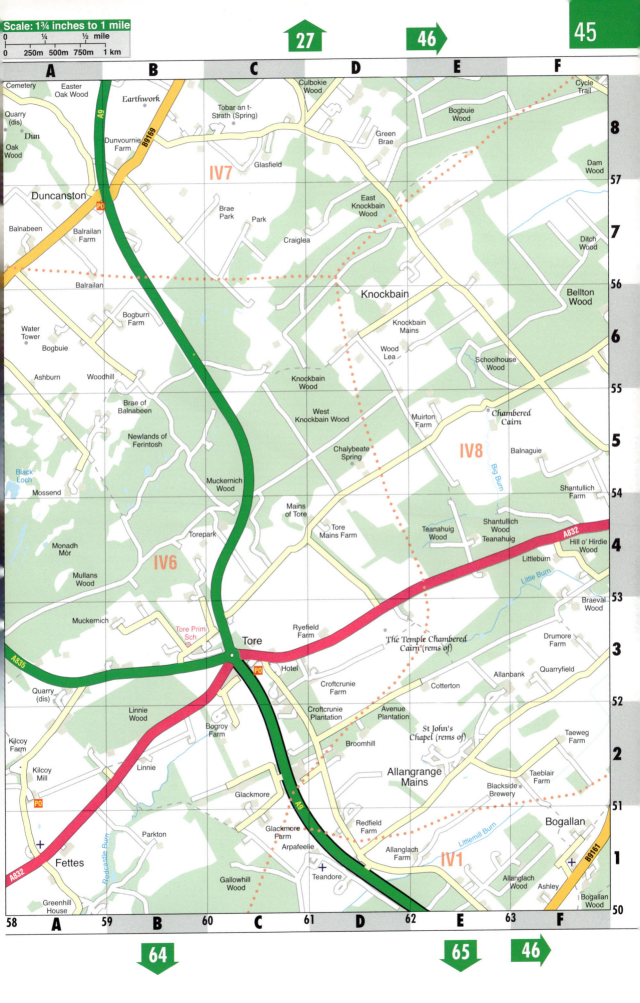

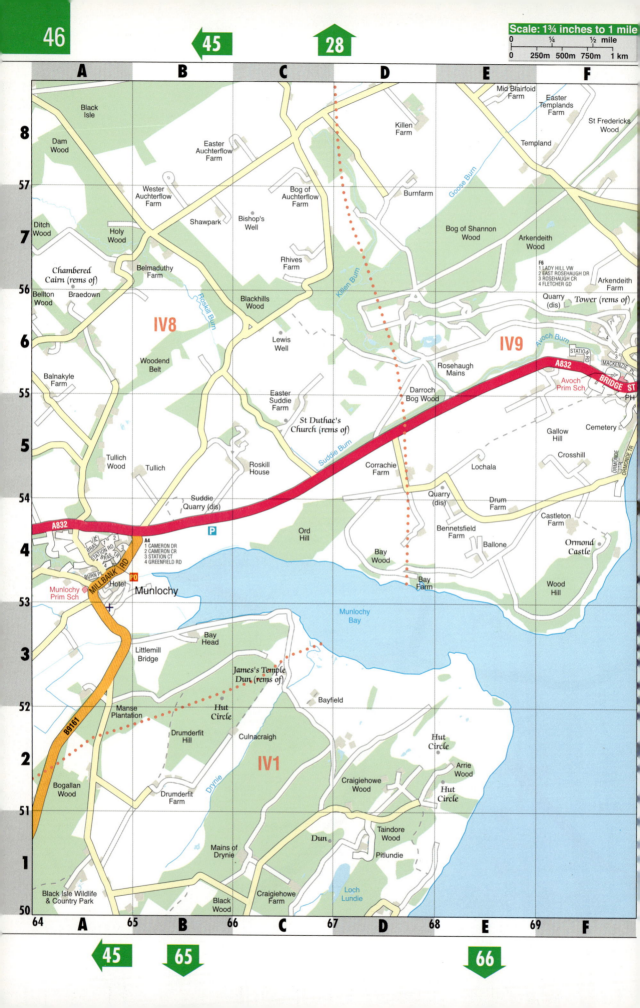

A   B   C   D   E   F

8

57

7

56

6

55

5

54

4

53

3

52

2

51

1

50

76   A   77   B   78   C   79   D   80   E   81   F

Fort George

Seaforth
Cameron
Mus

Sports
Gd

P

P

Rifle Ranges

ADAMS ROAD

SKINNER RD

DAWES ROAD

ALLAN RD

Kirkton

Wr Twr
Chy

Mast

Mast

Cemy

B9006

Macleod
Organics
Visitor Ctr

Hillhead
Farm

Cromal Mount

Football Gd

P

P

HIGH ST

HIGH ST

DUNMACGLAS

PO
Hotel

Ardersier

Ardersier
Prim Sch

STUART ST

HIGH ST

MANSE RD

PETER RD

STATION RD

Nairn Rd
Ind Est

Liby

B5
1 SCHOOL PL
2 CLACHAN RD
3 WEST END DR
4 CAMERON DR
5 REAYBANK RD
6 STUART AV
7 CAMPBELLTOWN
8 STATION DR

P

1

5

6

2

3

7

8

B9039

NAIRN RD

Milton of
Connage Farm

B9092

Treeton

Connage

Viewhill

Baddock

Carse of
Ardersier

Carse Wood

Cemy

Cemy

Aiten
Farm

Smithstown

Smithstown
Wood

Smithstown
Wood

Cairn

Muir of
Balnagowan

Milton of
Balnagowan

Hut Circles

Mains of
Balnagowan

Ballinreich

Flemington
House

Gollanfield

Pooltown

IV2

A96

Lochside

Wester
Lochend

Loch
Flemington

B9039

Industrial
Estate

Heliport

P

Inverness
Airport

Milton of
Gollanfield

Culblair

Balspardon

Cemy

Ballaggan

Polfalden

Brackley

Drumine

B9006

Balblair

Cairnglass

B9090

Woodend

A96

Mid Coul

Tornagrain
Wood

LC

War Mem

A96

Hillhead

Culaird

Little Croy
Farm

Tirfogrein

Heathfield

B9006

Clephanton

B9091

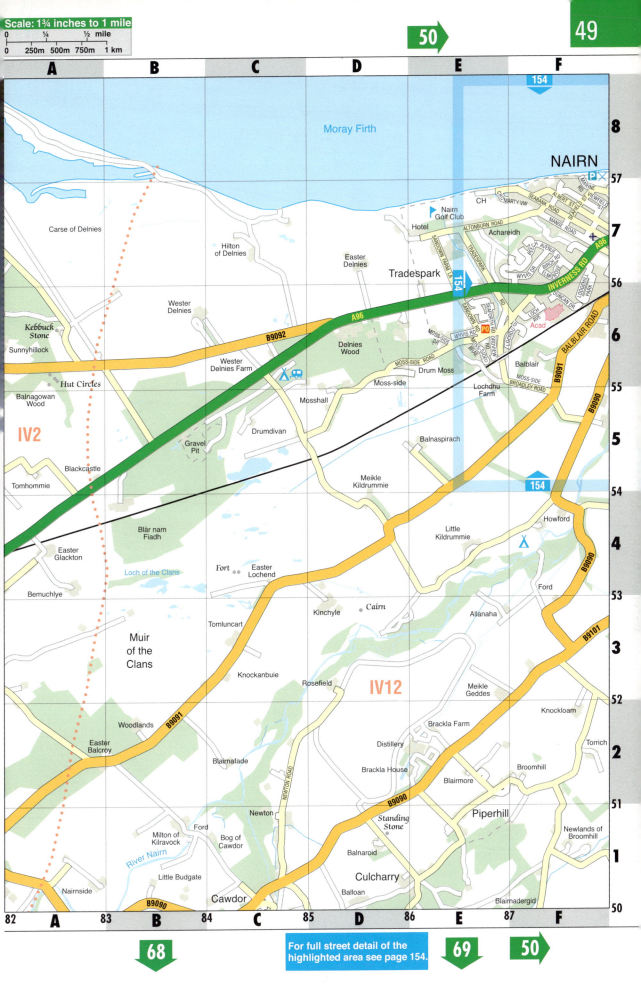

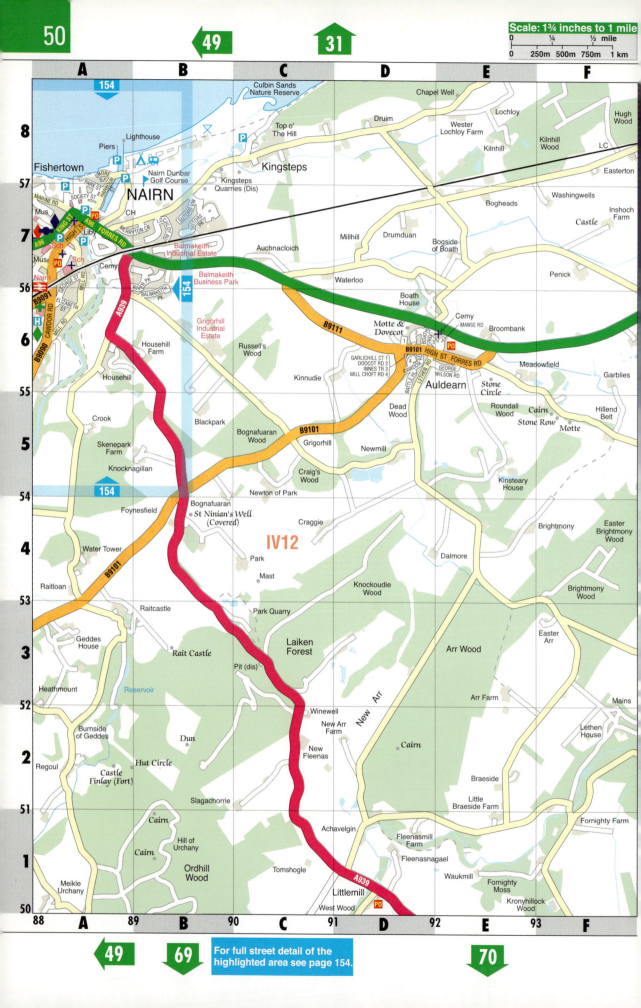

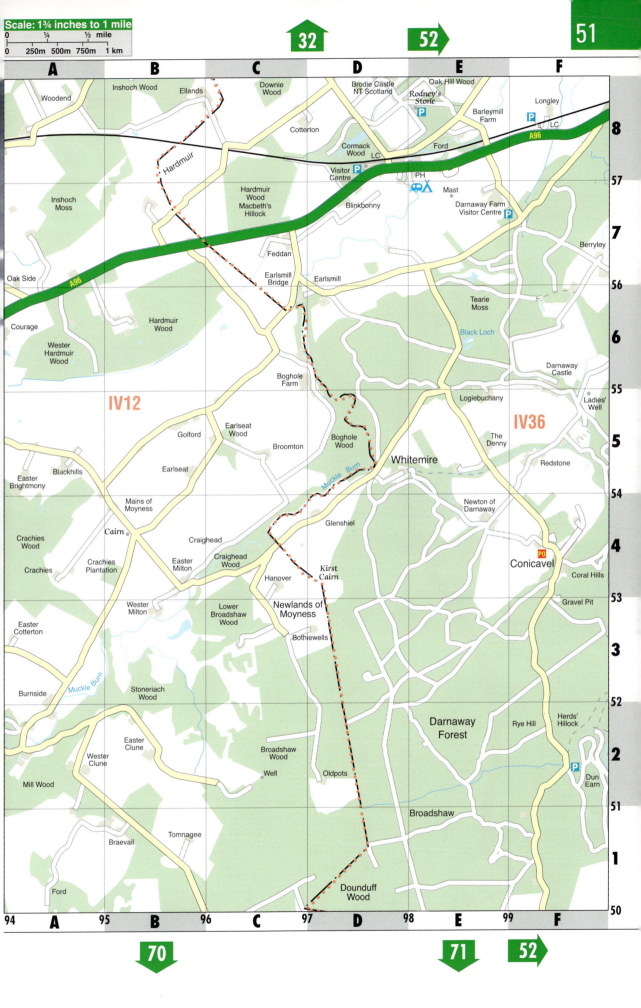

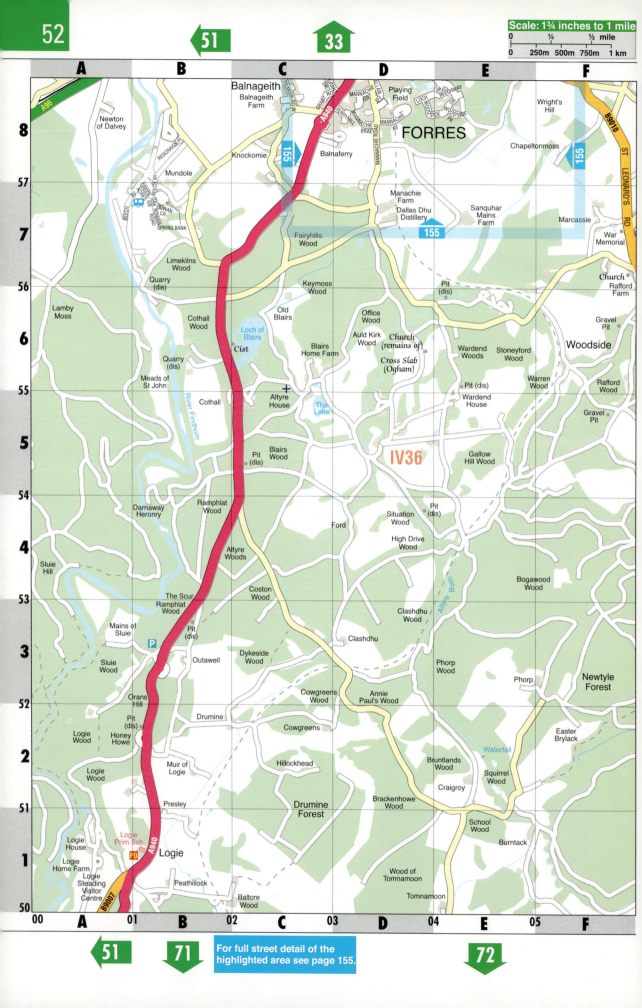

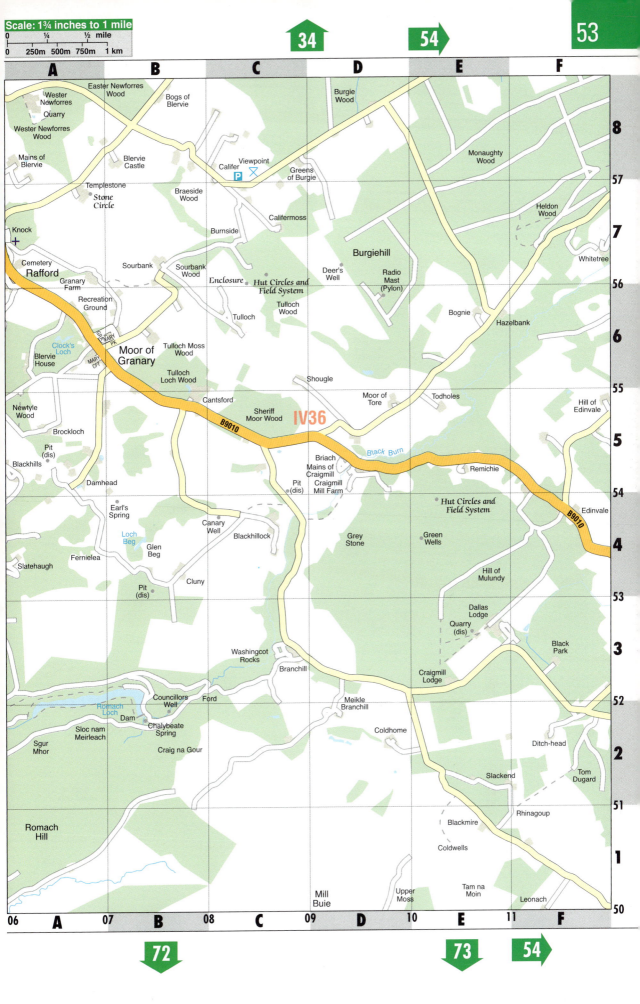

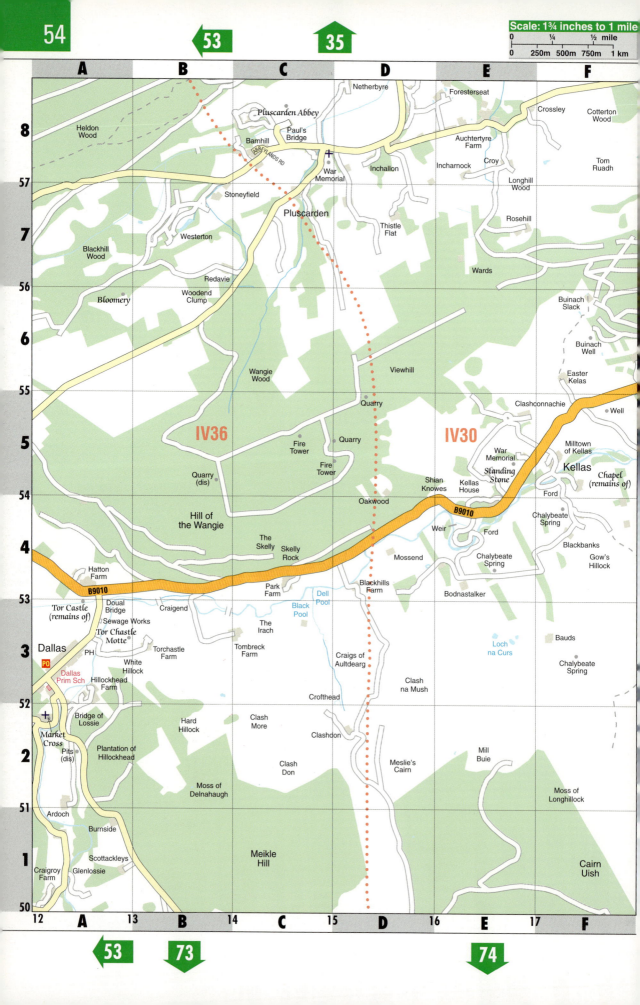

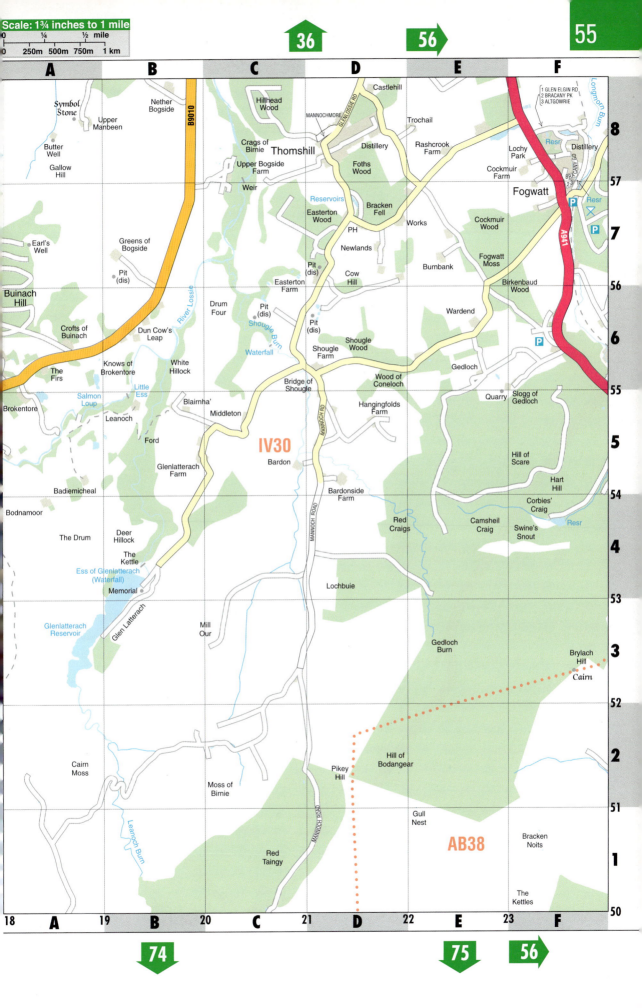

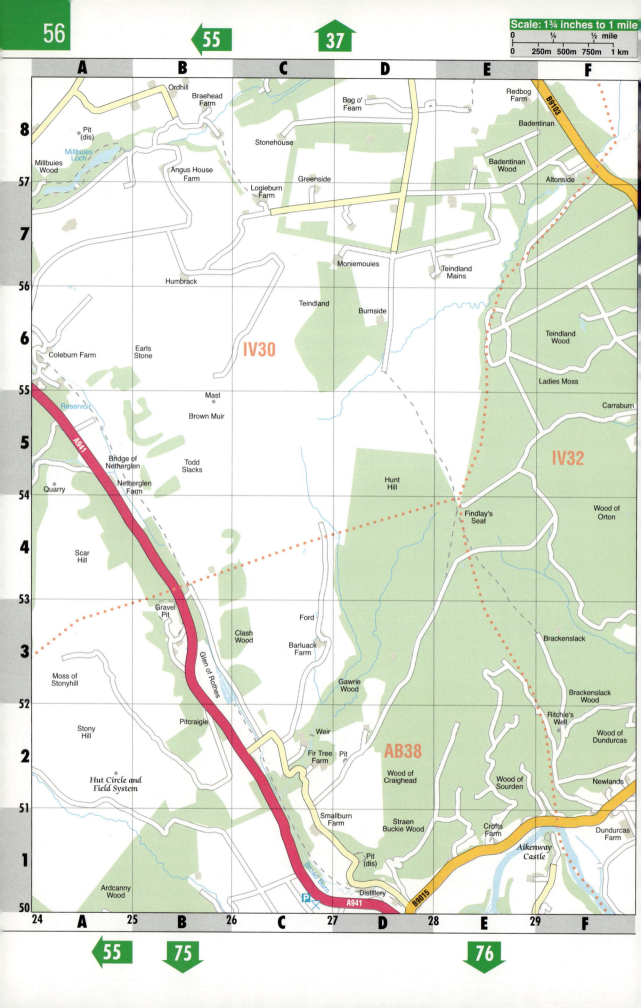

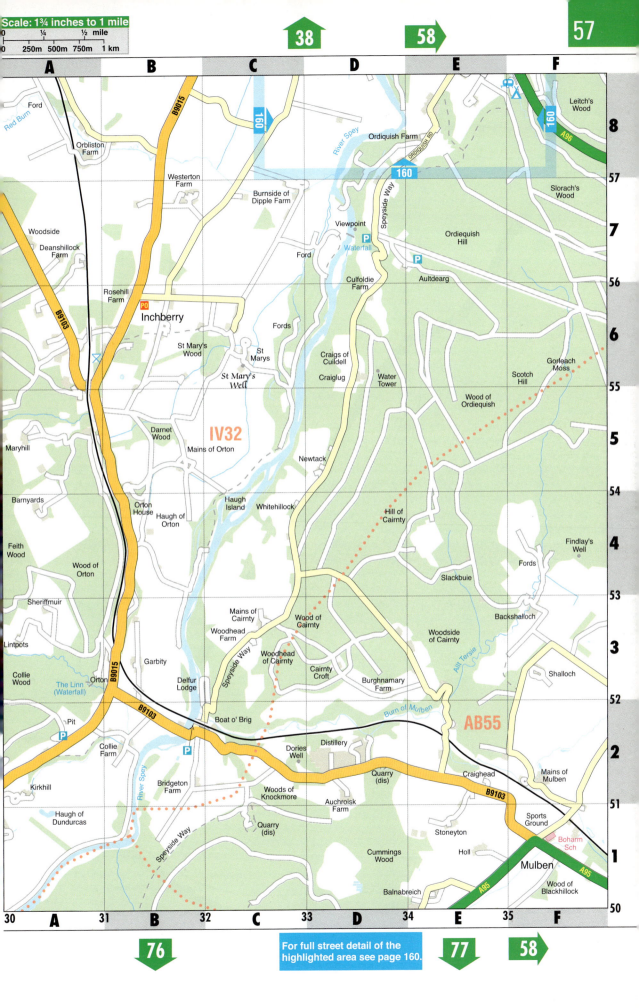

Scale: 1¾ inches to 1 mile

0   ¼   ½   mile
0   250m 500m 750m 1 km

A   B   C   D   E   F

8
57
7
56
6
55
5
54
4
53
3
52
2
51
1
50

Leitch's Wood
IV32
Whiteash Hill Wood
AB56
Corsekell Moss

Fire Tower
Monument
Whiteash Hill
Fire Tower
Raefin
B9016
Quarry (dis

Burn of Fochabers
Gallows Hill
Ryeriggs Croft
Henheads Moss

Aulthash
A96
Mast
Forgie Hill
Walkerstrough
Ryeriggs
Heads of Auchinderran

Pathside
Saughwells
Blackfold

Wood of Ordiequish
Douglasshiel Moss
Upper Drakemyres
AB55
Lower Drakemyres
Well
Oxwell

Thief's Hill
Forgie
Ardioch
Spring

P
Newton of Forgie
Tarrcroys
Auchairn

Sound Moor
Ford
Aultmore
Wells

Chy Distillery
Fieldhead

Gow Moss
North Bogbain
Yondertown
Loanhead

Knowhead
Croftmore
Little Forgie
Oakenhead
Tarmore

Lower Soundmoor
Ford
Malcolm Wood
South Bogbain
Crooks Mill
161
Haughs

Upper Mulben
Mossend Croft
Parkfoot
Hill of Mulderie
Burnside

Shandston
Bonded Warehouses
Wood of Mulderie
Bowlins
Allanbuie Farm

Hillockhead of Muldearie

The Tam
Bush Farm
A95

Garland
Cullieshangan
Muldearie Mains
Hillockhead Wood

A95
LC
Rosarie
A95

For full street detail of the highlighted area see page 161.

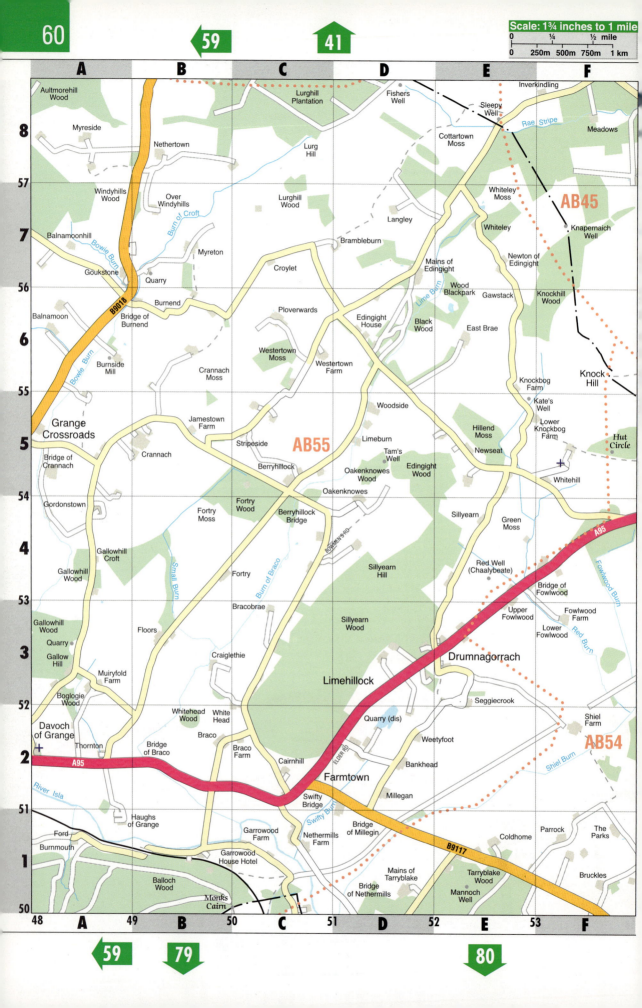

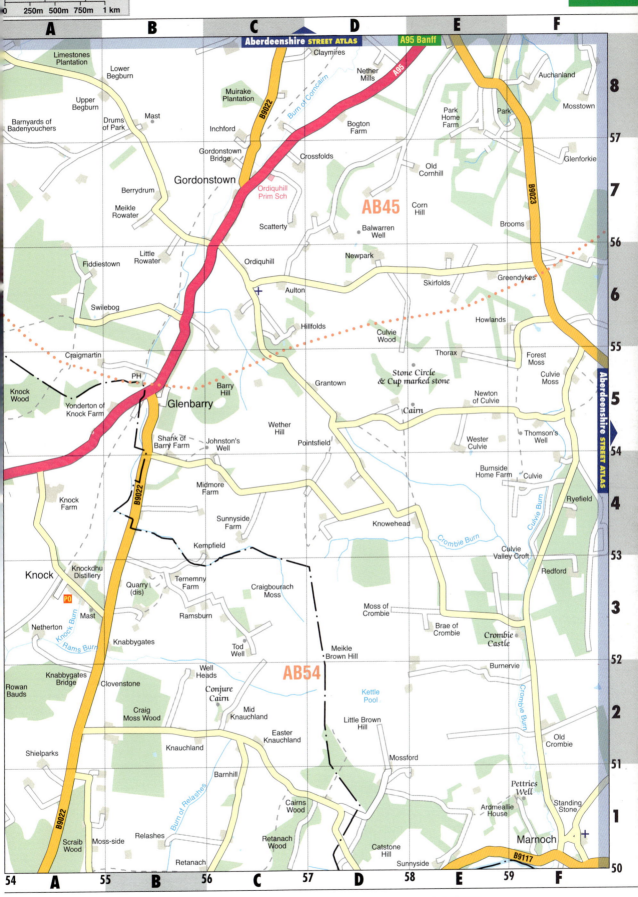

Scale: 1¾ inches to 1 mile

¼ ½ mile
0 250m 500m 750m 1 km

A95 Banff

A B C D E F

Limestones Plantation
Lower Begburn
Auchanland
Mosstown
8

Upper Begburn
Drums of Park
Mast
Muirake Plantation
Inchford
Claymires
Nether Mills
Park Home Farm
Park
57

Barnyards of Badenyouchers
Berrydrum
Gordonstown Bridge
Crossfolds
Old Cornhill
Glenforkie

Gordonstown
Ordiquhill Prim Sch
AB45
Corn Hill
Brooms
7

Meikle Rowater
Scatterty
Balwarren Well
56

Fiddiestown
Little Rowater
Ordiquhill
Newpark
Skirfolds
Greendykes

Swiebog
Aulton
Hillfolds
Howlands
6

Craigmartin
Culvie Wood
Thorax
Forest Moss
55

Knock Wood
PH
Barry Hill
Grantown
Stone Circle & Cup marked stone
Culvie Moss

Yonderton of Knock Farm
Glenbarry
Cairn
Newton of Culvie
5

Shank of Barry Farm
Johnston's Well
Wether Hill
Pointsfield
Wester Culvie
Thomson's Well

Knock Farm
Midmore Farm
Burnside Home Farm
Culvie
54

Sunnyside Farm
Knowehead
Crombie Burn
Ryefield
4

Kempfield
Culvie Valley Croft
Redford
53

Knock
Knockdhu Distillery
Quarry (dis)
Ternemny Farm
Craigbourach Moss
Moss of Crombie
Brae of Crombie
Crombie Castle

PO
Mast
Ramsburn
Meikle Brown Hill
3

Netherton
Knabbygates
Tod Well
AB54
Burnervie
52

Knabbygates Bridge
Clovenstone
Well Heads
Kettle Pool
Little Brown Hill

Rowan Bauds
Craig Moss Wood
Conjure Cairn
Mid Knauchland
Old Crombie
2

Shielparks
Knauchland
Easter Knauchland
Mossford
Pettries Well
Standing Stone

Barnhill
Ardmeallie House
Marnoch
1

Scraib Wood
Moss-side
Relashes
Retanach
Cairns Wood
Retanach Wood
Catstone Hill
Sunnyside
B9117
50

54 A 55 B 56 C 57 D 58 E 59 F

B9022
B9023
Burn of Corncairn
Knock Burn
Rams Burn
Burn of Relashes
Crombie Burn

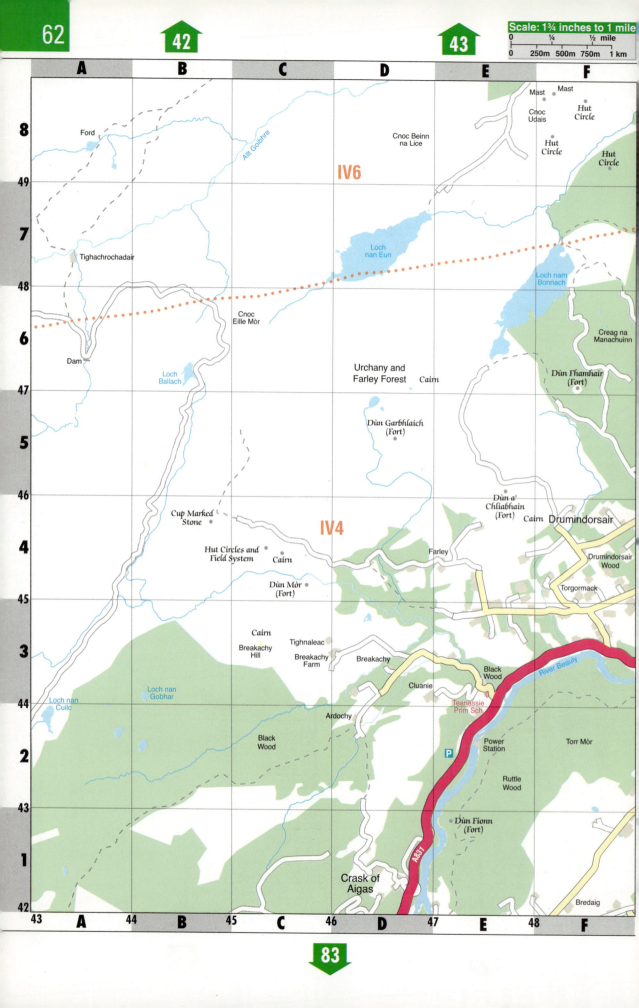

A   B   C   D   E   F

8

49

7

48

6

47

5

46

4

45

3

44

2

43

1

42

Ford

Allt Goibhre

IV6

Cnoc Beinn
na Lice

Mast   Mast
Cnoc
Udais
Hut
Circle
Hut
Circle
Hut
Circle

Tighachrochadair

Loch
nan Eun

Loch nam
Bonnach

Dam

Cnoc
Eille Mòr

Loch
Ballach

Urchany and
Farley Forest   Cairn

Creag na
Manachuinn

Dùn Fhamhair
(Fort)

Dùn Garbhlaich
(Fort)

Cup Marked
Stone

IV4

Dùn a'
Chliabhain
(Fort)   Cairn   Drumindorsair

Hut Circles and
Field System   Cairn

Farley

Drumindorsair
Wood

Dùn Mòr
(Fort)

Torgormack

Cairn
Breakachy
Hill

Tighnaleac

Breakachy
Farm   Breakachy

Black
Wood

River Beauly

Loch nan
Cuilc

Loch nan
Gobhar

Cluanie

Teanassie
Prim Sch

Black
Wood

Ardochy

P

Power
Station

Torr Mòr

Ruttle
Wood

A831

Dùn Fionn
(Fort)

Crask of
Aigas

Bredaig

43   A   44   B   45   C   46   D   47   E   48   F

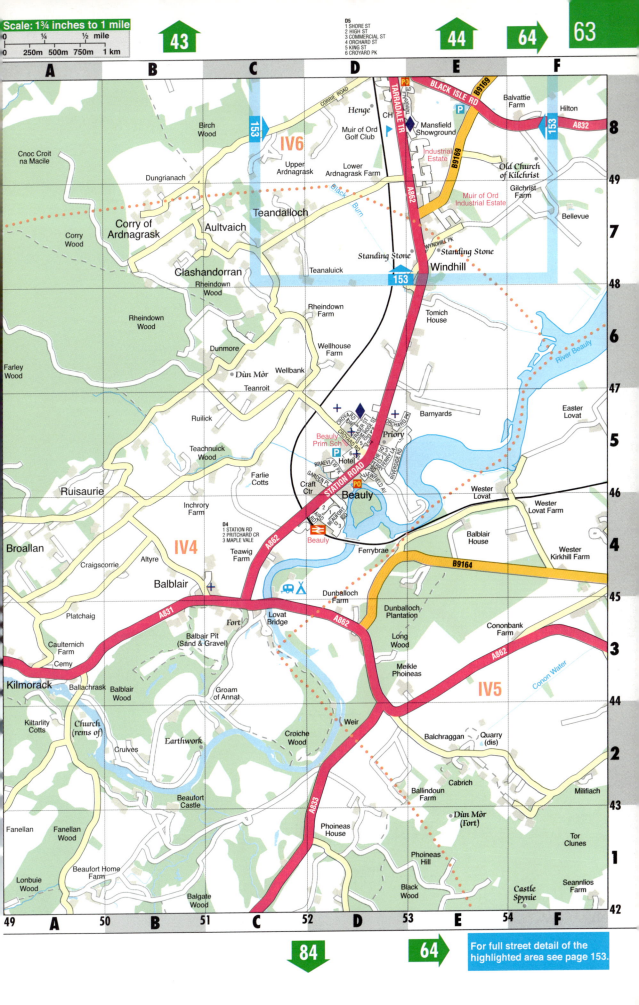

Scale: 1¾ inches to 1 mile

0   ¼   ½ mile
0   250m 500m 750m 1 km

St Mary's Church

Kilmuir

8

49

163

Moray Firth

7

48

6

47

IV1

Caledonian Stadium
(Inverness Caledonian
Thistle FC)

A9

LONGMAN RD

SEAFIELD RD
SEAFIELD RD
HARBOUR RD
HARBOUR ROAD

46

Seafield

MILLBURN RD

LC B865

A96

5

Hotel

Barracks

Millburn
Acad

VICTORIA

OLD PERTH RD

Sch

Raigmore

IV2

Hotel

Inverness Business
Park

4

CASTLE WY

Ashton

Coll

CROWN DR
UNION RD

Beechwood

Beechwood
Farm

45

PO Sch

Crown

KINGSMILLS RD
LEYS DR

B9006

Raigmore
H

Cradlehall

B8082

CULCABOCK RD OLD PERTH RD

CH

Inshes

Castlehill

3

ANNFIELD RD

B853

Inverness Golf Club

Police HQ

PO

Cradlehall Business
Park

B9006 CULLODEN ROAD

Hilton

CULDUTHEL RD

Sch

Culcabock

HARRIS RD

DRUMMOND

SIR WALTER SCOTT DR

Mill Burn

Easterfield

165

Easter
Muckovie

Lower
Muckovie

PO

MACKAY RD
CAULDEEN RD
OLDTOWN RD
KINTAIL RD

Sch

TEAL AV

MASON RD

STEVENSON RD

Balvonie
of Inshes

Upper
Muckovie

2

B8082

CH

Castle Heather

OLD EDINBURGH ROAD SOUTH

Parks

Balvonie
Wood

B9177

Drumossie
Hotel

Dam

Easter
Bogbain

Balvraid

43

Fairways
L Ctr

Druid Temple
Farm

Chambered
Cairn

A9

Drumossie Muir

Daviot
Wood

1

42

67   68   69   70   71   72

A   B   C   D   E   F

For full street detail of the highlighted area see pages 163 and 165.

65

165

87

E5
1 BIRCH PL
2 LARCH PL
3 ALDER PL
4 ASPEN PL
5 CULLODEN PK
6 MACGILLIVARY CT
7 MACDONALD CT
8 FRASER CT
9 MACLEAN CT
10 STEWART CT
11 ALLTAN PL
12 CULLODEN CN
13 FERNTOWER CT

F5
1 MORAYPARK LA
2 MORAY PARK PL
3 MORAY PARK CR
4 MORAY PARK WYND
5 OAKDENE CT
6 BLACKWELL AV
7 BLACKWELL RD
8 BLACKWELL CT
9 FERNTOWER PL
10 DOVECOTE PK

D3
1 CRADLEHALL GD
2 CAULFIELD TR
3 CAULFIELD PL
4 CAULFIELD GD
5 CAULFIELD PK
6 ORCHARD PK
7 INSHES CT

Alturlie
Point

Sand &
Gravel
Pit

Bothyhill

Gravel Pit

Redhill

Brecknish

LC

Lower
Cullernie

Blackhill

Chambered Cairn
(rems of)

A96

Ring Carn

LC

Sewage
Works

Balloch
Prim Sch

Allanfearn

LC

CAULFIELD ROAD

Milton

Culloden Acad

HAZEL AVE
KEPPOCH RD

Culloden

Duncan Forbes
Prim Sch

Hotel

MORAY PK
MORAY PK TR

GALLOWAY RD
CAULFIELD WALKER CR

Liby
PO

Cairnlaw Burn

Stratton

Ind Est

FERNTOWER RD

REDBURN AV

Smithton

Resaurie

GRAMMORE

CAULFIELD RD
MURRAY RD

PO

Culloden Wood

St Mary's Well

P

Smithton Prim Sch

Cradlehall

TOWERHILL AV

TOWER BRAE

BURN BRAE AV
BURN BRAE CR

Westhill

Blackpark

Woodside

Cradlehall Prim Sch

CRADLEHALL RD
INSHES RD

CAULFIELD RD
CHALK

CULLODEN ROAD

BRINKMAN

Easter
Mucklovie
Farm

BIRCHWOOD TR

Easter
Mucklovie

WOODLANDS LA

TOWER CT

JARBRIDGE VW

E3
1 TOWERHILL CR
2 TOWERHILL PL
3 TRENTHAM CT
4 TRENTHAM DR
5 TOWER CT
6 TOWER GD
7 LEANACH GD
8 LEANACH CT
9 BURN BRAE PL

10 MYRTLEFIELD LA
11 VIEWMOUNT BRAE

E4
1 SINCLAIR PK
2 SMITHTON VILLAS
3 MURRAY PL
4 FORBES PL
5 LOCH LANN TR
6 LOCH LANN CR
7 LOCH LANN AV
8 LOCH LANN CT
9 CAMERON CT

1 BIRCHWOOD PL
2 BIRCHWOOD BRAE
3 MURRAY PL
4 WOODLANDS PL
5 WOODLANDS TR
6 WOODLANDS RD

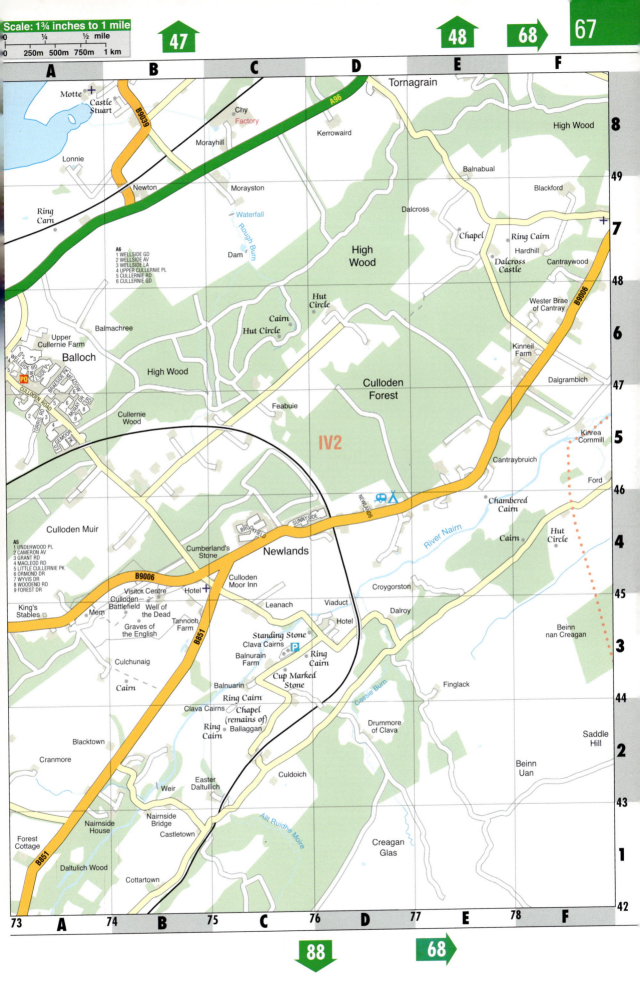

A B C D E F

Tornagrain

Motte
Castle Stuart
B9039
Lonnie
Newton
Morayhill
Morayston
Chy
Factory
Kerrowaird
A96
High Wood
Balnabual
Blackford
49
Ring Carn
Waterfall
Rough Burn
Dam
High Wood
Dalcross
Chapel
Ring Cairn
Hardhill
Dalcross Castle
Cantraywood
7
A6
1 WELLSIDE GD
2 WELLSIDE AV
3 WELLSIDE LA
4 UPPER CULLERNIE PL
5 CULLERNIE RD
6 CULLERNIE GD
Wester Brae of Cantray
B9006
48
Balmachree
Cairn
Hut Circle
Hut Circle
Kinneil Farm
Dalgrambich
6
Upper Cullernie Farm
Balloch
PO
High Wood
Culloden Forest
47
Cullernie Wood
Feabuie
IV2
Cantraybruich
Kinrea Cornmill
5
Chambered Cairn
Ford
46
NEWLANDS
River Nairn
Cairn
Hut Circle
Culloden Muir
A5
1 UNDERWOOD PL
2 CAMERON AV
3 GRANT RD
4 MACLEOD RD
5 LITTLE CULLERNIE PK
6 ORMOND DR
7 WYVIS DR
8 WOODEND RD
9 FOREST DR
BROCKFIELD
SUNNYSIDE
Newlands
Croygorston
4
Cumberland's Stone
Culloden Moor Inn
Leanach
Viaduct
Hotel
Dalroy
Beinn nan Creagan
45
B9006
Hotel
King's Stables
Visitor Centre
Culloden Battlefield
Well of the Dead
Mem
Graves of the English
Tannoch Farm
Standing Stone
Clava Cairns
Balnurain Farm
Ring Cairn
Cup Marked Stone
Finglack
3
B851
Culchunaig
Cairn
Balnuarin
Ring Cairn
Clava Cairns
Ring Cairn
Chapel (remains of)
Ballaggan
Drummore of Clava
Cassie Burn
Saddle Hill
44
Blacktown
Cranmore
Weir
Easter Daltullich
Culdoich
Beinn Uan
2
43
Nairnside House
Nairnside Bridge
Castletown
Allt Ruidhe Moire
Creagan Glas
1
Forest Cottage
B851
Daltulich Wood
Cottartown
42

73 A 74 B 75 C 76 D 77 E 78 F

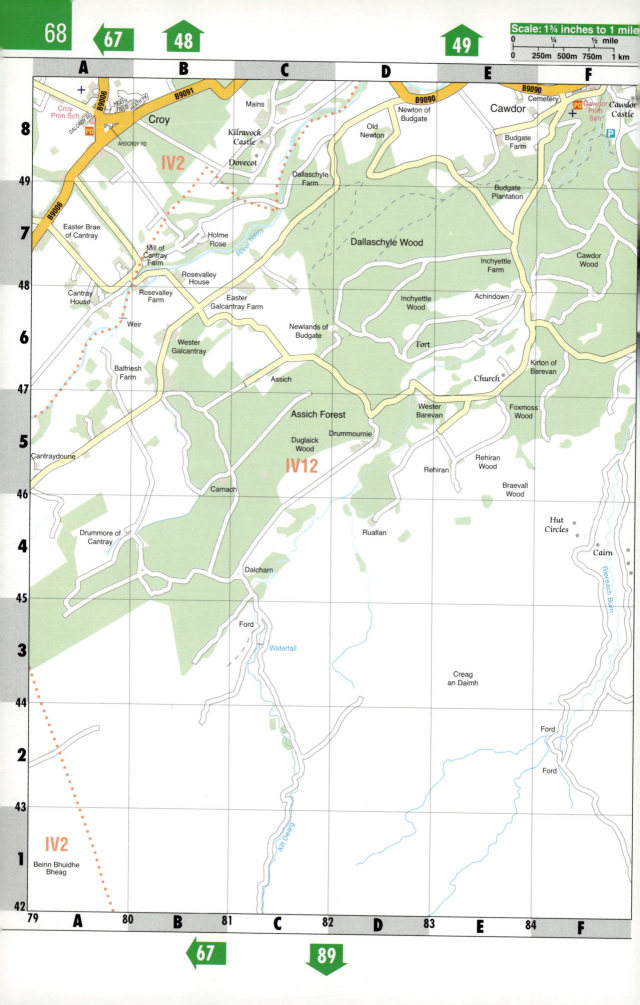

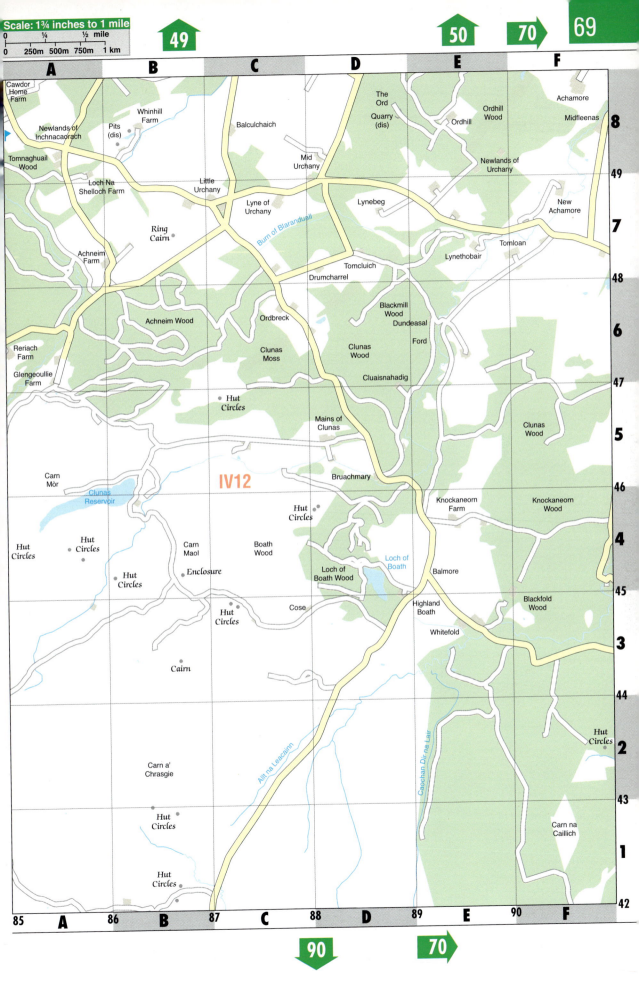

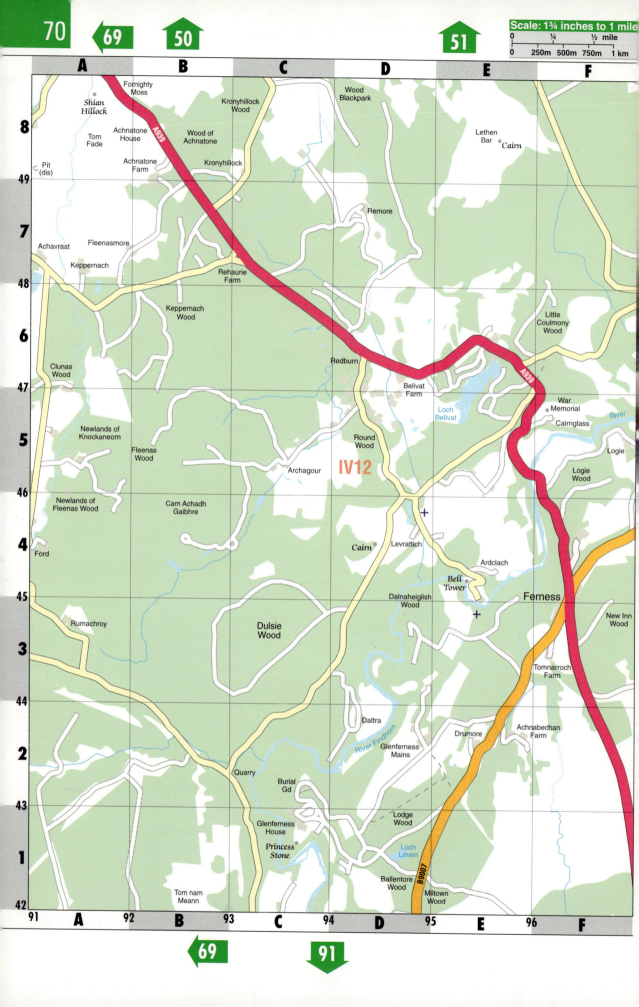

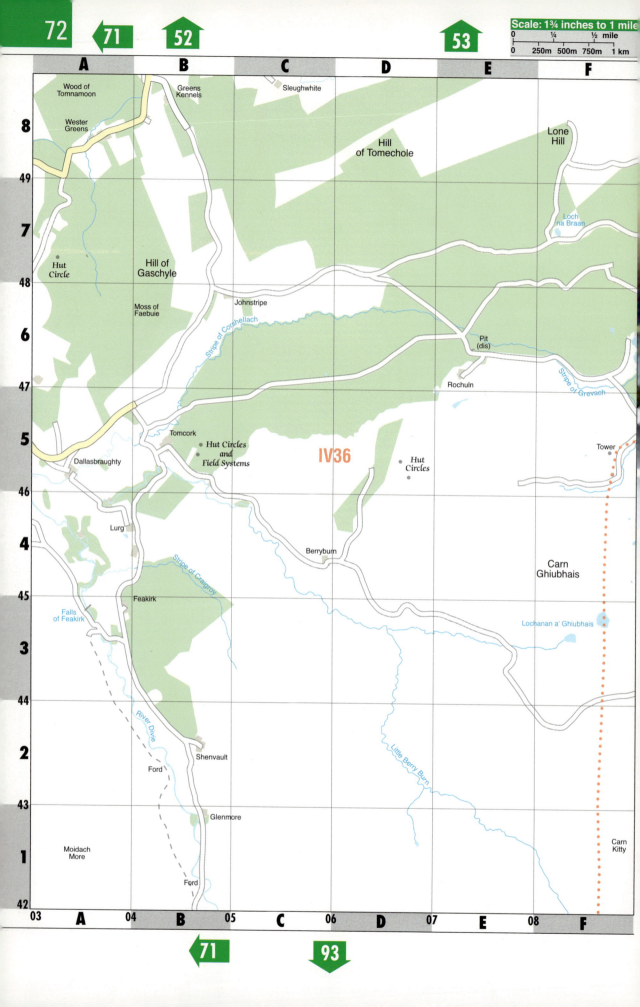

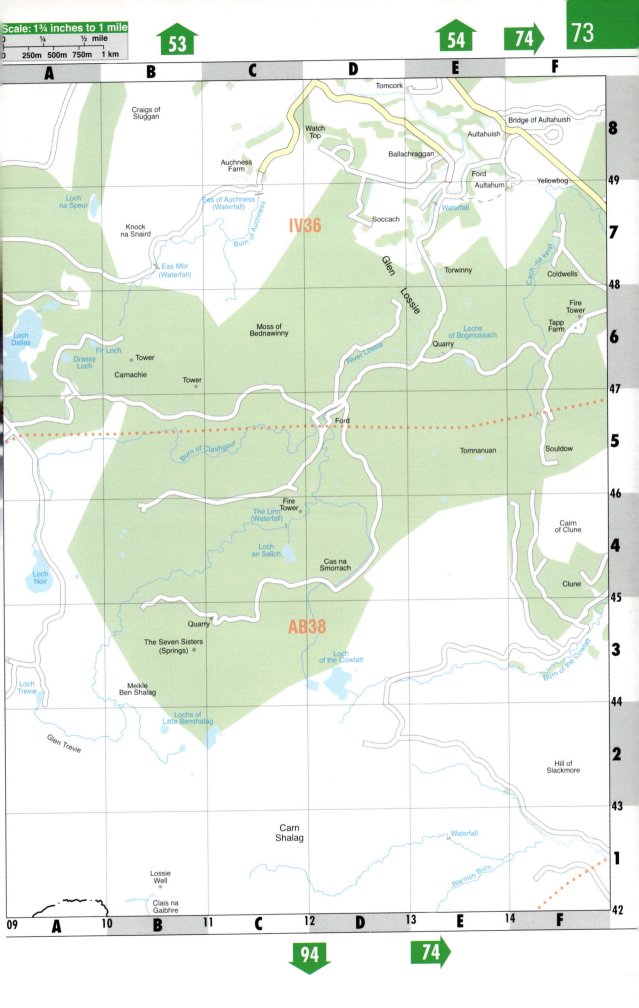

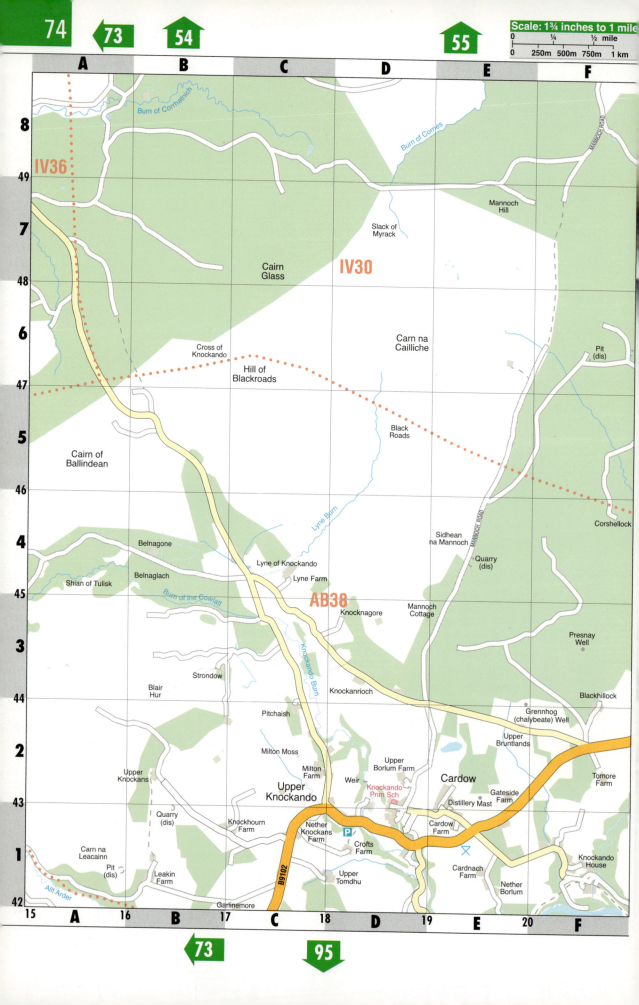

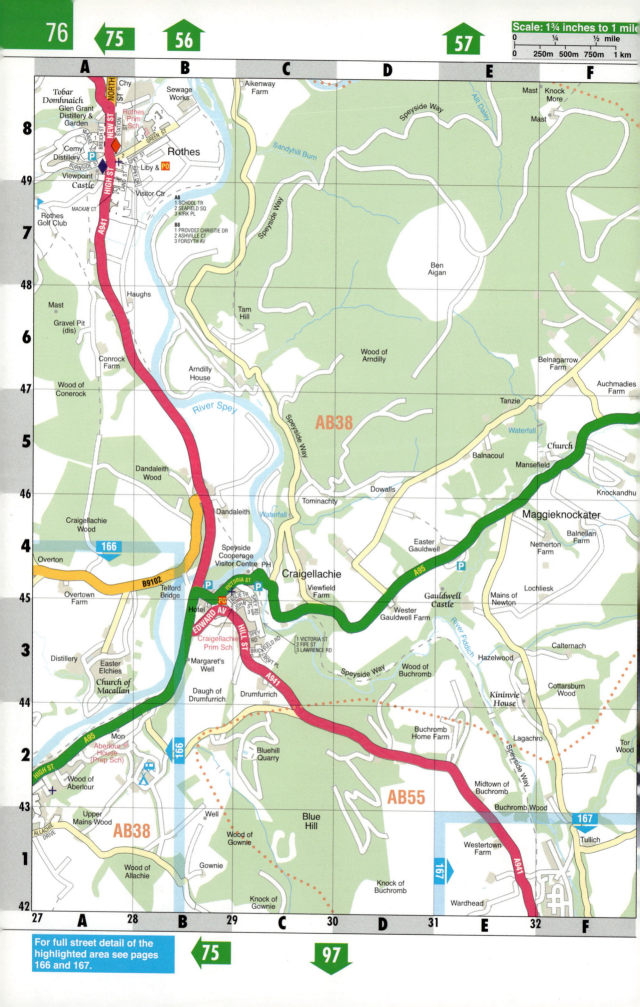

Scale: 1¾ inches to 1 mile

0   ¼   ½ mile
0   250m   500m   750m   1 km

Tobar Domhnaich
Glen Grant Distillery & Garden
Rothes Prim Sch
Sewage Works
Chy
NEW ST
STATION
BREICH ST
GREEN ST
Rothes
Cemy Distillery
Viewpoint Castle
BURNSIDE ST
HIGH ST
A941
Liby & PO
Visitor Ctr

A8
1 SCHOOL TR
2 SEAFIELD SQ
3 KIRK PL

B8
1 PROVOST CHRISTIE DR
2 ASHVILLE CT
3 FORSYTH AV

MACKAY CT
Rothes Golf Club

Aikenway Farm
Speyside Way
Allt Daley
Mast
Knock More
Mast
Mast

Sandyhill Burn

Haughs

Mast
Gravel Pit (dis)
Conrock Farm

Speyside Way

Tam Hill
Ben Aigan

Wood of Conerock

River Spey

Wood of Arndilly

Arndilly House

AB38

Belnagarrow Farm
Auchmadies Farm

Tanzie

Waterfall
Church
Mansefield
Knockandhu

Dandaleith Wood

Balnacoul

Craigellachie Wood

Dowalls

Maggieknockater

166
B9102
Overton

Dandaleith

Tominachty

Waterfall

Speyside Way

Easter Gauldwell
P

Netherton Farm
Balnellan Farm

Overtown Farm
Overton
Telford Bridge

Speyside Cooperage Visitor Centre
P
PH
VICTORIA ST
P

Craigellachie
Viewfield Farm

Gauldwell Castle
Wester Gauldwell Farm

A95

Mains of Newton
Lochliesk

Distillery
Easter Elchies
Church of Macallan

Hotel
EDWARD AV
PO
Craigellachie Prim Sch
Margaret's Well

HILL ST

LESLIE TR
SPEY RD
1
2
3

1 VICTORIA ST
2 FIFE ST
3 LAWRENCE RD

Speyside Way

River Fiddich

Hazelwood

Calternach

Cottarsburn Wood

A95
HIGH ST
Mon
Aberlour House (Prep Sch)

166

Daugh of Drumfurrich
Drumfurrich

A941

Wood of Buchromb

Kininvie House

Wood of Aberlour

Bluehill Quarry

Buchromb Home Farm

Lagachro

Midtown of Buchromb

Tor Wood

Speyside Way

Upper Mains Wood
ALLACHIE DRIVE

AB38

Well

Blue Hill

AB55

Buchromb Wood

167

Tullich

Wood of Gownie

Westertown Farm

167

A941

Wardhead

Wood of Allachie

Gownie

Knock of Gownie

Knock of Buchromb

For full street detail of the highlighted area see pages 166 and 167.

75   97

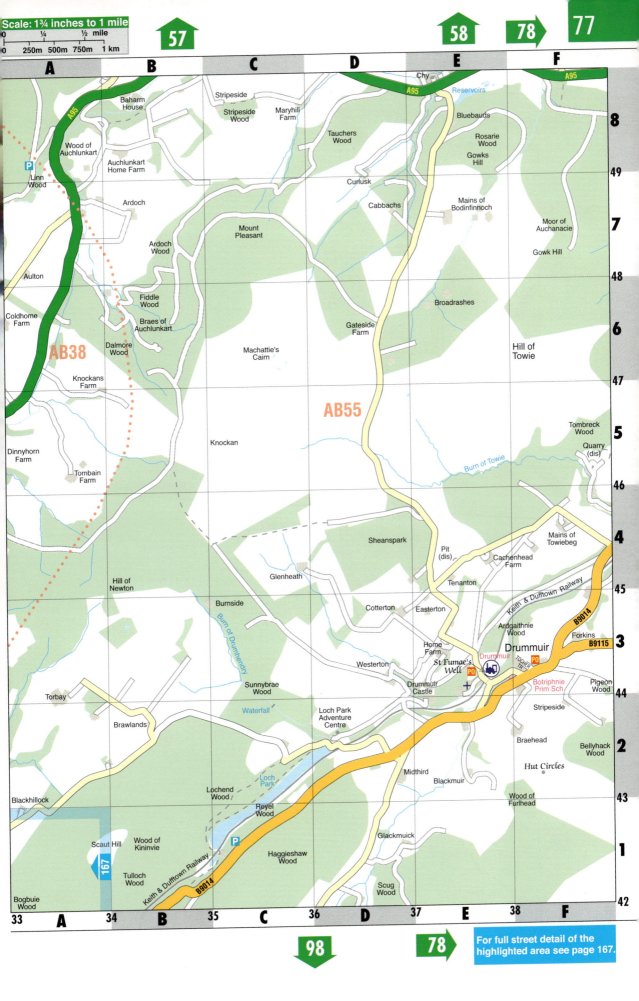

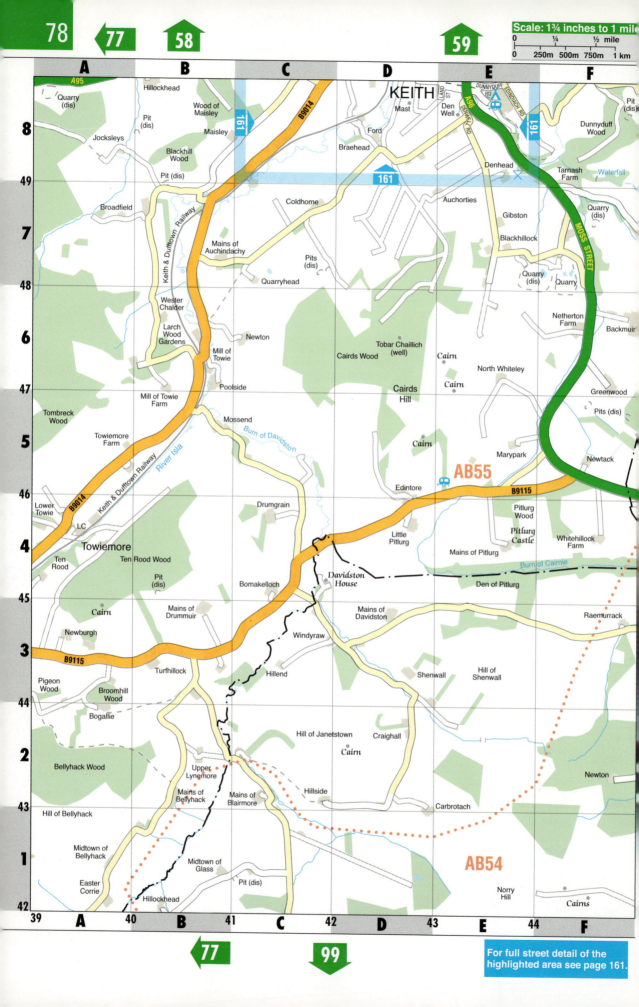

A B C D E F

8

49

7

48

6

47

5

46

4

45

3

44

2

43

1

42

39 A 40 B 41 C 42 D 43 E 44 F

A95

Quarry (dis)

Hillockhead

Wood of Maisley

Maisley

161

B9014

KEITH

Mast

LAND ST

Den Well

DUNNYDUFF RD

EDINDACH RD

161

Dunnyduff Wood

Quarry (dis)

Jocksleys

Pit (dis)

Blackhill Wood

Ford

Braehead

A96

DENWELL RD

Denhead

MOSS STREET

Tarnash Farm

Waterfall

Pit (dis)

Coldhome

161

Auchorties

Gibston

Quarry (dis)

Broadfield

Keith & Dufftown Railway

Mains of Auchindachy

Blackhillock

Quarry (dis)

Quarry

Netherton Farm

Backmuir

Pits (dis)

Wester Chalder

Quarryhead

Pits (dis)

Cairds Wood

Tobar Chaillich (well)

Cairn

North Whiteley

Cairn

Greenwood

Pits (dis)

Larch Wood Gardens

Newton

Mill of Towie

Cairds Hill

Cairn

Poolside

Mill of Towie Farm

Mossend

Burn of Davidston

Cairn

Marypark

Newtack

Tombreck Wood

Towiemore Farm

River Isla

Keith & Dufftown Railway

AB55

Edintore

B9115

Pitlurg Wood

Pitlurg Castle

Whitehillock Farm

Drumgrain

Little Pitlurg

Mains of Pitlurg

Lower Towie

B9014

LC

Ten Rood

Towiemore

Ten Rood Wood

Pit (dis)

Bomakelloch

Davidston House

Den of Pitlurg

Burn of Cairnie

Raemurrack

Cairn

Mains of Drummuir

Mains of Davidston

Newburgh

Windyraw

Shenwall

Hill of Shenwall

B9115

Turfhillock

Hillend

Pigeon Wood

Broomhill Wood

Bogallie

Hill of Janetstown

Craighall

Cairn

Newton

Bellyhack Wood

Upper Lynemore

Hillside

Carbrotach

Mains of Bellyhack

Mains of Blairmore

AB54

Hill of Bellyhack

Midtown of Bellyhack

Midtown of Glass

Pit (dis)

Norry Hill

Easter Corrie

Hillockhead

Cairns

For full street detail of the highlighted area see page 161.

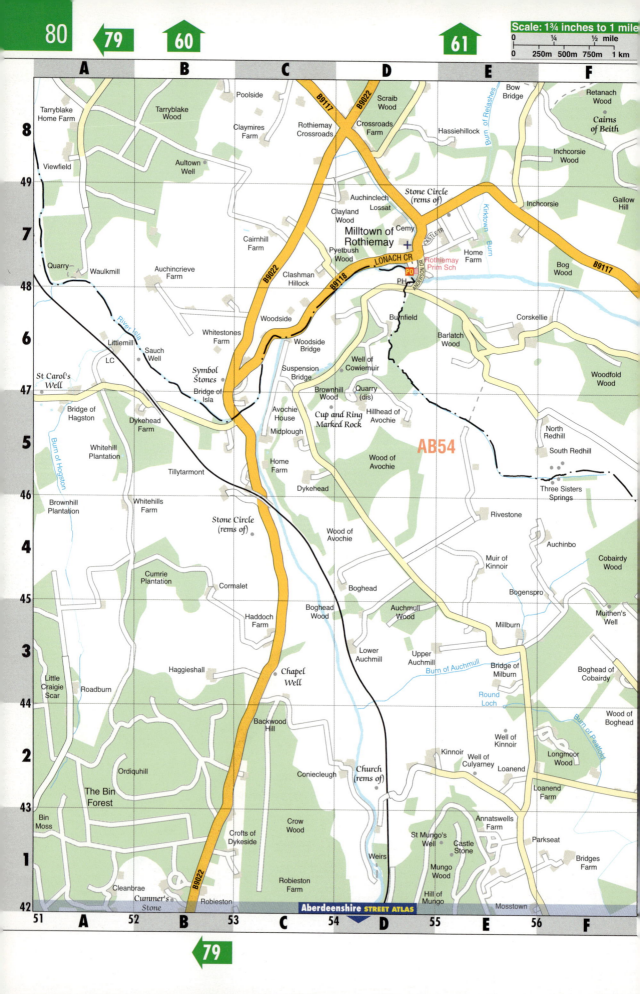

A   B   C   D   E   F

8
Tarryblake Home Farm
Tarryblake Wood
Poolside
Claymires Farm
Rothiemay Crossroads
Scraib Wood
Crossroads Farm
Hassiehillock
Bow Bridge
Retanach Wood
Cairns of Beith
Inchcorsie Wood

49
Viewfield
Aultown Well
Auchinclech
Lossat
Clayland Wood
Stone Circle (rems of)
Inchcorsie
Gallow Hill

7
Quarry
Waulkmill
Auchincrieve Farm
Cairnhill Farm
Pyetbush Wood
Milltown of Rothiemay
Cemy
LONACH CR
PO
Rothiemay Prim Sch
Home Farm
Bog Wood
B9117

48
Clashman Hillock
B9022
B9118
PH
Burnfield
Corskellie

6
Littlemill
LC
Sauch Well
Whitestones Farm
Woodside
Woodside Bridge
Well of Cowiemuir
Barlatch Wood
Woodfold Wood

47
St Carol's Well
Bridge of Hagston
Symbol Stones
Bridge of Isla
Suspension Bridge
Brownhill Wood
Quarry (dis)
Cup and Ring Marked Rock
Hillhead of Avochie

5
Whitehill Plantation
Dykehead Farm
Avochie House
Midplough
Wood of Avochie
AB54
North Redhill
South Redhill
Three Sisters Springs

46
Brownhill Plantation
Whitehills Farm
Tillytarmont
Home Farm
Dykehead
Wood of Avochie
Rivestone

4
Cumrie Plantation
Cormalet
Stone Circle (rems of)
Boghead
Muir of Kinnoir
Auchinbo
Cobairdy Wood

45
Haddoch Farm
Boghead Wood
Auchmull Wood
Millburn
Bogenspro
Muithen's Well

3
Haggieshall
Roadburn
Lower Auchmill
Upper Auchmill
Burn of Auchmull
Bridge of Milburn
Boghead of Cobairdy

44
Little Craigie Scar
Chapel Well
Round Loch
Wood of Boghead

2
The Bin Forest
Ordiquhill
Backwood Hill
Coniecleugh
Church (rems of)
Kinnoir
Well of Kinnoir
Well of Culyarney
Loanend
Longmoor Wood
Loanend Farm

1
Bin Moss
Crofts of Dykeside
Crow Wood
Weirs
St Mungo's Well
Castle Stone
Mungo Wood
Annatswells Farm
Parkseat
Bridges Farm

42
Cleanbrae
Cummer's Stone
B9022
Robieston
Robieston Farm
Hill of Mungo
Mosstown

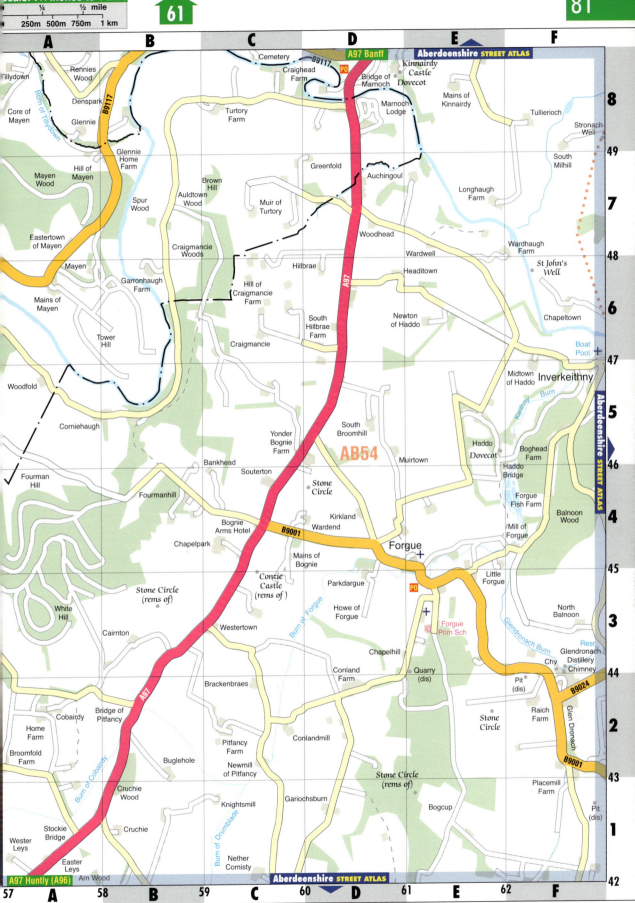

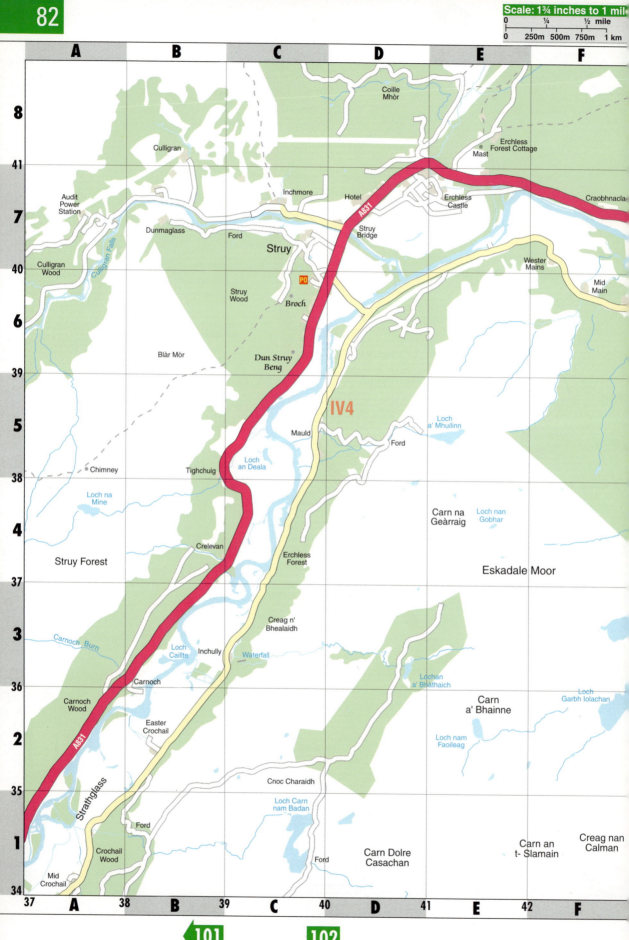

Scale: 1¾ inches to 1 mile

0   ¼   ½   mile
0   250m   500m   750m   1 km

Columns: A B C D E F

Rows (left): 8 41 7 40 6 39 5 38 4 37 3 36 2 35 1 34

Bottom grid: 37 A 38 B 39 C 40 D 41 E 42 F

Coille Mhòr

Erchless Forest Cottage
Mast

Culligran

Inchmore

Hotel

A831

Erchless Castle

Craobhnacla

Audit Power Station

Dunmaglass

Ford

Struy Bridge

Struy

Culligran Falls

Culligran Wood

Wester Mains

Mid Main

Struy Wood

PO

Broch

Blàr Mòr

Dun Struy Beng

IV4

Loch a' Mhuilinn

Mauld

Ford

Loch an Deala

Chimney

Tighchuig

Loch na Mine

Carn na Geàrraig

Loch nan Gobhar

Eskadale Moor

Struy Forest

Crelevan

Erchless Forest

Creag n' Bhealaidh

Carnoch Burn

Loch Caillte

Inchully

Waterfall

Lochan a' Bhàthaich

Carn a' Bhainne

Loch Garbh Iolachan

Carnoch

Carnoch Wood

Easter Crochail

Loch nam Faoileag

A831

Strathglass

Cnoc Charaidh

Ford

Loch Carn nam Badan

Carn Dolre Casachan

Ford

Carn an t- Slamain

Creag nan Calman

Mid Crochail

Crochail Wood

101   102

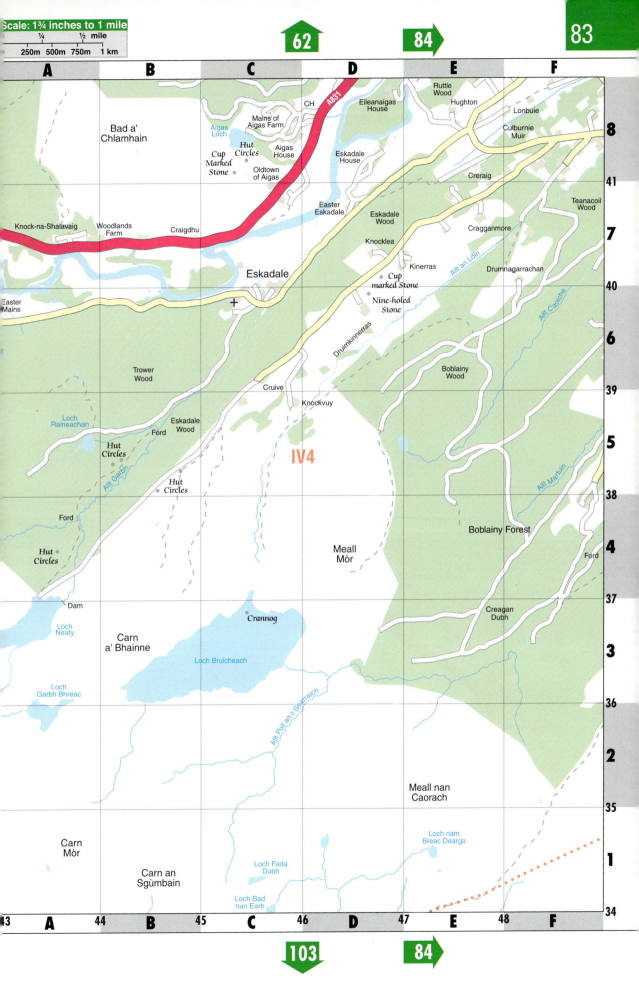

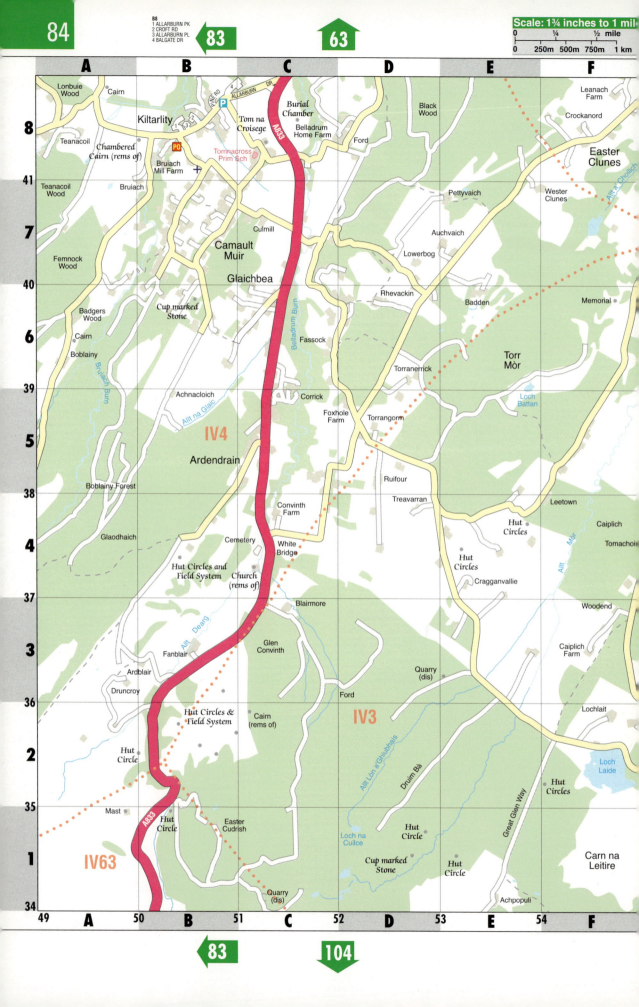

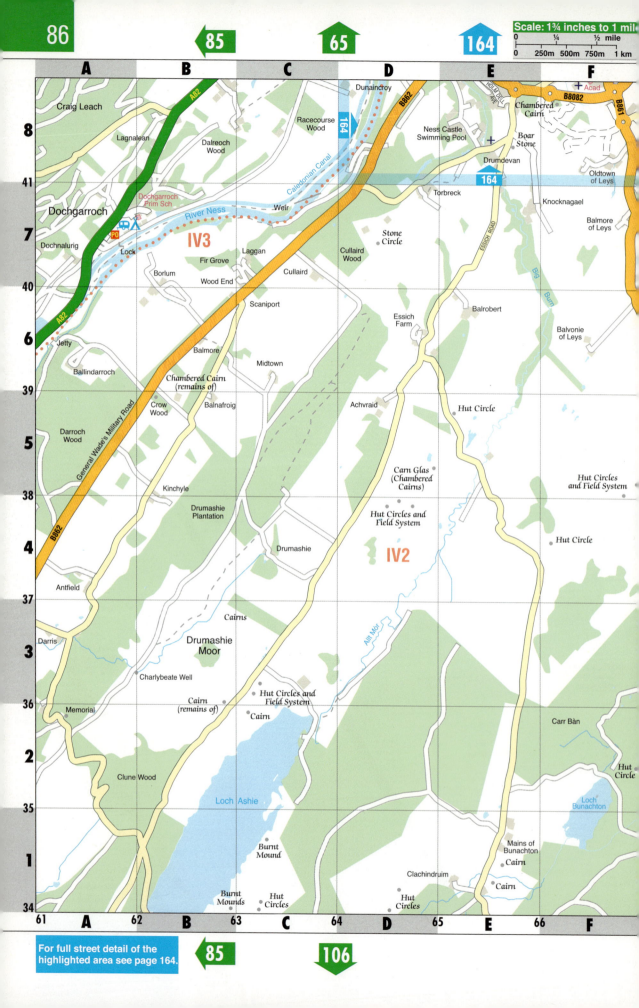

Scale: 1¾ inches to 1 mile

Craig Leach

Lagnalean

Dochgarroch
Prim Sch

Dochgarroch

Dochnalurig

Lock

Jetty

Ballindarroch

Darroch
Wood

Antfield

Darris

Memorial

Clune Wood

A82

Dalreoch
Wood

River Ness

IV3

Borlum

Fir Grove

Wood End

Balmore

Chambered Cairn
(remains of)

Crow
Wood

Balnafroig

Kinchyle

Drumashie
Plantation

Drumashie

Cairns

Drumashie
Moor

Charlybeate Well

Cairn
(remains of)

Cairn

Loch Ashie

General Wade's Military Road

B862

Dunaincroy

Racecourse
Wood

Caledonian Canal

Weir

Laggan

Cullaird

Scaniport

Midtown

Stone
Circle

Cullaird
Wood

Essich
Farm

Achvraid

Carn Glas
(Chambered
Cairns)

Hut Circles and
Field System

IV2

Allt Mòr

Hut Circles and
Field System

Cairn

Burnt
Mound

Burnt
Mounds

Hut
Circles

B862

Ness Castle
Swimming Pool

Torbreck

Drumdevan

Balrobert

Hut Circle

ESSICH ROAD

Big Burn

Chambered
Cairn

Boar
Stone

Oldtown
of Leys

Knocknagael

Balmore
of Leys

Balvonie
of Leys

Hut Circle

Hut Circles
and Field System

Hut Circle

Carr Bàn

Hut
Circle

Loch
Bunachton

Mains of
Bunachton

Cairn

Clachindruim

Cairn

Hut
Circles

B8082

Acad

B861

164

164

85
65
164
85
106
For full street detail of the highlighted area see page 164.

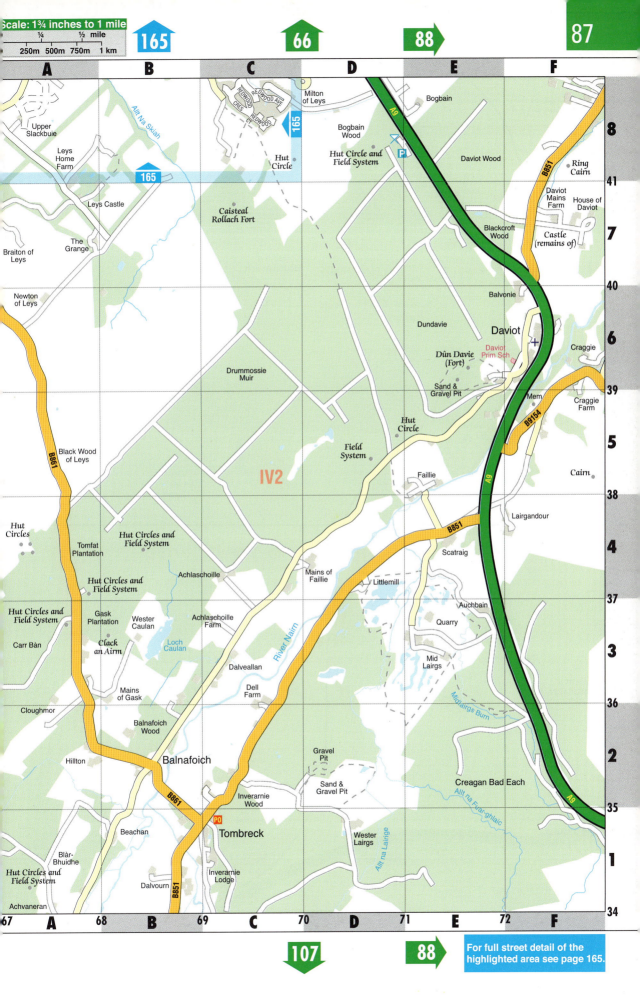

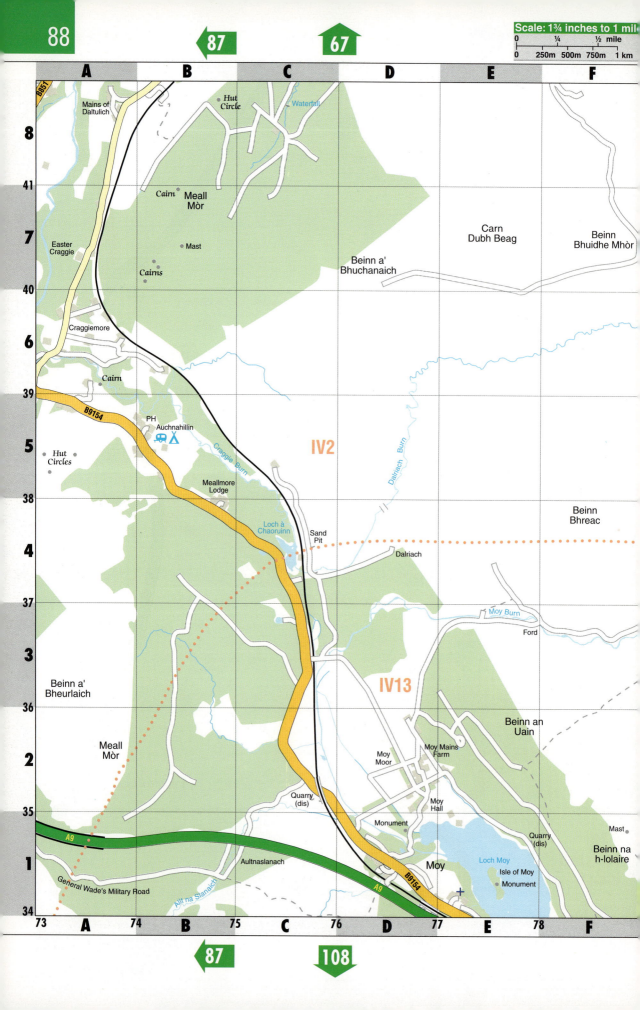

87
67

Scale: 1¾ inches to 1 mile

0   ¼   ½   mile
0   250m   500m   750m   1 km

B851

Mains of Daltulich

Hut Circle

Waterfall

Cairn

Meall Mòr

Easter Craggie

Mast

Carn Dubh Beag

Beinn Bhuidhe Mhòr

Cairns

Beinn a' Bhuchanaich

Craggiemore

Cairn

B9154

PH
Auchnahillin

Hut Circles

Craggie Burn

IV2

Dalriach Burn

Meallmore Lodge

Beinn Bhreac

Loch à Chaoruinn

Sand Pit

Dalriach

Moy Burn

Ford

Beinn a' Bheurlaich

Beinn an Uain

Meall Mòr

Moy Moor

Moy Mains Farm

IV13

Quarry (dis)

Moy Hall

Monument

Quarry (dis)

Mast

Beinn na h-Iolaire

A9

Loch Moy

Aultnaslanach

Moy

B9154

Isle of Moy Monument

General Wade's Military Road

Allt na Slanaich

A9

87
108

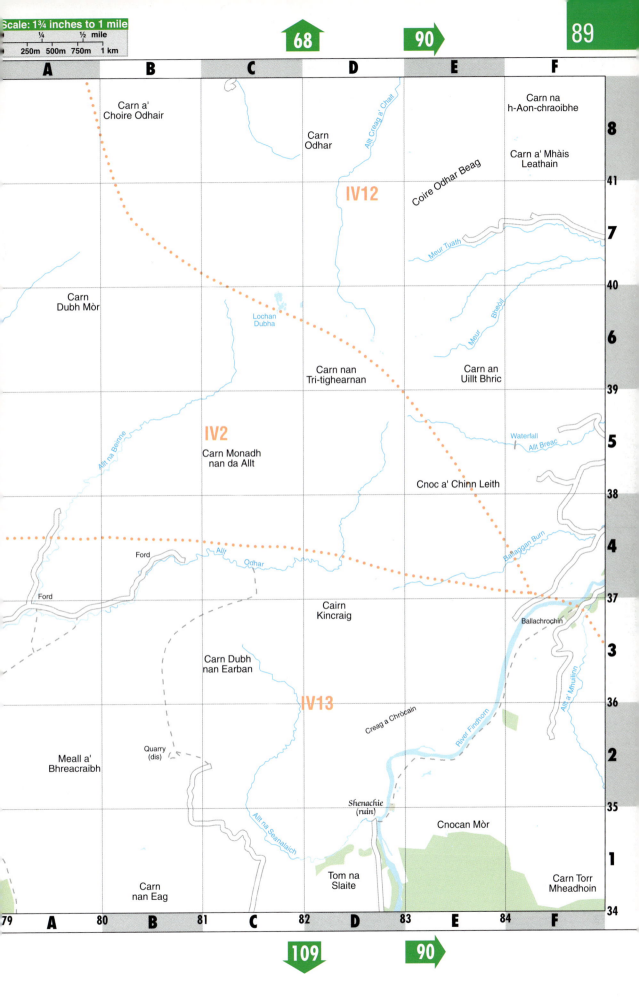

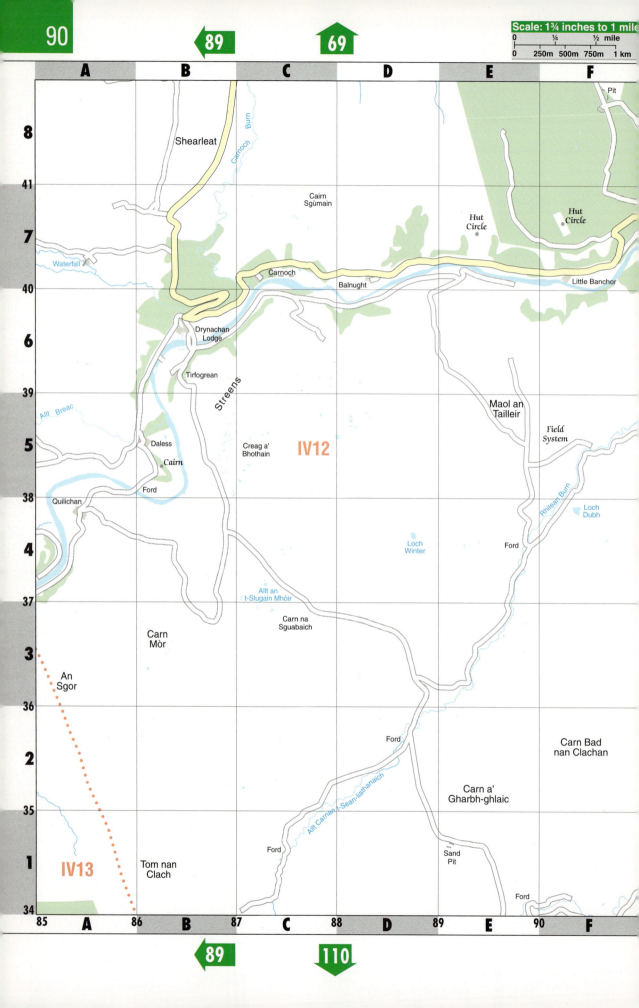

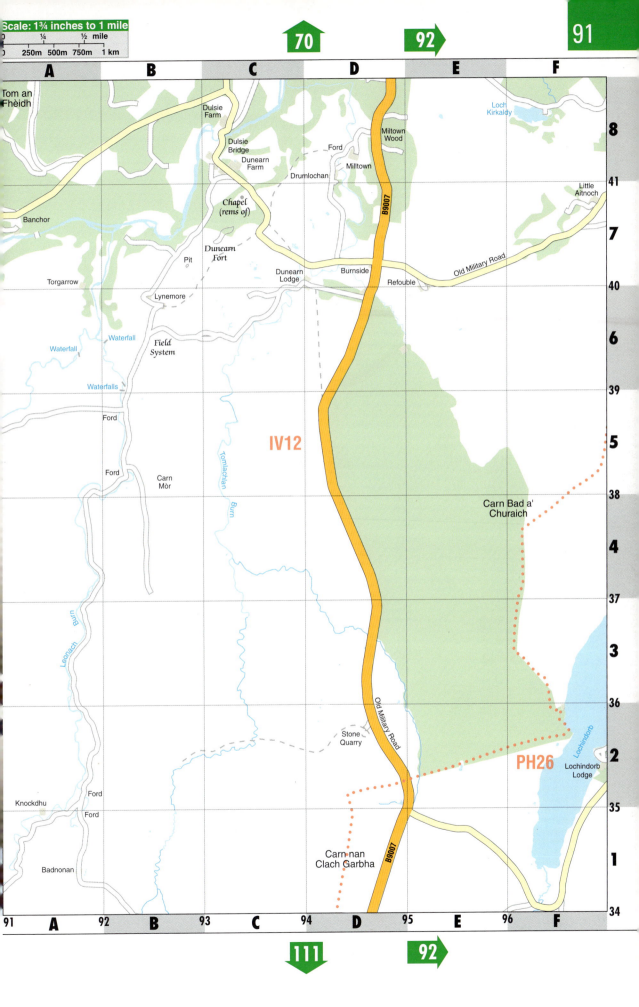

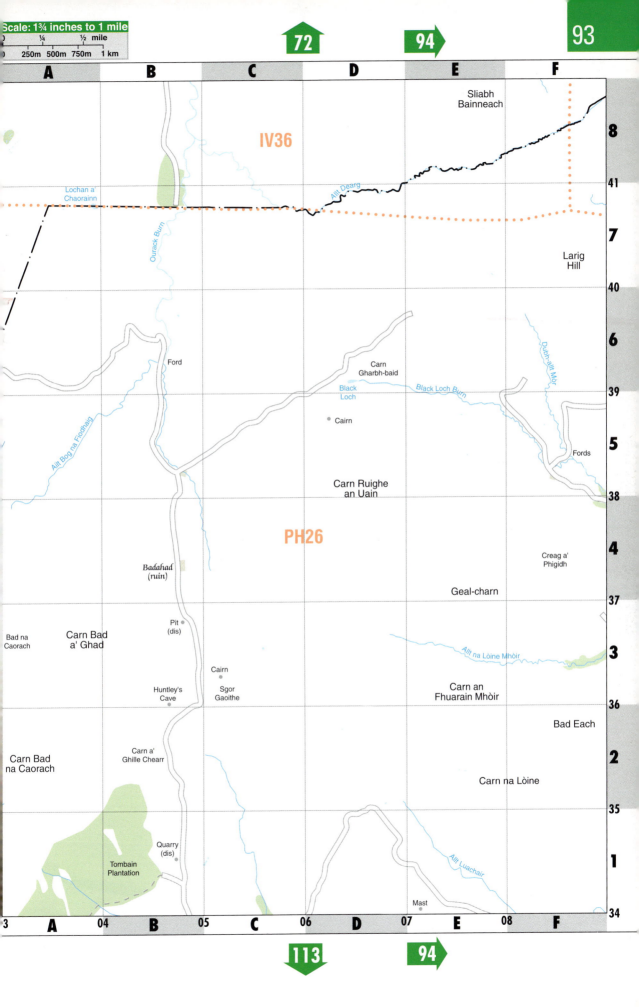

Scale: 1¾ inches to 1 mile

0   ¼   ½   mile

0   250m   500m   750m   1 km

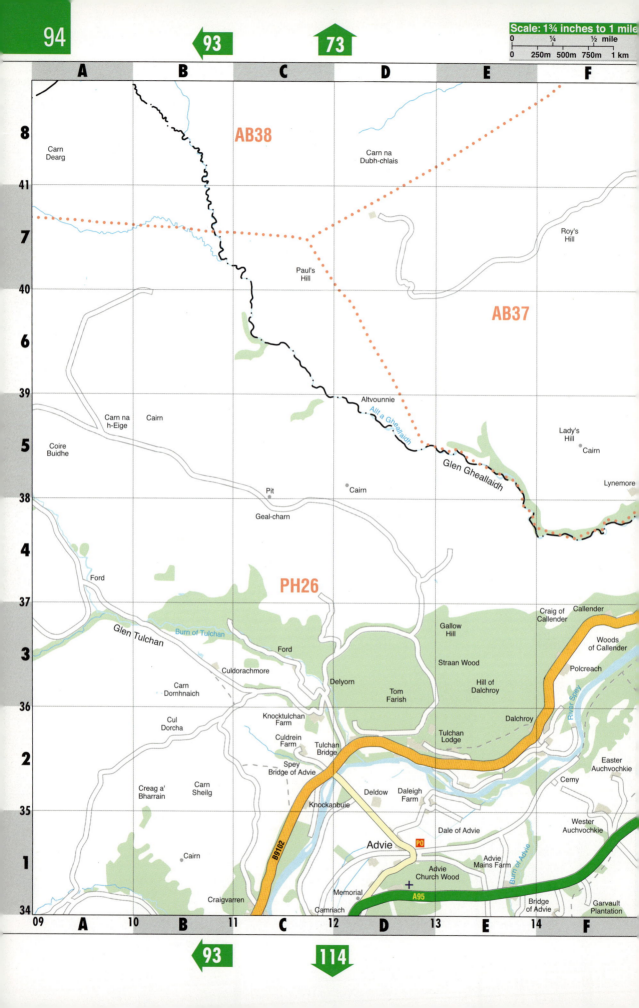

A   B   C   D   E   F

8

Carn Dearg

AB38

Carn na Dubh-chlais

41

7

Roy's Hill

Paul's Hill

40

AB37

6

39

Carn na h-Eige

Cairn

Altvounnie

Allt a Gheallaidh

5

Coire Buidhe

Lady's Hill

Cairn

Glen Gheallaidh

Lynemore

38

Pit

Cairn

Geal-charn

4

Ford

PH26

37

Glen Tulchan

Burn of Tulchan

Ford

Craig of Callender

Callender

Gallow Hill

Woods of Callender

3

Culdorachmore

Straan Wood

Polcreach

River Spey

Carn Dornhnaich

Delyorn

Tom Farish

Hill of Dalchroy

36

Cul Dorcha

Knocktulchan Farm

Dalchroy

2

Culdrein Farm

Tulchan Bridge

Tulchan Lodge

Easter Auchvochkie

Creag a' Bharrain

Carn Sheilg

Spey Bridge of Advie

Cemy

35

Knockanbuie

Deldow

Daleigh Farm

Dale of Advie

Wester Auchvochkie

B9102

Advie

PO

Advie Mains Farm

Burn of Advie

Cairn

Advie Church Wood

1

Craigvarren

Memorial

A95

Bridge of Advie

Garvault Plantation

Camriach

34

09   A   10   B   11   C   12   D   13   E   14   F

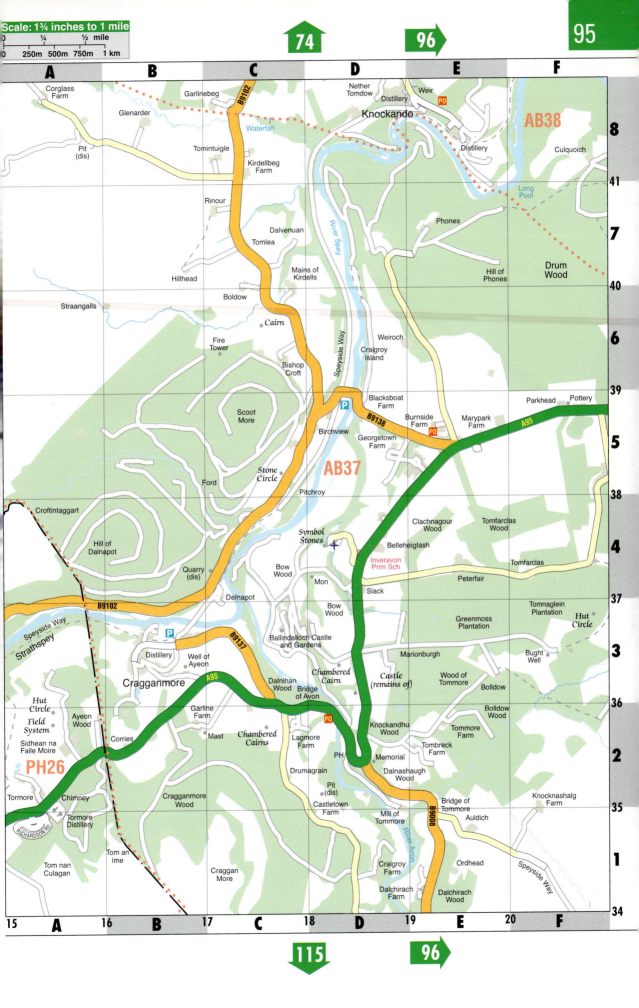

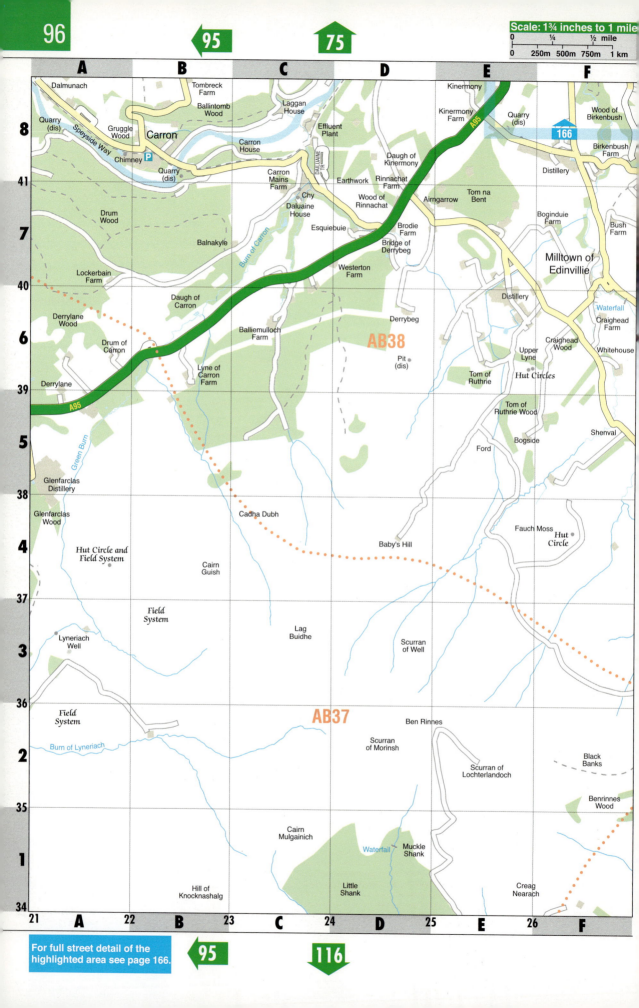

95

75

Scale: 1¾ inches to 1 mile

0   ¼   ½   mile
0 250m 500m 750m 1 km

A   B   C   D   E   F

Dalmunach
Tombreck Farm
Ballintomb Wood
Laggan House

Quarry (dis)
Speyside Way
Gruggle Wood
Carron
Carron House
Effluent Plant

Wood of Birkenbush
Kinermony
Kinermony Farm
Quarry (dis)

8

Chimney
P
Quarry (dis)
Carron Mains Farm
Daugh of Kinermony
Earthwork
Rinnachat Farm
A95
Distillery
Birkenbush Farm

41

Chy
Daluaine House
Wood of Rinnachat
Airngarrow
Tom na Bent

Drum Wood
Balnakyle
Burn of Carron
Esquiebuie
Brodie Farm
Boginduie Farm
Bush Farm

7

Lockerbain Farm
Westerton Farm
Bridge of Derrybeg
Milltown of Edinvillie

40

Derrylane Wood
Daugh of Carron
Balliemulloch Farm
Derrybeg
Distillery
Craighead Farm
Waterfall

6

Drum of Carron
Lyne of Carron Farm
AB38
Pit (dis)
Upper Lyne
Craighead Wood
Whitehouse

Derrylane
A95
Tom of Ruthrie
Hut Circles

39

Tom of Ruthrie Wood
Shenval

Green Burn
Bogside
Ford

5

Glenfarclas Distillery

38

Glenfarclas Wood
Cadha Dubh
Fauch Moss
Hut Circle

4

Hut Circle and Field System
Cairn Guish
Baby's Hill

37

Field System
Lag Buidhe
Scurran of Well

3

Lyneriach Well

36

Field System
AB37
Ben Rinnes

Burn of Lyneriach
Scurran of Morinsh
Black Banks

2

Scurran of Lochterlandoch
Benrinnes Wood

35

Cairn Mulgainich
Waterfall
Muckle Shank
Creag Nearach

1

Hill of Knocknashalg
Little Shank

34

21   A   22   B   23   C   24   D   25   E   26   F

166

For full street detail of the highlighted area see page 166.

95

116

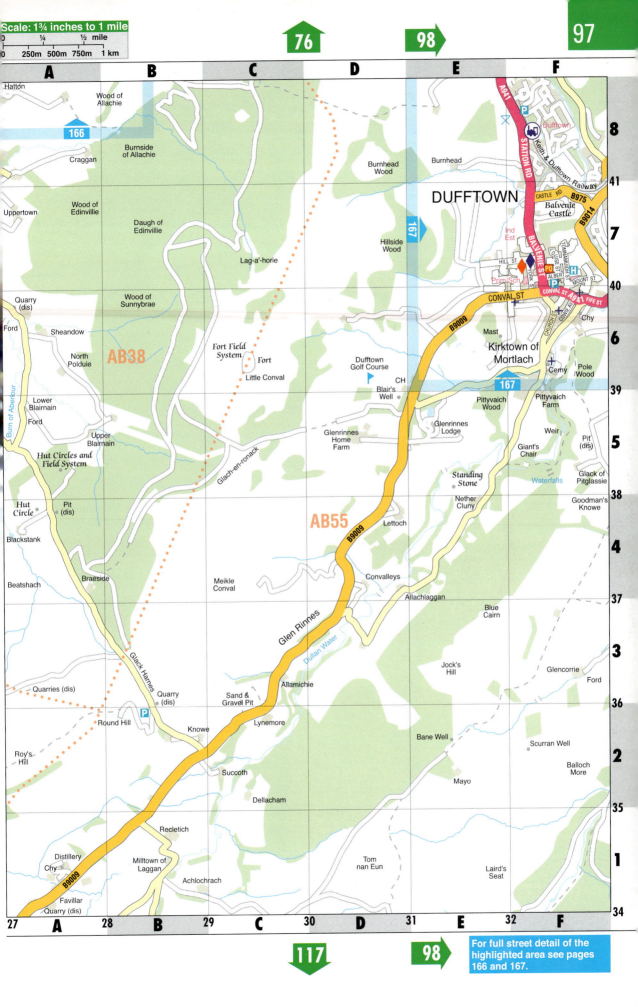

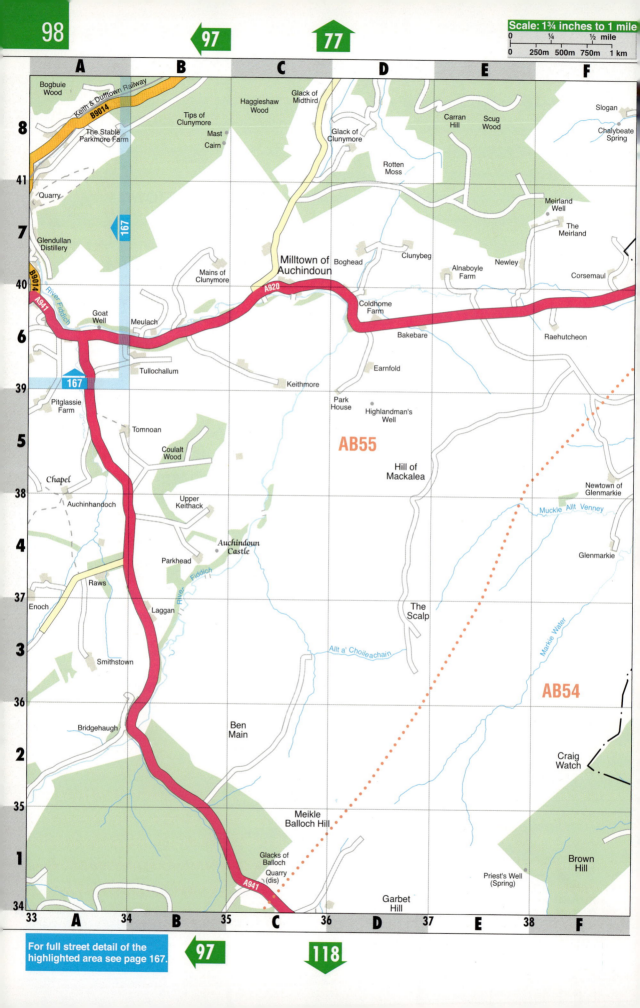

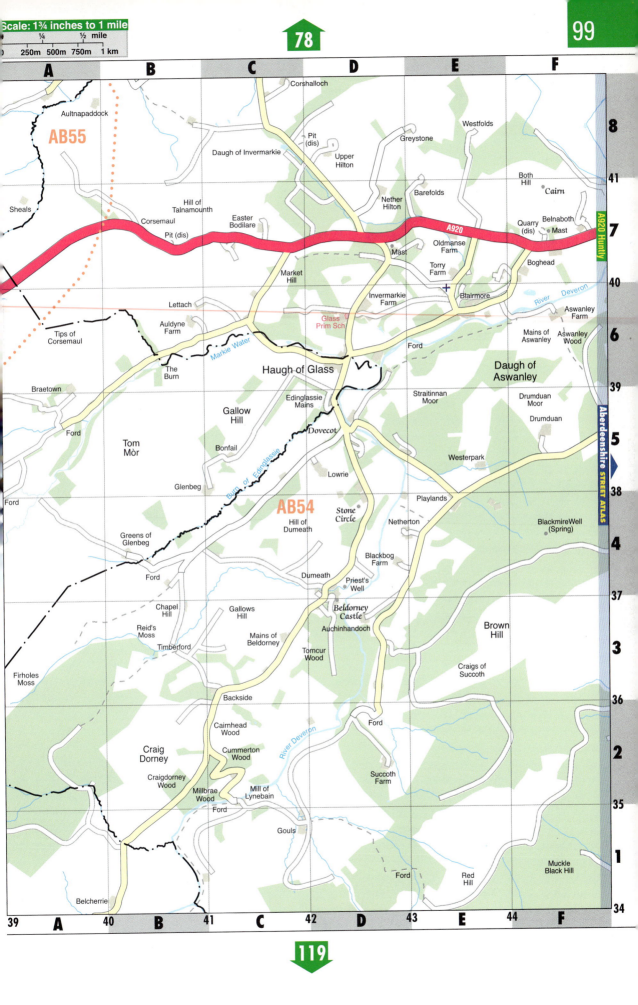

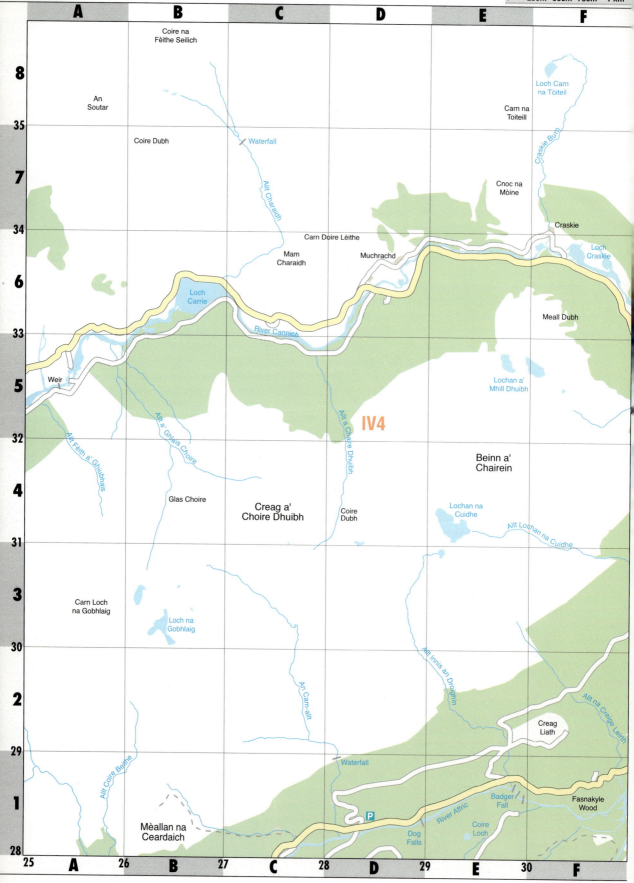

Scale: 1¾ inches to 1 mile

0   ¼   ½ mile
0   250m 500m 750m 1 km

A   B   C   D   E   F

8
35
7
34
6
33
5
32
4
31
3
30
2
29
1
28

An Soutar

Coire na Fèithe Seilich

Coire Dubh

Waterfall

Allt Charaidh

Carn Doire Lèithe

Mam Charaidh

Muchrachd

Loch Carn na Tòiteil

Carn na Toiteill

Cnoc na Mòine

Craskie Burn

Craskie

Loch Craskie

Loch Carrie

River Cannich

Meall Dubh

Weir

Allt a' Ghlais Choire

Allt a Chaire Dhuibh

IV4

Lochan a' Mhill Dhuibh

Beinn a' Chairein

Allt Fèith a' Ghiubhais

Glas Choire

Creag a' Choire Dhuibh

Coire Dubh

Lochan na Cuidhe

Allt Lochan na Cuidhe

Carn Loch na Gobhlaig

Loch na Gobhlaig

An Carn-allt

Allt Innis an Droighin

Allt na Creige Lèirth

Creag Liath

Allt Coire Beithe

Mèallan na Ceardaich

Waterfall

P

River Affric

Badger Fall

Fasnakyle Wood

Dog Falls

Coire Loch

25   A   26   B   27   C   28   D   29   E   30   F

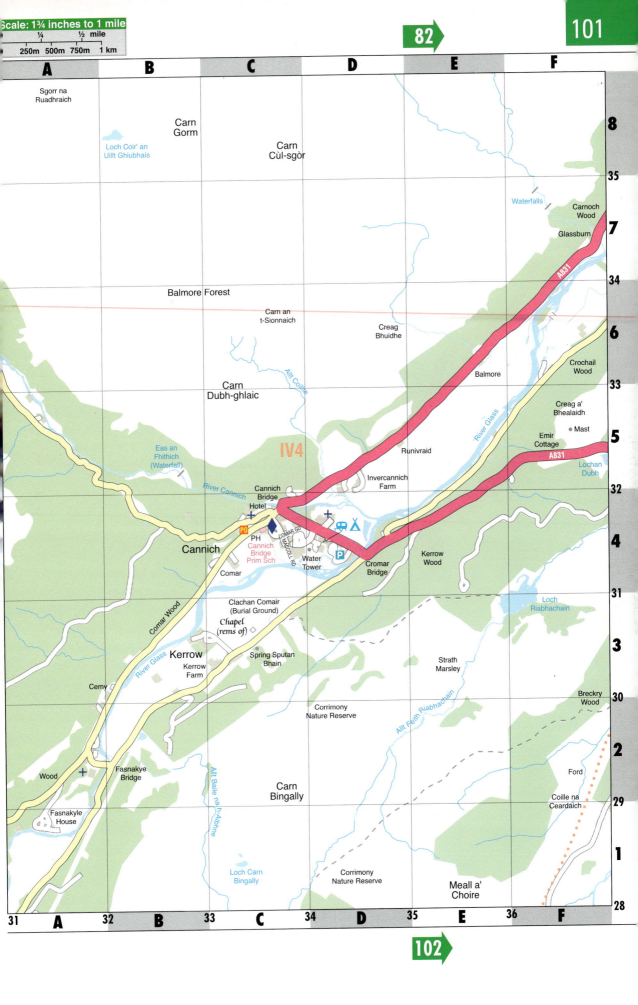

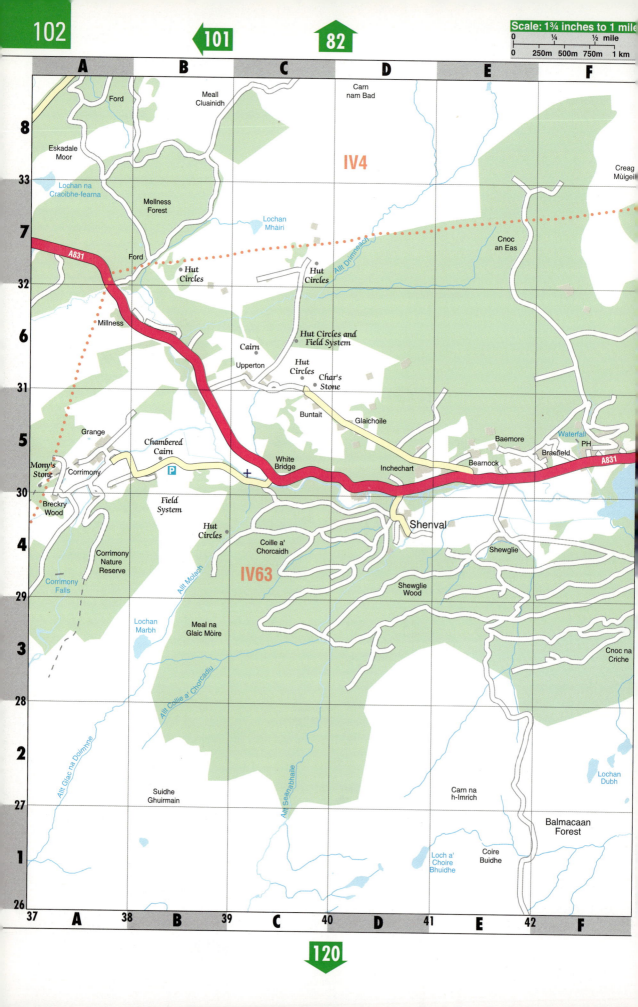

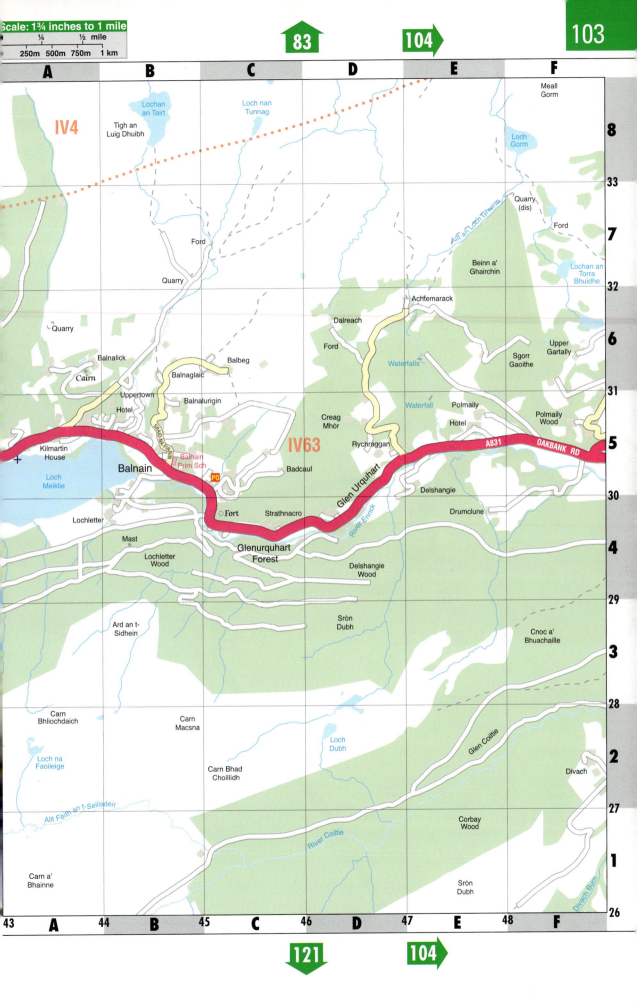

Scale: 1¾ inches to 1 mile
¼ ½ mile
250m 500m 750m 1 km

A   B   C   D   E   F

IV4

Meall Gorm

Lochan an Tairt

Loch nan Tunnag

Loch Gorm

8

Tigh an Luig Dhuibh

33

Allt an Loch Ghuirm

Quarry (dis)

Ford

7

Ford

Beinn a' Ghairchin

Lochan an Torra Bhuidhe

Quarry

Achtemarack

32

Dalreach

Upper Gartally

Quarry

Balnalick

Balbeg

Ford

Waterfalls

Sgorr Gaoithe

6

Cairn

Balnaglaic

Creag Mhòr

Waterfall

Polmaily

Polmaily Wood

31

Uppertown

Balnalurigin

IV63

Hotel

Kilmartin House

Hotel

Rychraggan

A831

OAKBANK RD

5

SRÒN-NA-FÀIRN

Balnain Prim Sch

Balnain

PO

Badcaul

Glen Urquhart

Delshangie

Loch Meiklie

Fort

Strathnacro

River Enrick

Drumclune

30

Lochletter

Glenurquhart Forest

4

Mast

Lochletter Wood

Delshangie Wood

29

Ard an t-Sidhein

Sròn Dubh

Cnoc a' Bhuachaille

3

28

Carn Bhliochdaich

Carn Macsna

Loch Dubh

Glen Coiltie

Divach

2

Loch na Faoileige

Carn Bhad Choillidh

27

Allt Fèith an t-Seilisdeir

River Coiltie

Corbay Wood

1

Carn a' Bhainne

Sròn Dubh

Divach Burn

26

43   A   44   B   45   C   46   D   47   E   48   F

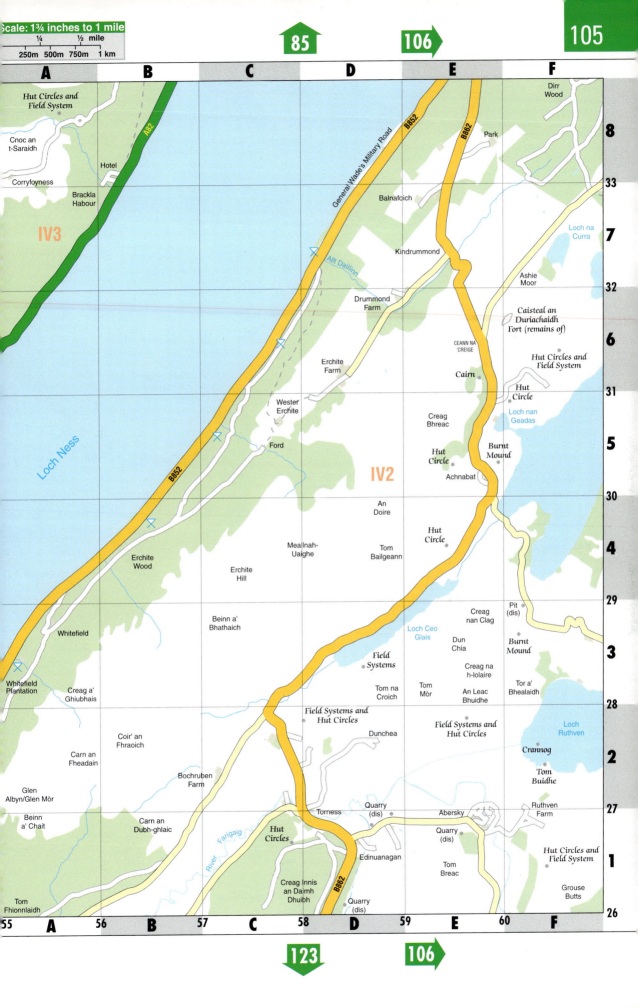

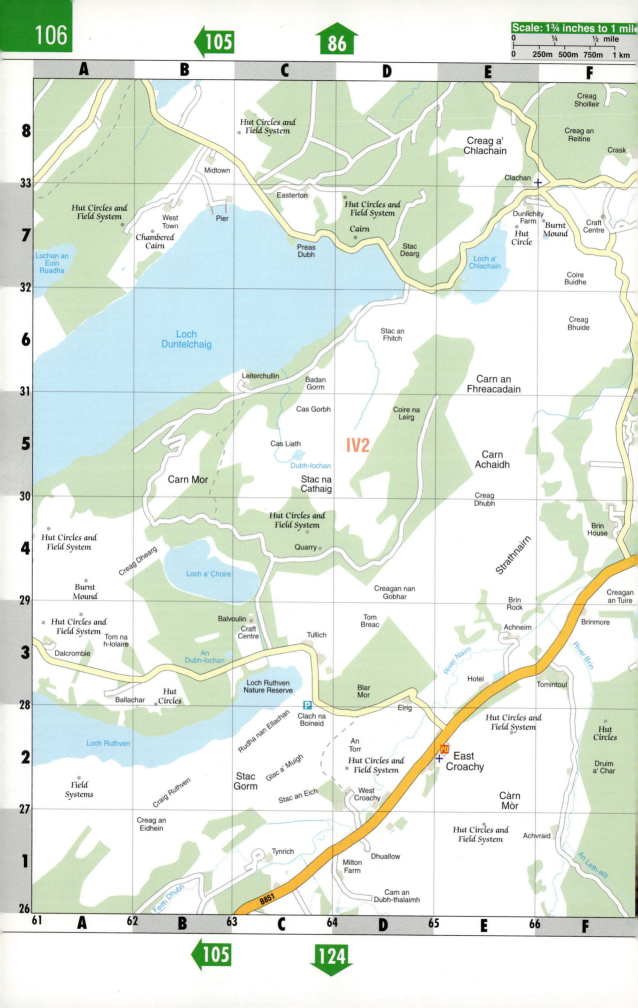

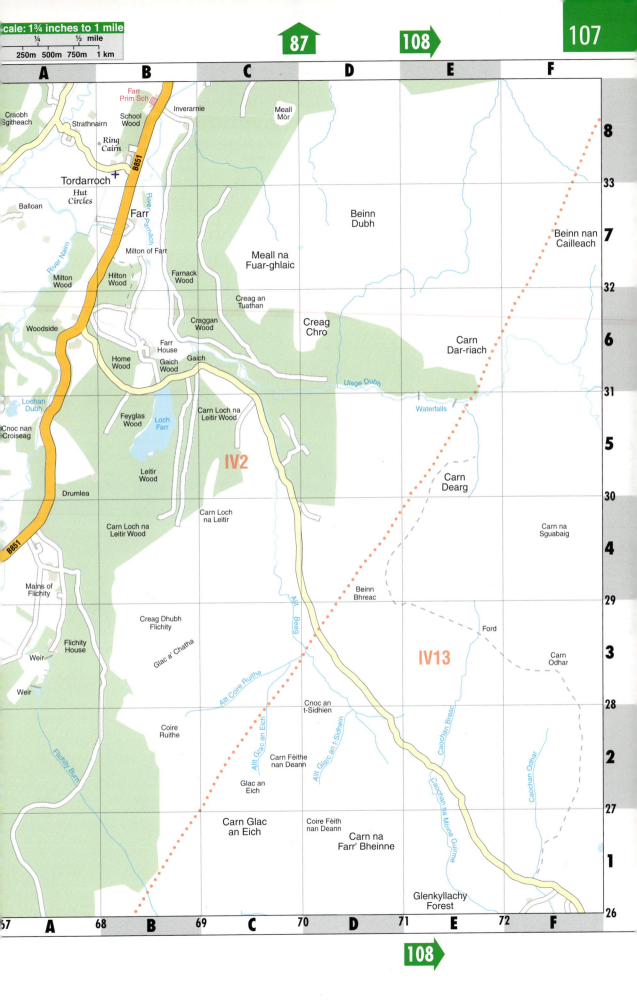

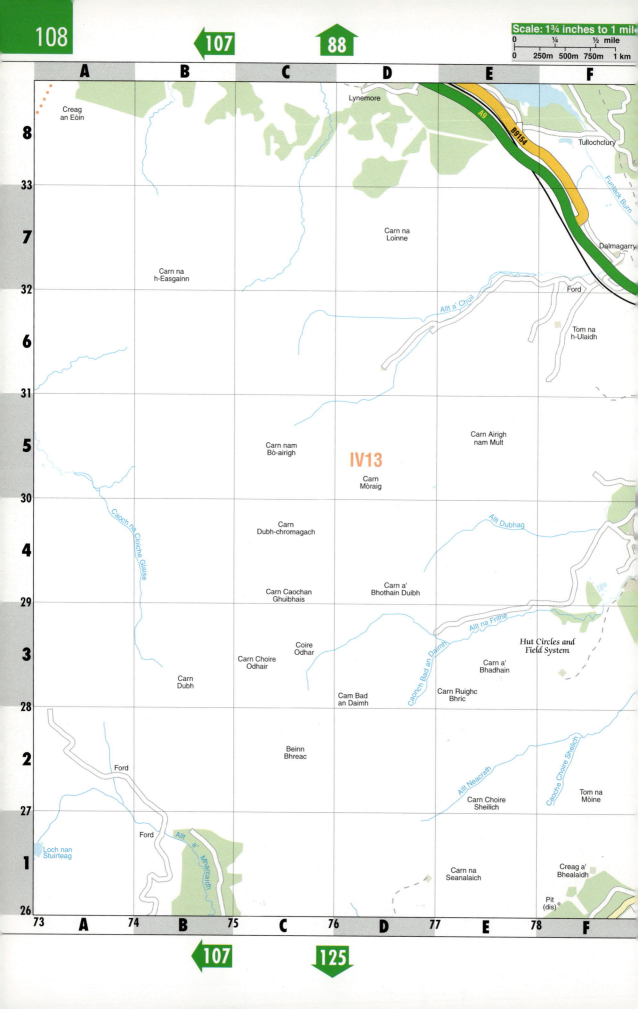

107
88

Scale: 1¾ inches to 1 mile

0   ¼   ½   mile
0   250m   500m   750m   1 km

A   B   C   D   E   F

8

Creag
an Eòin

Lynemore

A9

B9154

Tullochclury

33

7

Carn na
Loinne

Dalmagarry

Carn na
h-Easgainn

32

Allt a' Chuil

Ford

6

Tom na
h-Ulaidh

31

Caoch na Cloiche Glaise

Carn Airigh
nam Mult

5

Carn nam
Bò-airigh

IV13

Carn
Mòraig

Allt Dubhag

30

Carn
Dubh-chromagach

4

29

Carn Caochan
Ghuibhais

Carn a'
Bhothain Duibh

Allt na Frithe

Coire
Odhar

Hut Circles and
Field System

3

Carn Choire
Odhair

Caonch Bad an Daimh

Carn a'
Bhadhain

Carn
Dubh

Cam Bad
an Daimh

Carn Ruighe
Bhric

28

2

Beinn
Bhreac

Allt Neacrath

Carn Choire
Sheilich

Caoche Choire Sheilich

Tom na
Mòine

27

Ford

1

Loch nan
Stuirteag

Ford

Allt a' Mharcaidh

Carn na
Seanalaich

Creag a'
Bhealaidh

Pit
(dis)

26

73   A   74   B   75   C   76   D   77   E   78   F

107
125

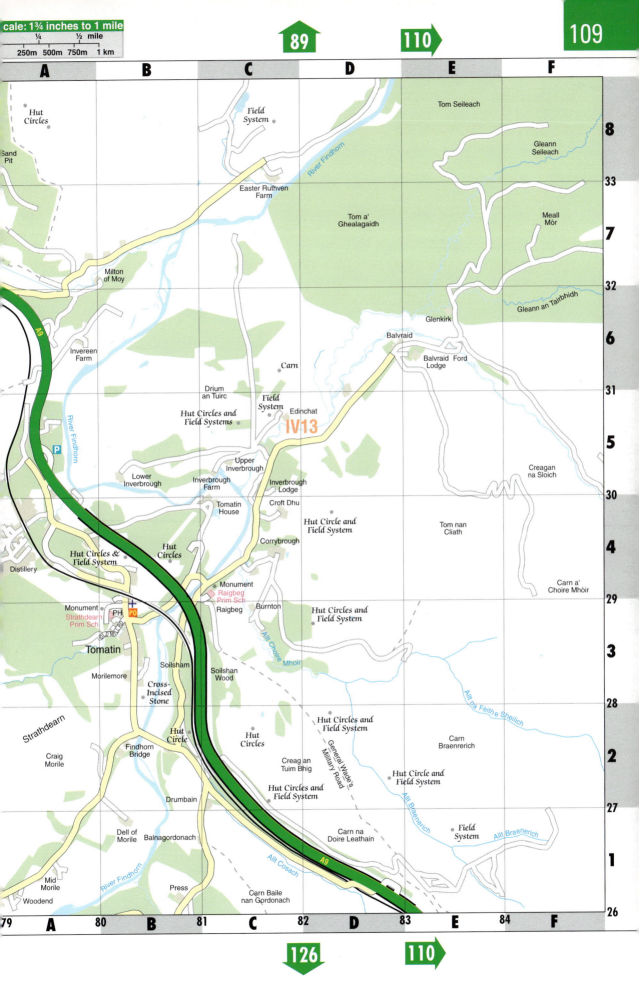

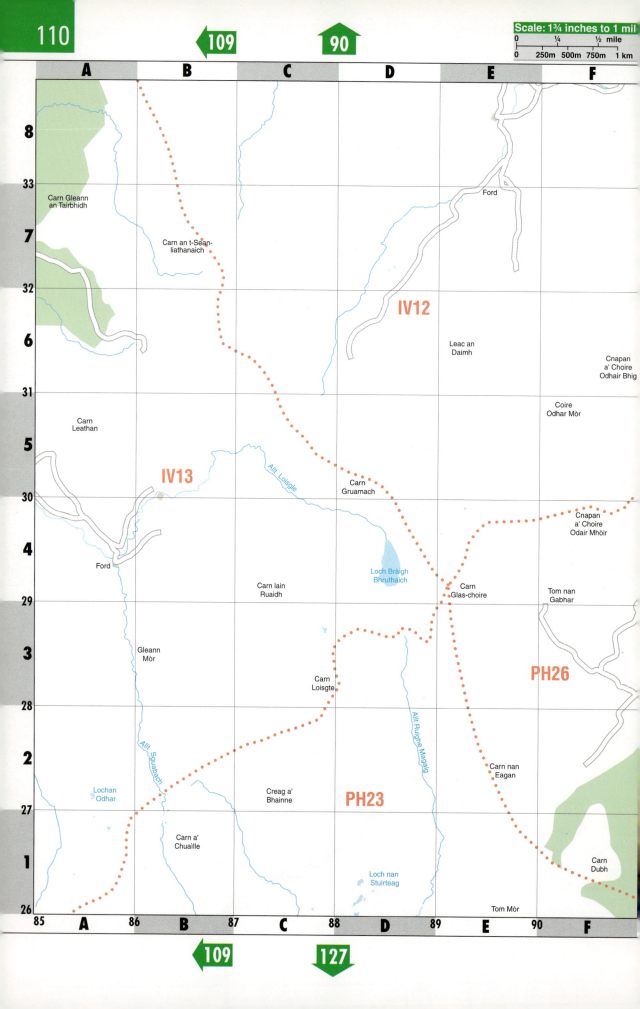
Scale: 1¾ inches to 1 mil

0   ¼   ½   mile
0   250m 500m 750m 1 km

A   B   C   D   E   F

8

33

Carn Gleann
an Tairbhidh

7

Carn an t-Sean-
liathanaich

Ford

32

IV12

6

Leac an
Daimh

Cnapan
a' Choire
Odhair Bhig

31

Carn
Leathan

Coire
Odhar Mòr

5

IV13

Allt Loisgte

Carn
Gruamach

Cnapan
a' Choire
Odair Mhòir

30

Ford

Loch Bràigh
Bhruthaich

Carn Iain
Ruaidh

Carn
Glas-choire

Tom nan
Gabhar

29

4

Gleann
Mòr

PH26

3

Carn
Loisgte

Allt Ruighe Magaig

28

Allt Sguabach

Creag a'
Bhainne

PH23

Carn nan
Eagan

2

Lochan
Odhar

27

Carn a'
Chuaille

Loch nan
Stuirteag

Carn
Dubh

1

Tom Mòr

26

85   A   86   B   87   C   88   D   89   E   90   F

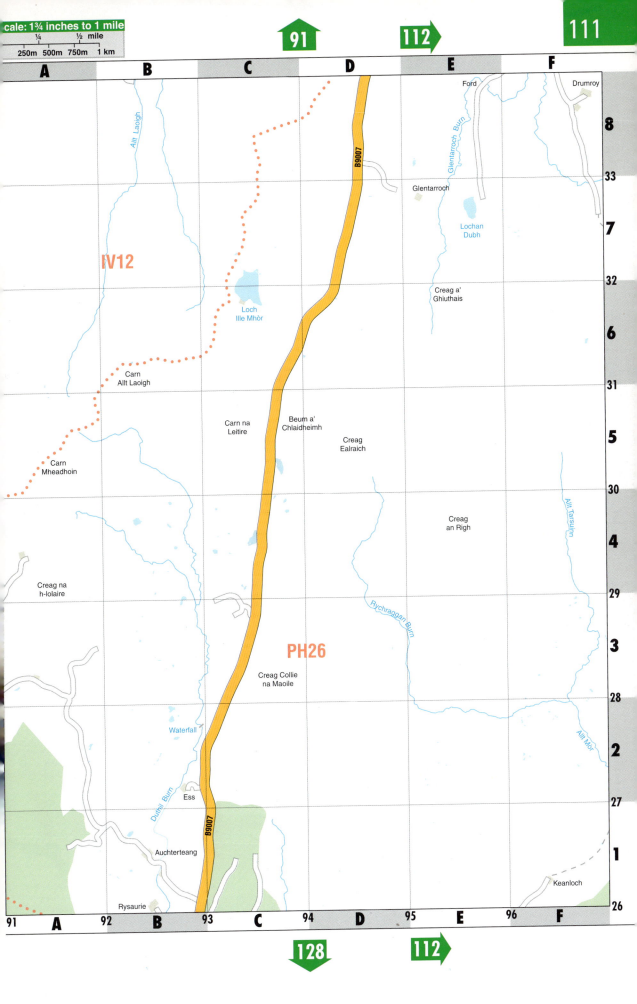

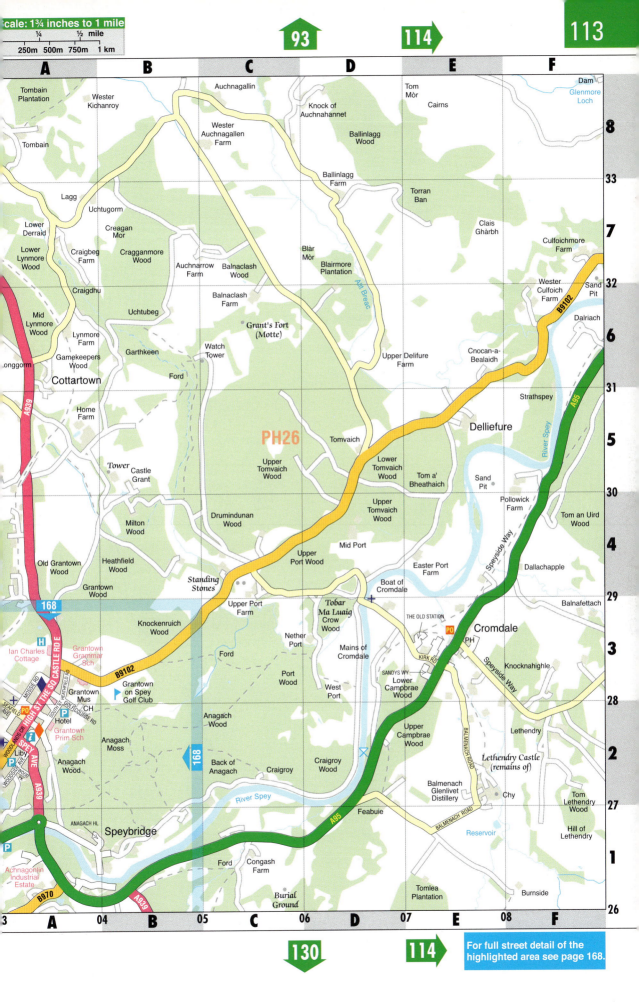

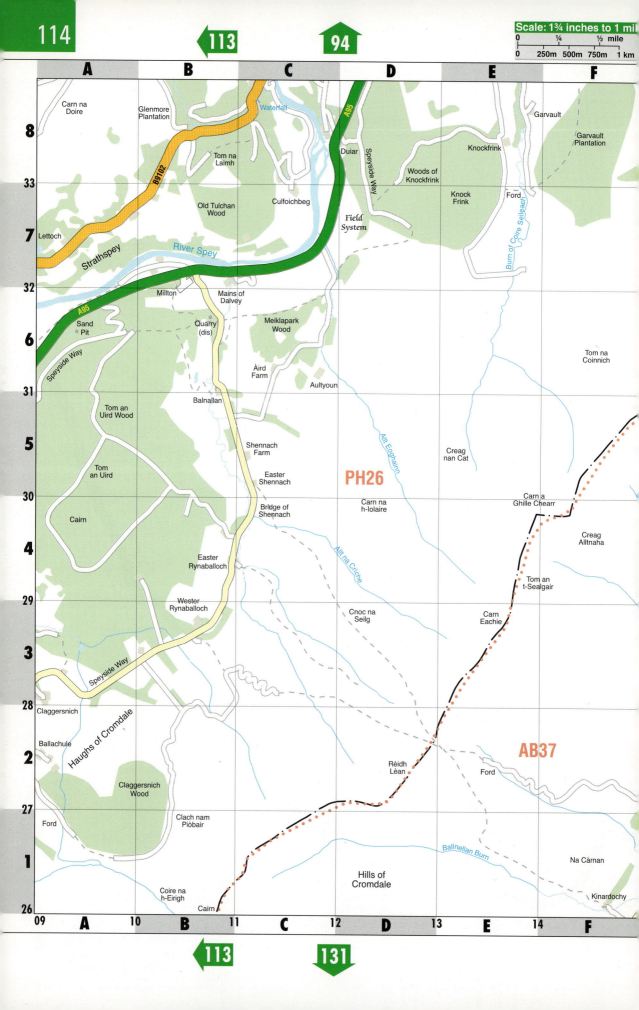

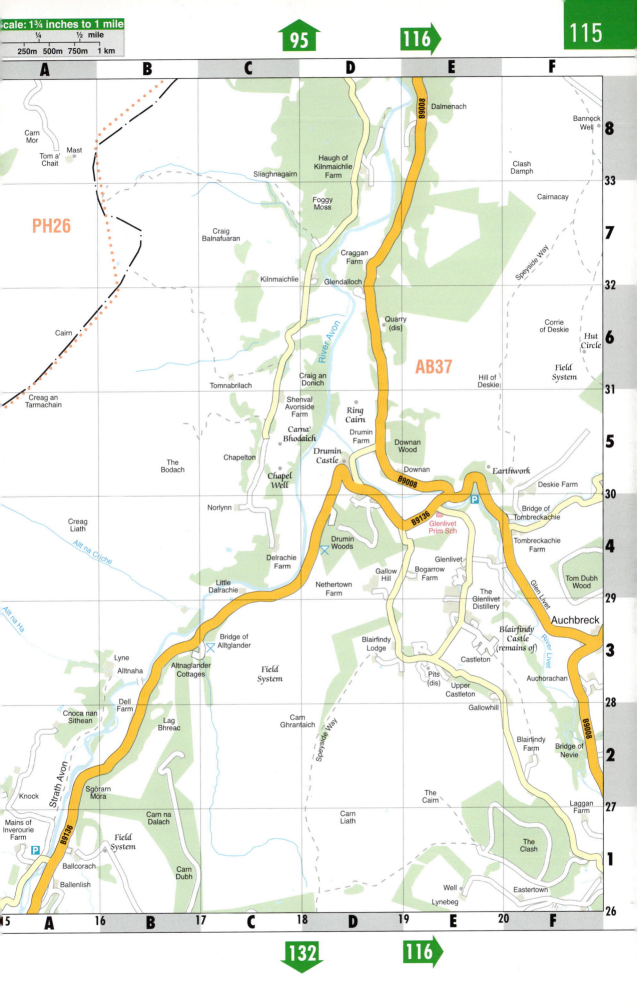

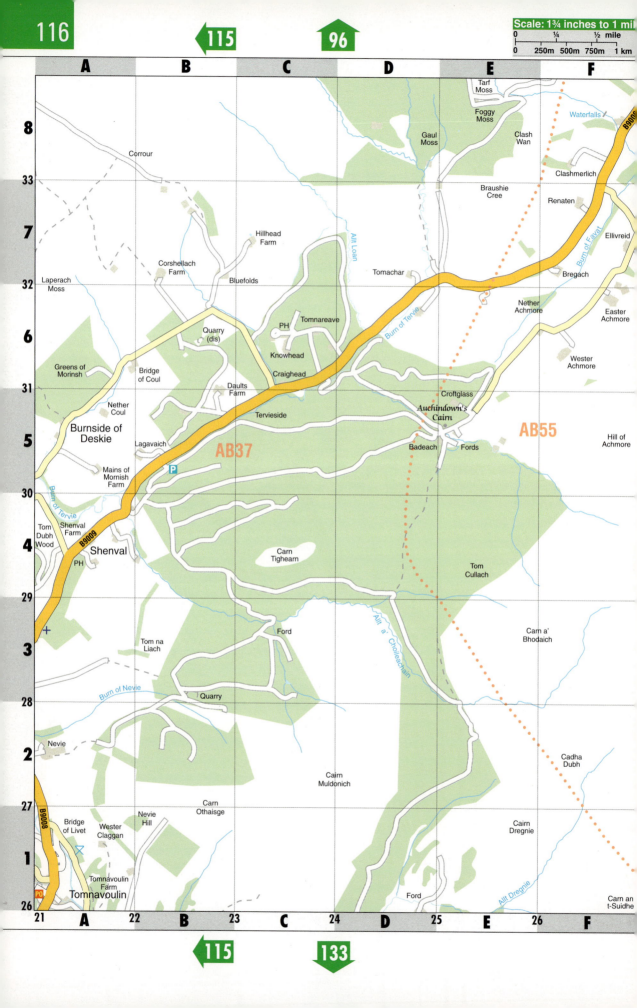

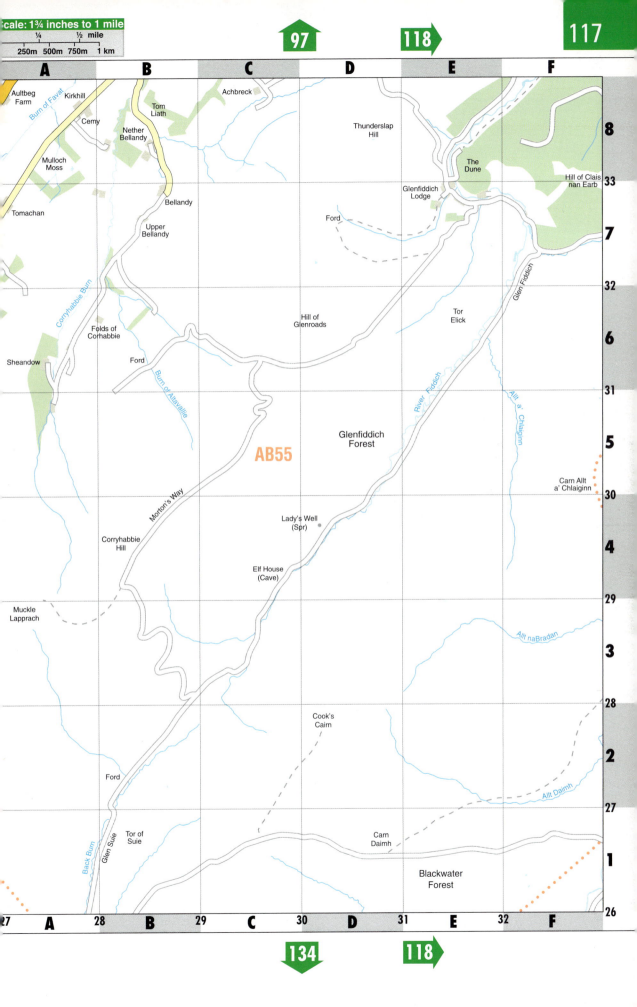

A B C D E F

Aultbeg Farm
Burn of Favat
Kirkhill
Cemy
Tom Liath
Nether Bellandy
Mulloch Moss
Tomachan
Bellandy
Upper Bellandy
Corryhabbie Burn
Folds of Corhabbie
Sheandow
Ford
Burn of Altavaille

Achbreck

Thunderslap Hill

Ford

The Dune
Glenfiddich Lodge
Hill of Clais nan Earb

Glen Fiddich

Hill of Glenroads

Tor Elick

River Fiddich

Allt a' Chlaiginn

Glenfiddich Forest

AB55

Carn Allt a' Chlaiginn

Morton's Way

Lady's Well (Spr)

Corryhabbie Hill

Elf House (Cave)

Muckle Lapprach

Allt naBradan

Cook's Cairn

Allt Daimh

Ford

Back Burn
Glen Suie
Tor of Suie

Carn Daimh

Blackwater Forest

8
33
7
32
6
31
5
30
4
29
3
28
2
27
1
26

27 A 28 B 29 C 30 D 31 E 32 F

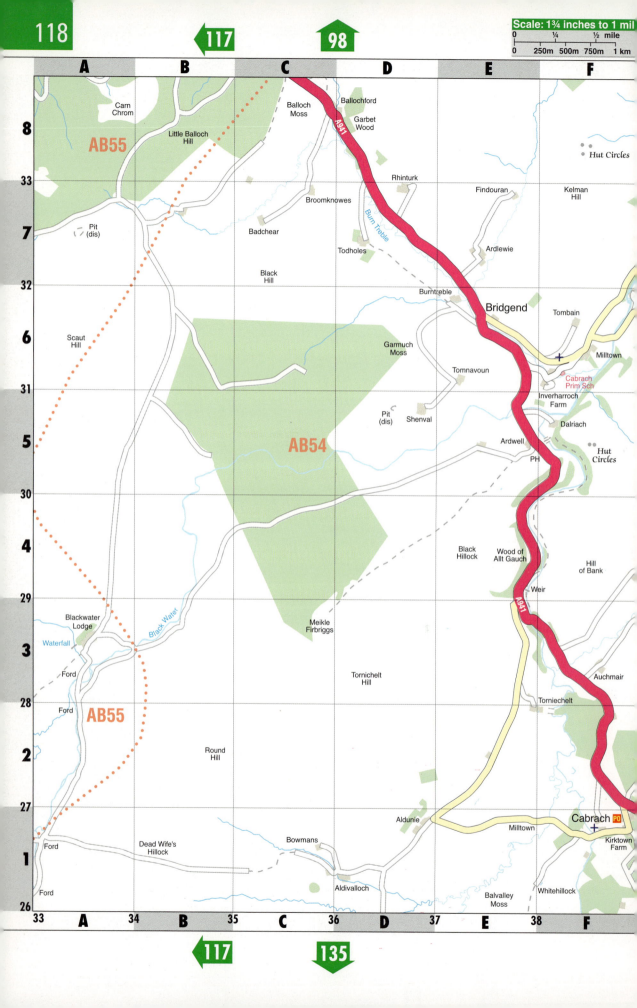

Scale: 1¾ inches to 1 mile

0   ¼   ½   mile

0   250m   500m   750m   1 km

Carn Chrom

AB55

Little Balloch Hill

Balloch Moss

Ballochford

Garbet Wood

Hut Circles

Pit (dis)

Broomknowes

Rhinturk

Findouran

Kelman Hill

Badchear

Todholes

Ardlewie

Black Hill

Burntreble

Bridgend

Tombain

Scaut Hill

Garmuch Moss

Tomnavoun

Cabrach Prim Sch

Milltown

AB54

Pit (dis)

Shenval

Inverharroch Farm

Dalriach

Ardwell

PH

Hut Circles

Blackwater Lodge

Black Water

Black Hillock

Wood of Allt Gauch

Hill of Bank

Waterfall

Weir

Ford

Meikle Firbriggs

A941

Ford

AB55

Ford

Tornichelt Hill

Auchmair

Torniechelt

Round Hill

Aldunie

Milltown

Cabrach PO

Ford

Dead Wife's Hillock

Bowmans

Kirktown Farm

Ford

Aldivalloch

Balvalley Moss

Whitehillock

117   98   117   135

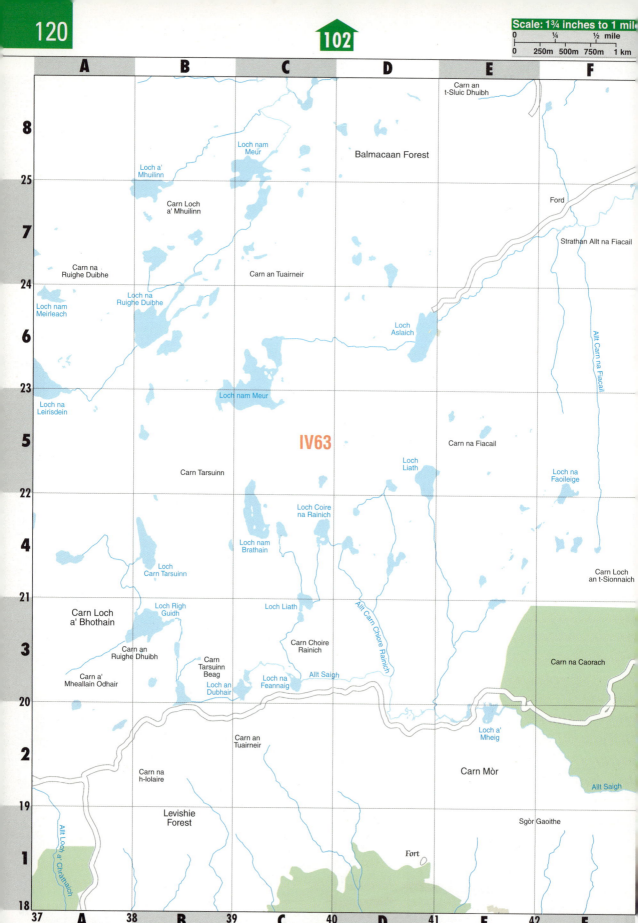

A   B   C   D   E   F

8

25

7

24

6

23

5

22

4

21

3

20

2

19

1

18

Carn an t-Sluic Dhuibh

Balmacaan Forest

Loch nam Meur

Loch a' Mhuilinn

Carn Loch a' Mhuilinn

Ford

Strathan Allt na Fiacail

Carn na Ruighe Duibhe

Carn an Tuairneir

Loch na Ruighe Duibhe

Loch nam Meirleach

Loch Aslaich

Allt Carn na Fiacail

Loch na Leirisdein

Loch nam Meur

IV63

Carn na Fiacail

Loch Liath

Carn Tarsuinn

Loch na Faoileige

Loch Coire na Rainich

Loch nam Brathain

Loch Carn Tarsuinn

Carn Loch an t-Sionnaich

Carn Loch a' Bhothain

Loch Righ Guidh

Loch Liath

Allt Carn Chlore Rainich

Carn na Caorach

Carn an Ruighe Dhuibh

Carn Tarsuinn Beag

Carn Choire Rainich

Carn a' Mheallain Odhair

Loch an Dubhair

Loch na Feannaig

Allt Saigh

Loch a' Mheig

Carn an Tuairneir

Carn Mòr

Carn na h-Iolaire

Allt Saigh

Levishie Forest

Sgòr Gaoithe

Allt Loch a' Chràttaich

Fort

37   A   38   B   39   C   40   D   41   E   42   F

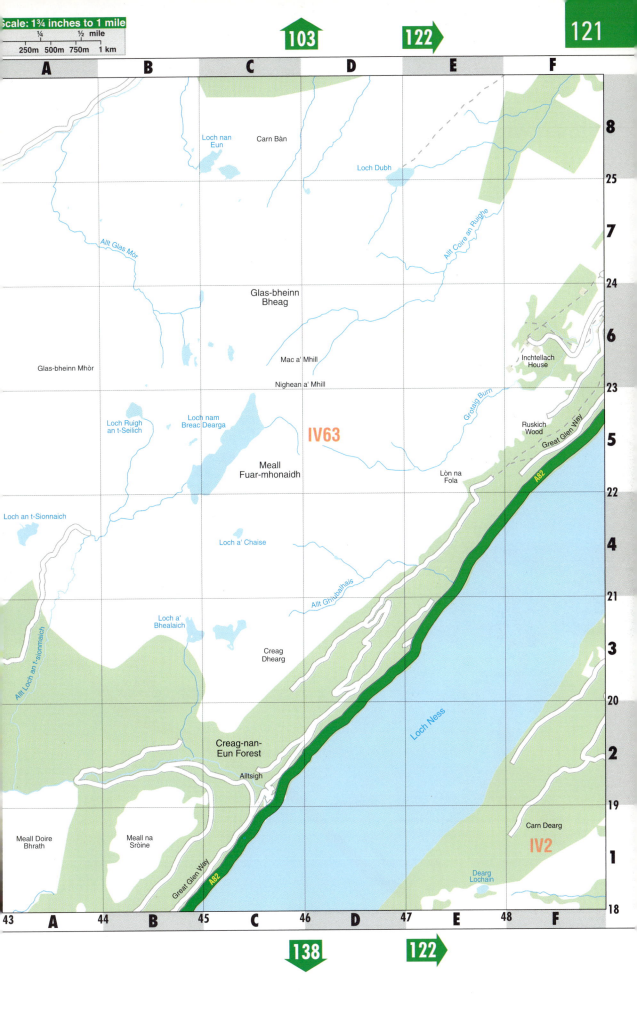

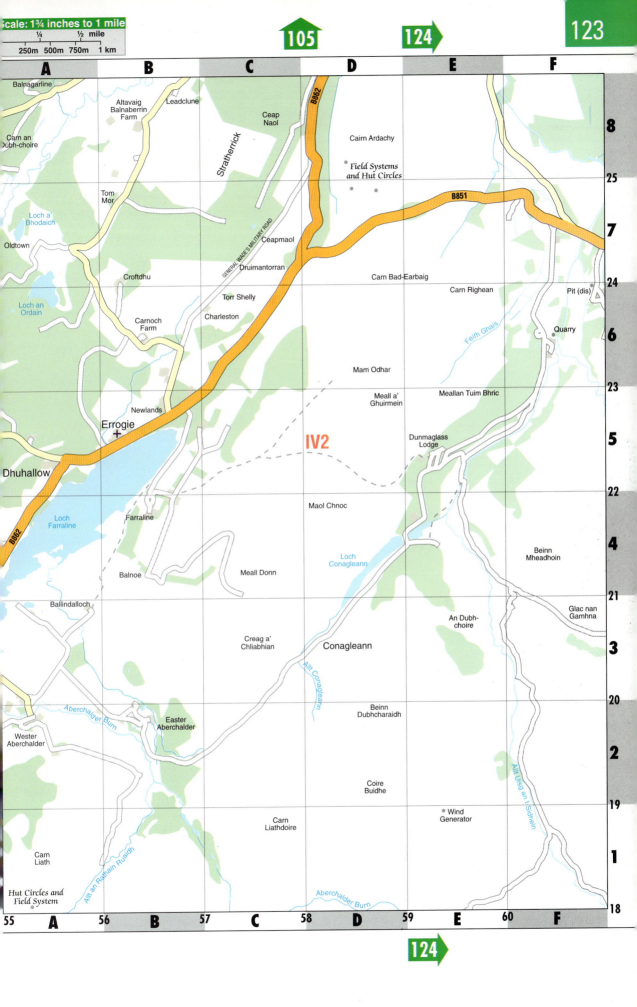

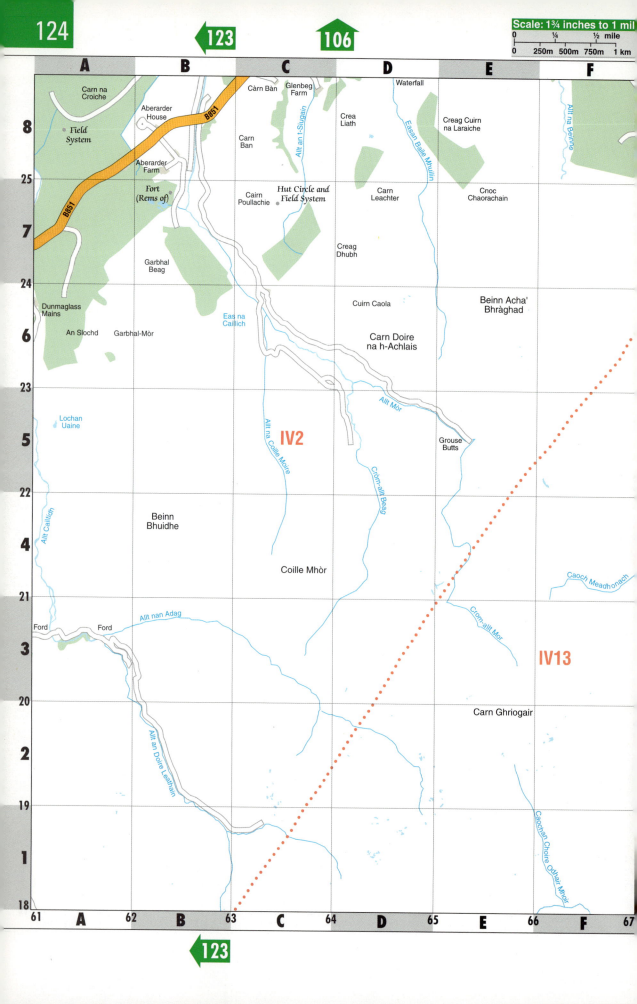

123
106

Scale: 1¾ inches to 1 mil

0   ¼   ½   mile
0   250m 500m 750m 1 km

A   B   C   D   E   F

Carn na
Croiche

Aberarder
House

B851

Càrn Bàn

Glenbeg
Farm

Waterfall

8

Field
System

Allt an t-Siugain

Crea
Liath

Creag Cuirn
na Laraiche

Allt na Beinne

25

Aberarder
Farm

Fort
(Rems of)

Cairn
Poullachie

Hut Circle and
Field System

Carn
Leachter

Easan Baile Mhuilin

Cnoc
Chaorachain

7

B851

Garbhal
Beag

Creag
Dhubh

24

Dunmaglass
Mains

Garbhal-Mòr

Eas na
Caillich

Cuirn Caola

Beinn Acha'
Bhràghad

6

An Slochd

Carn Doire
na h-Achlais

23

Allt Mòr

Allt Cailltich

Lochan
Uaine

Allt na Coille Moire

IV2

Grouse
Butts

5

22

Beinn
Bhuidhe

Cròm-allt Beag

Caoch Meadhonach

4

Coille Mhòr

Cròm-allt Mòr

21

Ford

Ford

Allt nan Adag

IV13

3

Allt an Doire Leathain

Carn Ghriogair

20

2

19

Caochan Choire Odhair Mhoir

1

18

61   A   62   B   63   C   64   D   65   E   66   F   67

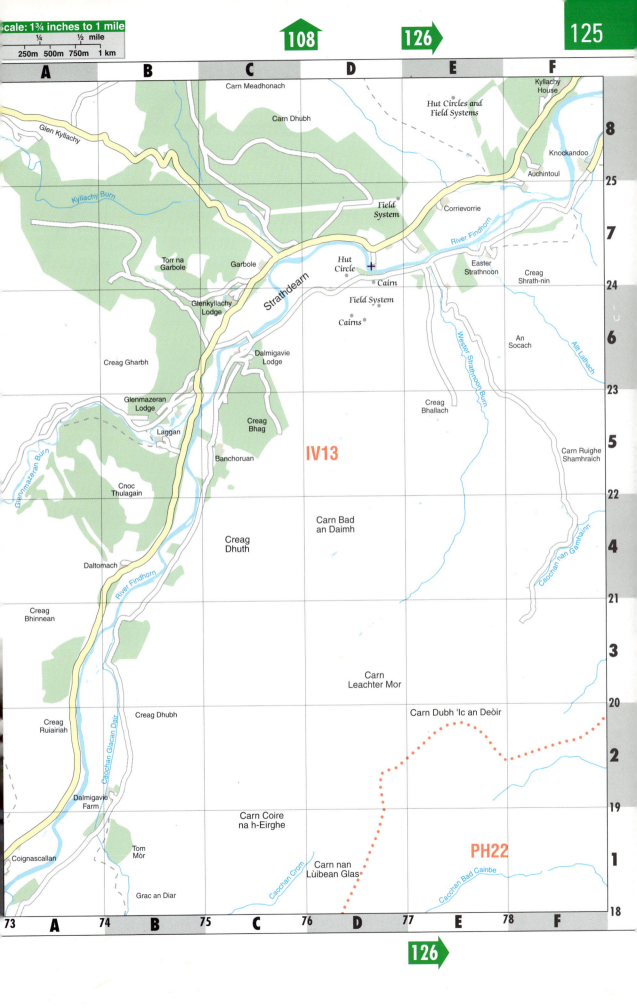

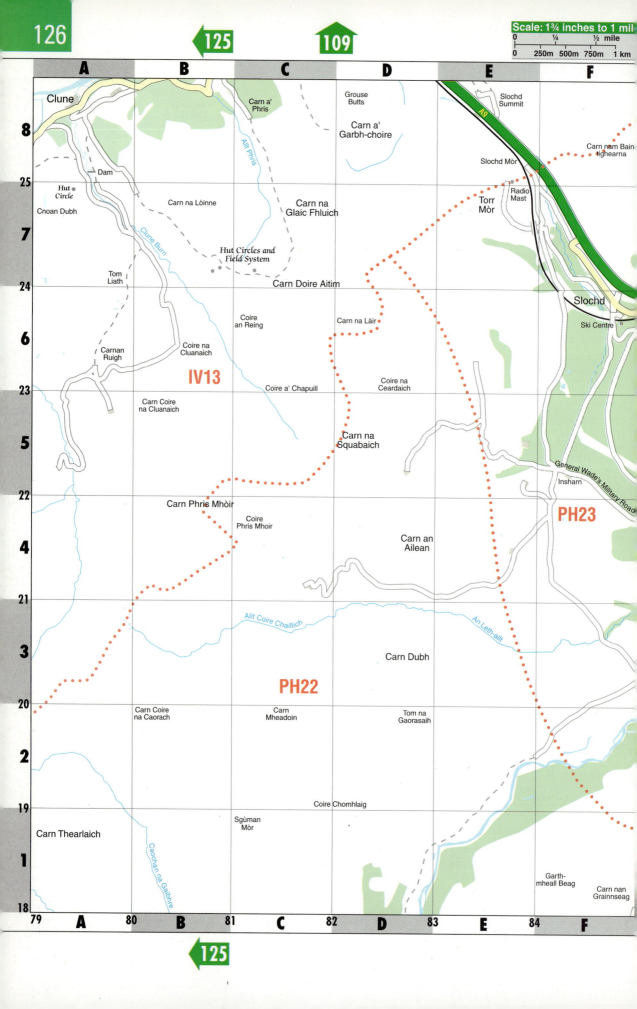

Scale: 1¾ inches to 1 mil

0   ¼   ½   mile
0   250m 500m 750m 1 km

Clune

A

Carn a'
Phris

Grouse
Butts

Carn a'
Garbh-choire

Slochd
Summit

A9

Carn nam Bain
tighearna

Hut
Circle

Cnoan Dubh

Allt Phris

Carn na Lòinne

Carn na
Glaic Fhluich

Slochd Mòr

Torr
Mòr

Radio
Mast

Dam

Clune Burn

Tom
Liath

Hut Circles and
Field System

Carn Doire Aitim

Slochd

Coire
an Reing

Carn na Làir

Ski Centre

Carnan
Ruigh

Coire na
Cluanaich

IV13

Coire a' Chapuill

Coire na
Ceardaich

Carn Coire
na Cluanaich

Carn na
Squabaich

General Wade's Military Road

Insharn

Carn Phris Mhòir

Coire
Phris Mhoir

Carn an
Ailean

PH23

Allt Coire Chaillich

An Leth-allt

Carn Dubh

PH22

Carn Coire
na Caorach

Carn
Mheadoin

Tom na
Gaorasaih

Coire Chomhlaig

Sgùman
Mòr

Carn Thearlaich

Caochan na Gaibhre

Garth-
mheall Beag

Carn nan
Grainnseag

79   A   80   B   81   C   82   D   83   E   84   F

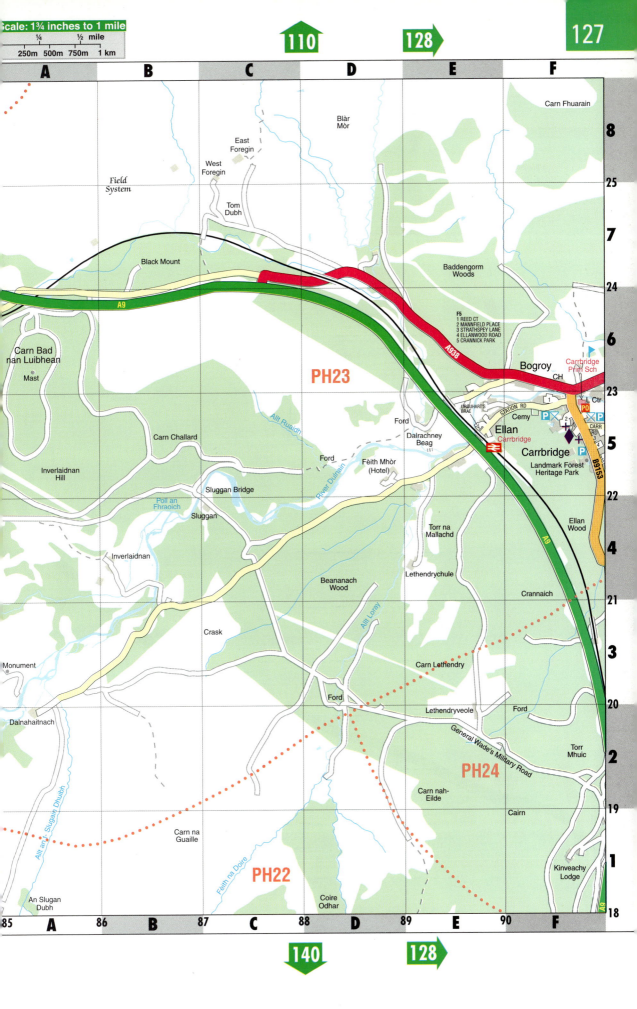

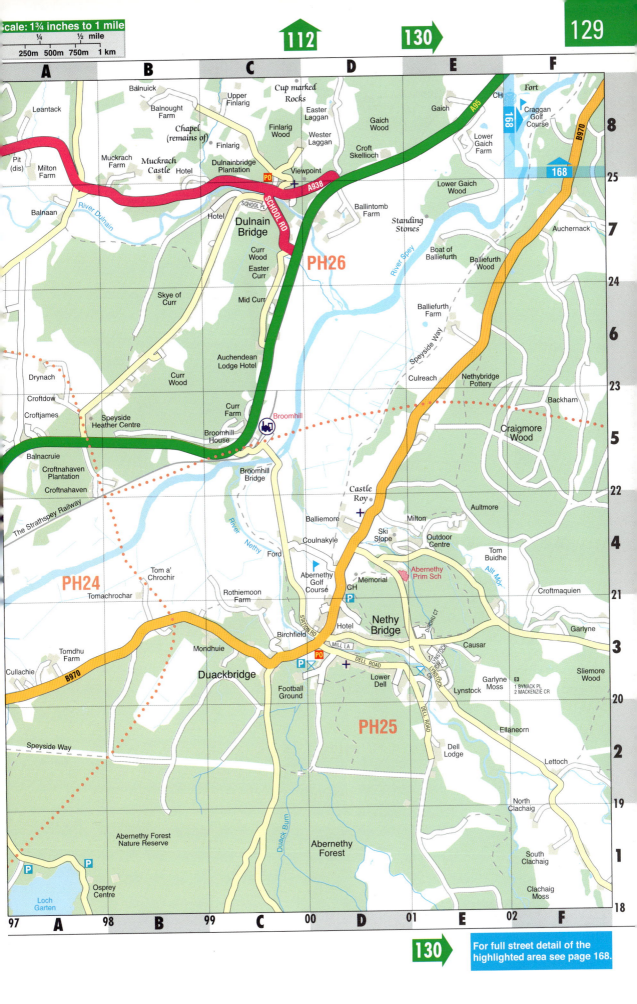

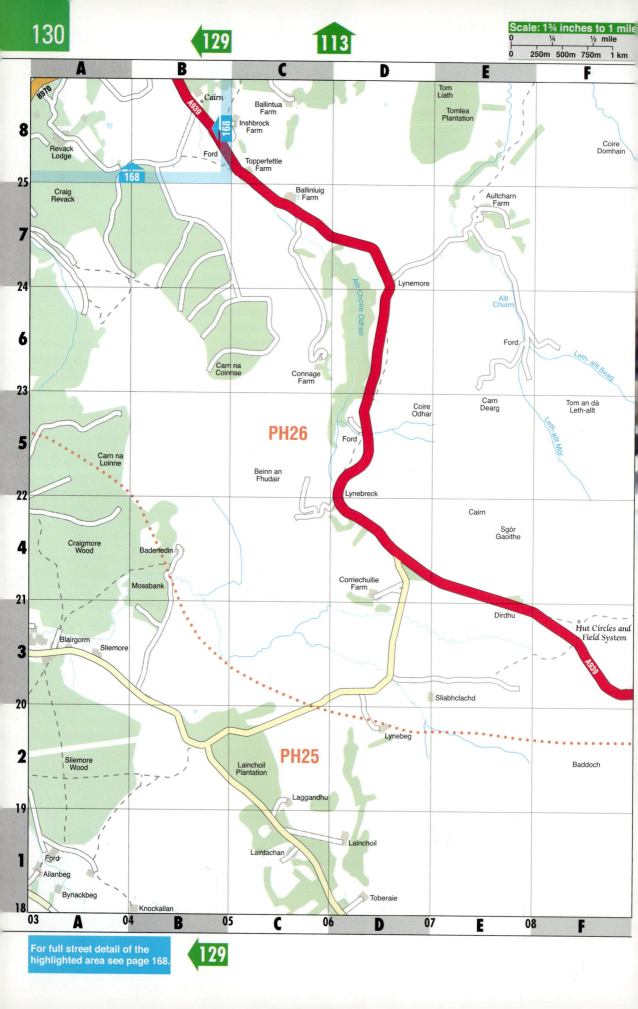

130
◄ 129
▲ 113
Scale: 1¾ inches to 1 mile
0   ¼   ½   mile
0   250m 500m 750m 1 km

B970

Cairn
A939
Revack
Lodge
168
Inshbrock
Farm
Ballintua
Farm
Tom
Liath
Tomlea
Plantation
Coire
Domhain

Ford
Topperfettle
Farm
Craig
Revack
168
Ballinluig
Farm
Aultcharn
Farm

Carn na
Coinnse
Connage
Farm
Allt Choire Odhair
Lynemore
Allt
Chuirn
Ford
Leth-allt Beag

PH26
Coire
Odhar
Carn
Dearg
Tom an dà
Leth-allt

Carn na
Loinne
Ford
Leth-allt Mòr

Beinn an
Fhudair
Lynebreck
Cairn
Sgòr
Gaoithe

Craigmore
Wood
Badenedin
Corriechullie
Farm
Dirdhu
Hut Circles and
Field System

Mossbank
A939

Blairgorm
Sliemore
Sliabhclachd

Sliemore
Wood
Lynebeg
Baddoch

Lainchoil
Plantation
PH25

Laggandhu

Laintachan
Lainchoil

Ford
Ailanbeg
Toberaie

Bynackbeg
Knockailan

For full street detail of the
highlighted area see page 168.
◄ 129

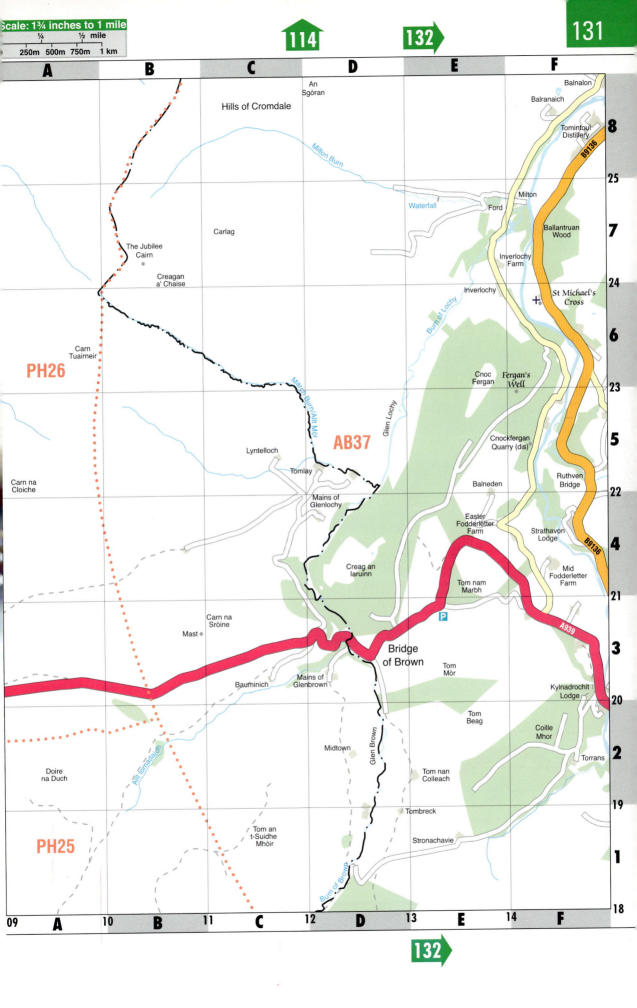

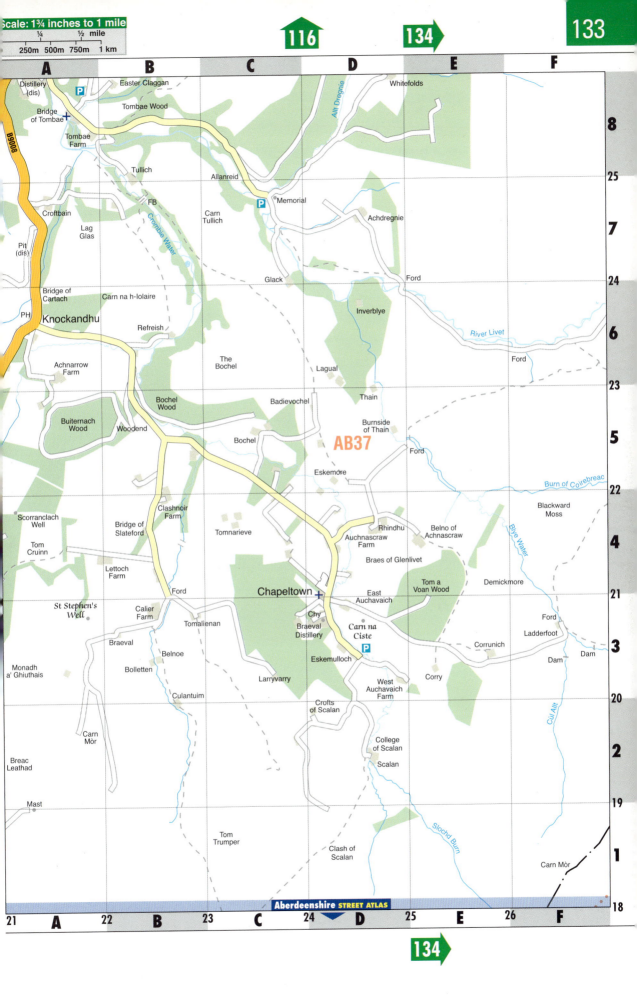

Scale: 1¾ inches to 1 mile

¼   ½ mile
250m 500m 750m 1 km

A   B   C   D   E   F

Distillery (dis)
P
Easter Claggan
Whitefolds
Allt Dregnie

Bridge of Tombae
Tombae Wood
8

Tombae Farm

Tullich
Allanreid
25

B9008
Croftbain
FB
P
Memorial
Achdregnie
7

Lag Glas
Carn Tullich

Pit (dis)
Glack
Ford
24

Bridge of Cartach
Carn na h-Iolaire
Inverblye
River Livet

PH
Refreish
Ford
6

Knockandhu

Achnarrow Farm
The Bochel
Lagual
Ford

Bochel Wood
Badievochel
Thain
23

Buiternach Wood
Woodend
Bochel
Burnside of Thain
5

AB37
Ford

Eskemore
Burn of Coirebreac

Clashnoir Farm
22

Scorranclach Well
Tomnarieve
Rhindhu
Belno of Achnascraw
Blackward Moss

Bridge of Slateford
Auchnascraw Farm
4

Tom Cruinn
Braes of Glenlivet
Blye Water

Lettoch Farm
Tom a Voan Wood
Demickmore

Ford
Chapeltown
East Auchavaich
21

St Stephen's Well
Calier Farm
Chy
Carn na Ciste
Corrunich
Ford
Ladderfoot
3

Braeval
Tomalienan
Braeval Distillery
Dam
Dam

Monadh a' Ghiuthais
Belnoe
P
Corry

Bolletten
Eskemulloch
West Auchavaich Farm
Corry

Culantuim
Larryvarry
20

Carn Mòr
Crofts of Scalan
Cùl Allt

Breac Leathad
College of Scalan
2

Scalan

Mast
19

Tom Trumper
Clash of Scalan
Slochd Burn
1

Carn Mòr
18

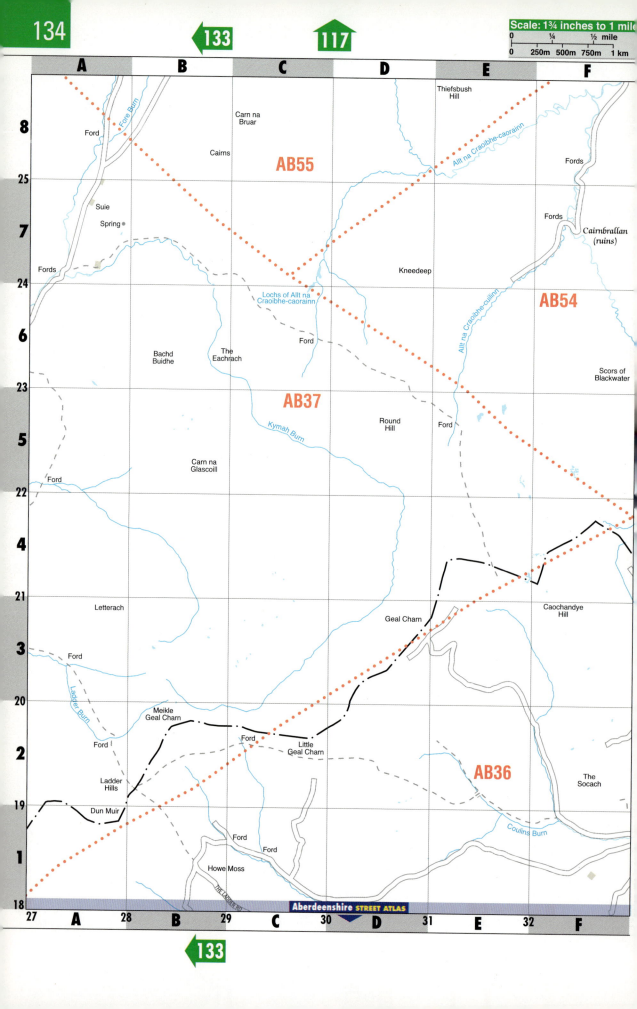

Scale: 1¾ inches to 1 mile

0   ¼   ½ mile
0   250m 500m 750m 1 km

A   B   C   D   E   F

8

25

7

24

6

23

5

22

4

21

3

20

2

19

1

18

Fore Burn

Ford

Suie

Spring

Fords

Carn na Bruar

Cairns

AB55

Thiefsbush Hill

Allt na Craoibhe-caorainn

Fords

Fords

Cairnbrallan (ruins)

Kneedeep

Lochs of Allt na Craoibhe-caorainn

Bachd Buidhe

The Eachrach

Ford

AB37

Kymah Burn

Allt na Craoibhe-cuilinn

AB54

Scors of Blackwater

Round Hill

Ford

Carn na Glascoill

Ford

Letterach

Geal Charn

Caochandye Hill

Ford

Ladder Burn

Meikle Geal Charn

Ford

Little Geal Charn

AB36

The Socach

Ladder Hills

Dun Muir

Coulins Burn

Ford

Ford

Howe Moss

THE LADDER RD

Aberdeenshire STREET ATLAS

27   A   28   B   29   C   30   D   31   E   32   F

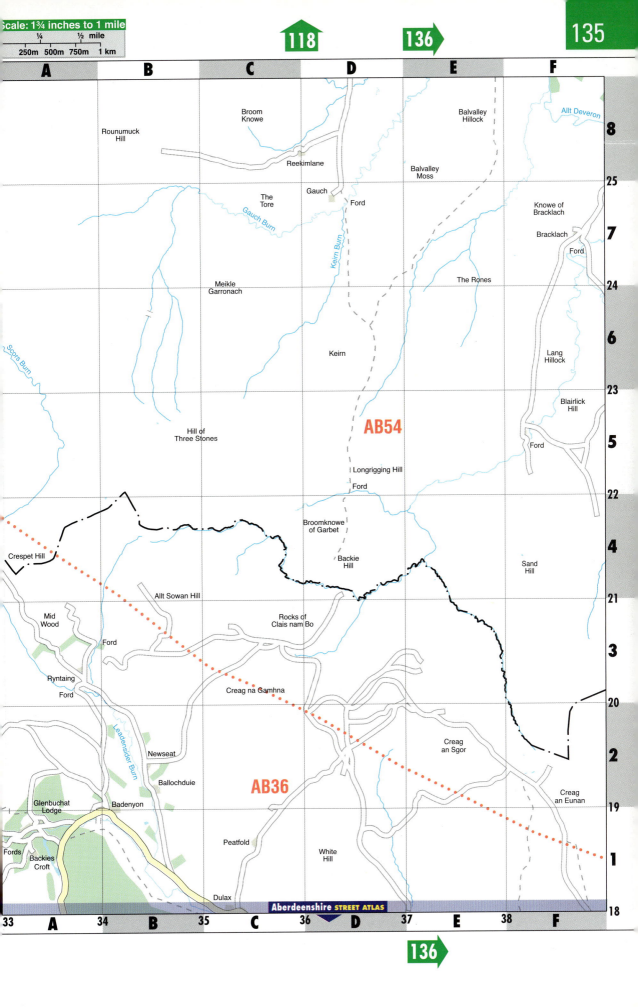

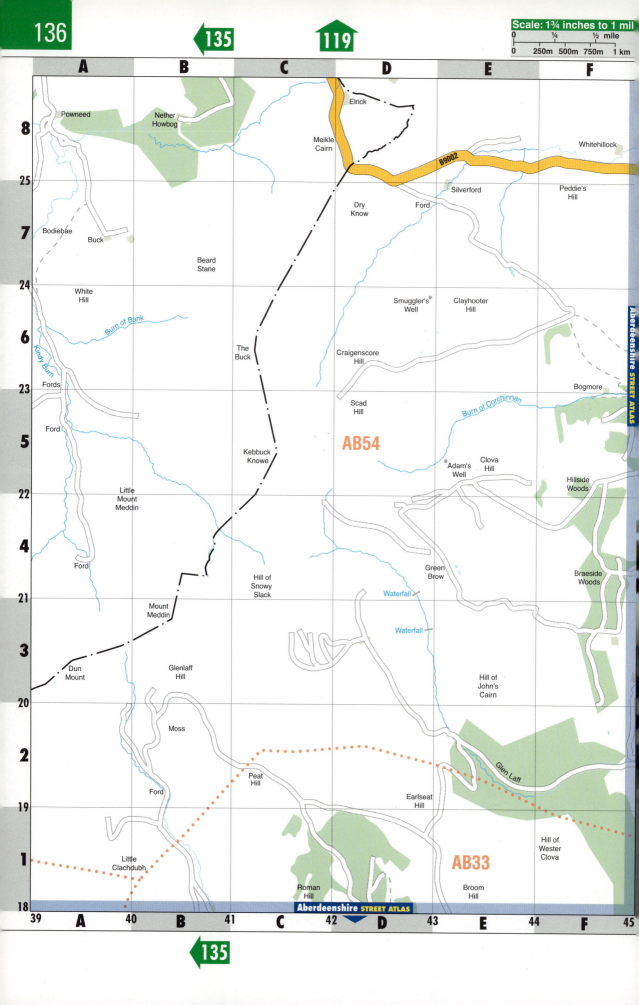

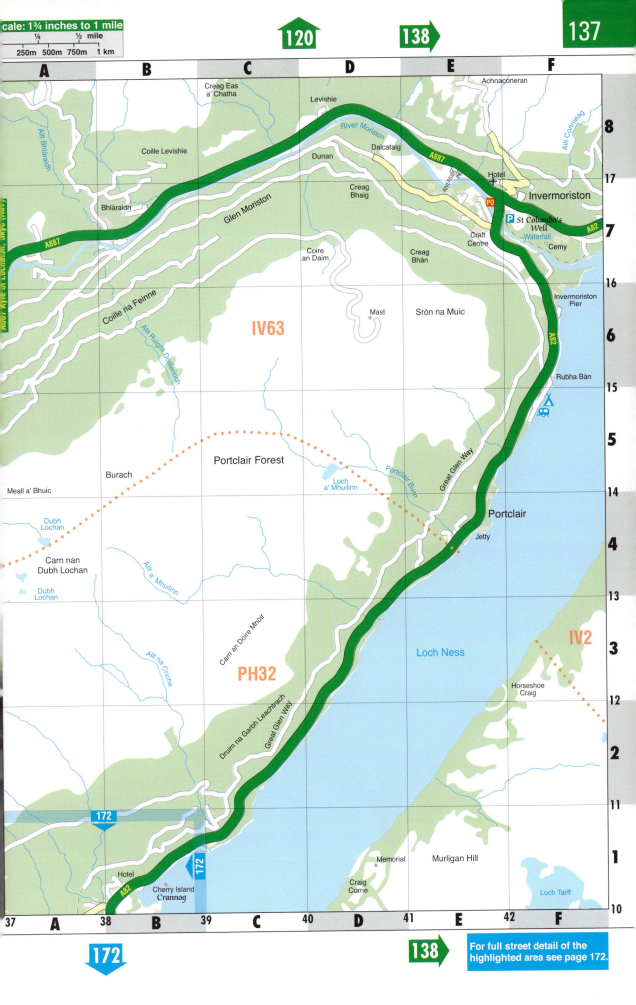

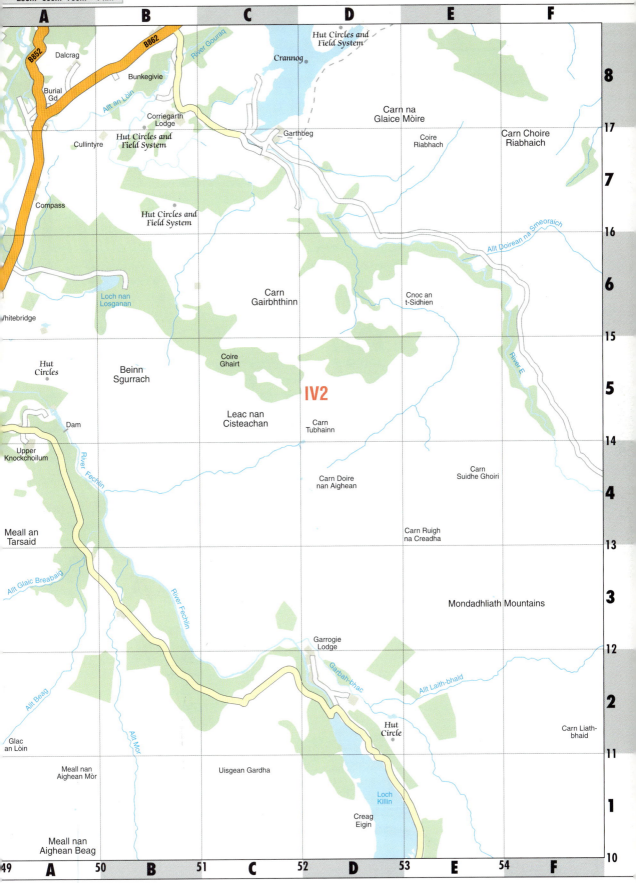

Scale: 1¾ inches to 1 mile

¼   ½   mile

250m 500m 750m 1 km

A   B   C   D   E   F

8
17
7
16
6
15
5
14
4
13
3
12
2
11
1
10

49   A   50   B   51   C   52   D   53   E   54   F   10

B852

Dalcrag

B862

Bunkegivie

River Gouraq

Hut Circles and
Field System

Crannog

Allt an Lòin

Corriegarth
Lodge

Carn na
Glaice Mòire

Garthbeg

Coire
Riabhach

Carn Choire
Riabhaich

Cullintyre

Hut Circles and
Field System

Compass

Hut Circles and
Field System

Allt Doirean na Smeoraich

Loch nan
Losganan

Whitebridge

Carn
Gairbhthinn

Cnoc an
t-Sidhien

River E

Hut
Circles

Beinn
Sgurrach

Coire
Ghairt

IV2

Leac nan
Cisteachan

Carn
Tubhainn

Dam

Carn Doire
nan Aighean

Carn
Suidhe Ghoiri

Upper
Knockchoilum

River Fechlin

Meall an
Tarsaid

Carn Ruigh
na Creadha

Allt Glaic Breabaig

Mondadhliath Mountains

River Fechlin

Garrogie
Lodge

Garbah-bhac

Allt Laith-bhaid

Allt Beag

Allt Mòr

Hut
Circle

Carn Liath-
bhaid

Glac
an Lòin

Meall nan
Aighean Mòr

Uisgean Gardha

Loch
Killin

Creag
Eigin

Meall nan
Aighean Beag

Scale: 1¾ inches to 1 mil

0   ¼   ½ mile
0   250m 500m 750m 1 km

A   B   C   D   E   F

Coire Shuilean Duibh

Carn Dearg

Glac na Ba' Duibhe

Cairn Beinn Ghuilbin

Fort

A9

Avielochan Farm

Avielochan

Sidhean Ruighe Sheumais

Kinveachy Forest

Carn Avie

An Leth chreag

Hut Circles & Field System

Loch nan Carraigean

Carn Sleamhuinn

Carn Mòr

A95

Grainish Farm

B9152

Ford

Milton Burn

Ford

Ford

Sluggangranish

Achantoul

The Shieling

Ford

Steallan Dubh

PH22

Ford

Milton

Ind Est

169

DALFABER DR

SPEY AV

Milton Park

Prim Sch

LC

Dalfaber

Creag nan Gabhar

CORROUR RD

Cairn

Dearg Mòr

Cairn

Dalfaber Golf & Country Club

CRAIG-NA GOWER AV

GRAMPIAN RD

CAFIELD PL

PO

P

Aviemore

Carn Fiaclach

Creag na h-Iolaire

Craigellachie National Nature Reserve

Chy

P

Liby

Aviemore

P

Coire na h-Uchdaich

Hotel

i

DALFABER RD

Fords

Lochan Dubh

Viewpoint

169

YH

Allt Dubh

An Gleannan

Creag Ghleannain

Caravan Park

B970

Dell of Rothiemurchus

Corrour House

Kinakyle

Rothiemurchus Visitor Centre

Inverdruie

P

Allt-na-Criche

Lynwilg

169

B970

B970

PH21

Waterfall

Ballinluig Farm

A9

B9152

Gravel Pit

Creag na h-Uamha

Fords

85   A   86   B   87   C   88   D   89   E   90   F

For full street detail of the highlighted area see page 169.

Scale: 1¾ inches to 1 mile
¼   ½   mile
250m 500m 750m 1 km

A   B   C   D   E   F

Loch Vaa
Cemy
Laggantygown

The Strathspey Railway

Speyside Way

Wester Dalvoult
Street of Kincardine
Knock of Kincardine
Auchgourish Gardens (Arboretum)

Loch Mallachie

PH24

Lochan Dubh

Glencairn

Loch Dallas

Kinchurdy Farm

Auchgourish

Blàr Mòr

Mhòr Cottage

Tomnagowhan

Speyside Way

West Croftmore

Loch an Eilein

Auchgourish Burn

Loch na Lair

Delbog

PH25

River Spey

Milton Ford

Hut Circles

Cairns (remains of)

Field System

Glac Mhòr

Craiggowrie Burn

Pityoulish Farm

Coire Sgamh

Creag Mheadhonach

B970

Loch Pityoulish

Creag Phitiulais

Stone

An Slugan

Milton Burn

Creag a' Ghreusaiche

Mast

Craiggowrie

Coire Bogha Choinnich

Callart Hill

PH22

169

Guislich Farm

Ford

Achnahatnich Farm

Druimintoul Lodge

Moormore

Cairngorm Sleddog Adventure Centre

Badaguish (Outdoor Centre)

Allt Feithe Moire

Allt na Doire

River Druie

Coylumbridge

Waterfall

Glen More Forest Park

Hotel

Aultnancaber Clay Pigeon Shooting

River Luineag

The Queen's Forest

91   A   92   B   93   C   94   D   95   E   96   F

8
17
7
16
6
15
5
14
4
13
3
12
2
11
1
10

144   For full street detail of the highlighted area see page 169.   145

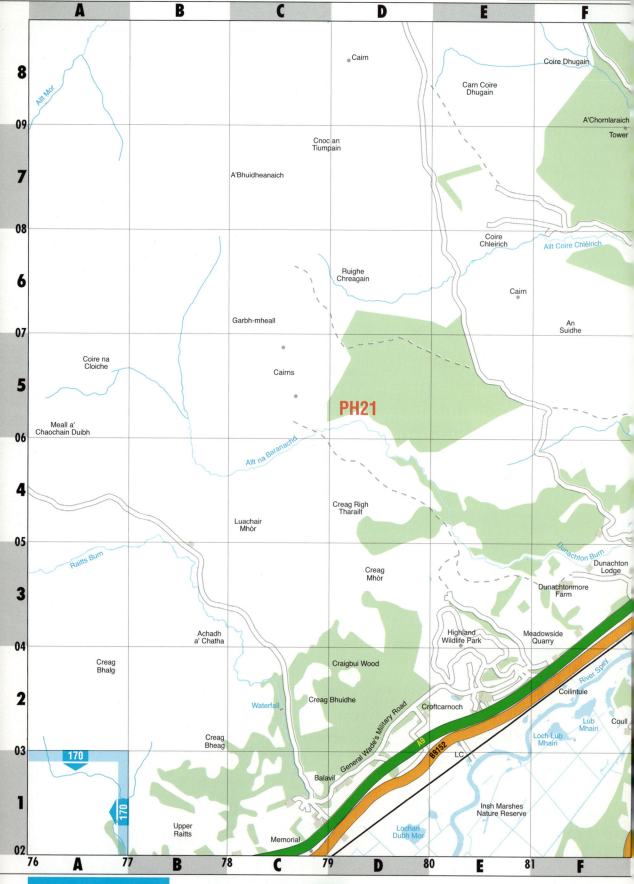

Scale: 1¾ inches to 1 mil
0   ¼   ½ mile
0 250m 500m 750m 1 km

PH21

For full street detail of the highlighted area see page 170.

170

147

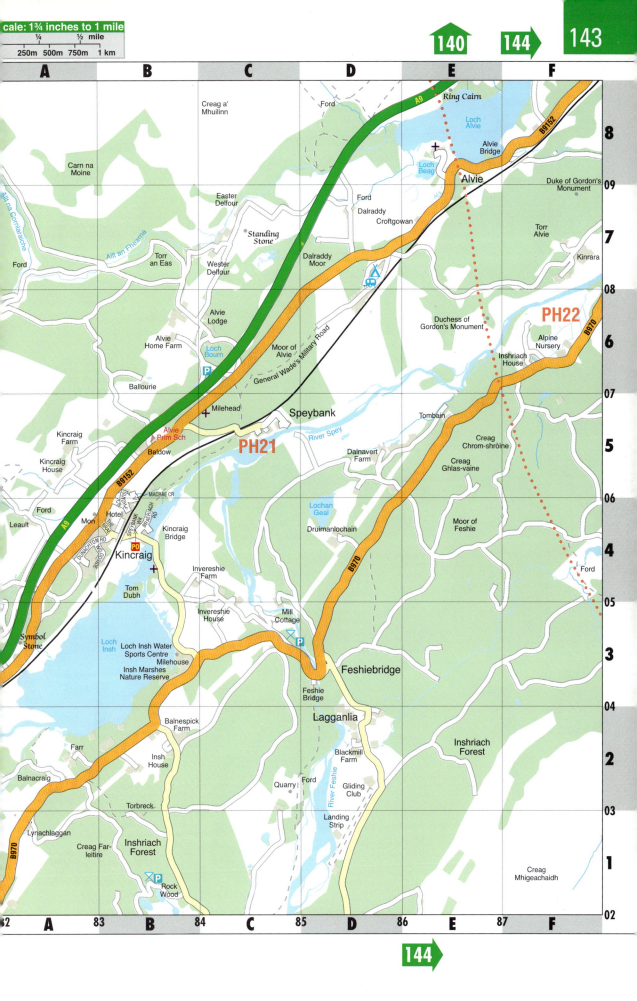

Scale: 1¾ inches to 1 mile

0   ¼   ½ mile
0   250m   500m   750m   1 km

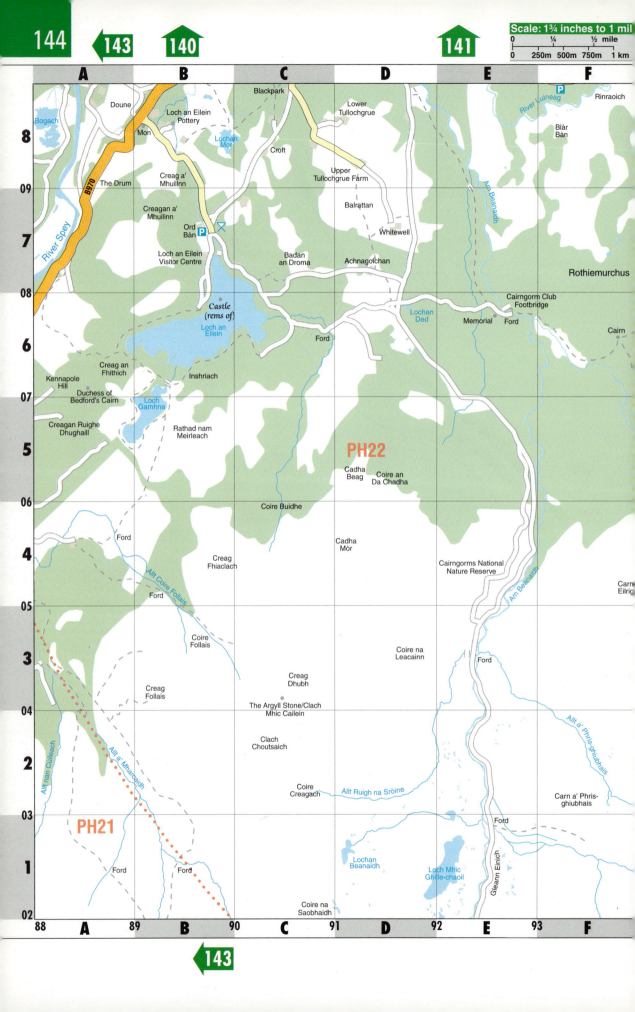

A   **B**   **C**   **D**   **E**   **F**

Doune
Loch an Eilein Pottery
Mon
Lochan Mòr
Bogach
River Spey
Blackpark
Croft
Lower Tullochgrue
River Luineag
Rinraoich
Blàr Bàn

B970
The Drum
Creag a' Mhuillnn
Creagan a' Mhuilinn
Ord Bàn
Loch an Eilein Visitor Centre
Upper Tullochgrue Farm
Balrattan
Whitewell
Badan an Droma
Achnagoichan
An Beanaidh

8
09
7
08

Castle (rems of)
Loch an Eilein
Ford
Lochan Ded
Memorial
Ford
Cairngorm Club Footbridge
Cairn
Rothiemurchus

6

Creag an Fhithich
Inshriach
Kennapole Hill
Duchess of Bedford's Cairn
Loch Gamhna
Creagan Ruighe Dhughaill
Rathad nam Meirleach

07
5

PH22

Cadha Beag
Coire an Da Chadha

06
Coire Buidhe
4

Ford
Allt Coire Follais
Creag Fhiaclach
Cadha Mòr
Cairngorms National Nature Reserve
Am Beanaidh
Carn Eilrig

05
Ford
3
Coire Follais
Coire na Leacainn
Ford

Allt nan Cùileach
Creag Follais
Creag Dhubh
The Argyll Stone/Clach Mhic Cailein
Allt a' Phris-ghiubhais

04

Clach Choutsaich
Allt a' Mharcaidh
2
Coire Creagach
Allt Ruigh na Sròine
Carn a' Phris-ghiubhais

03
Ford
Gleann Einich
PH21
1
Ford
Ford
Lochan Beanaidh
Loch Mhic Ghille-chaoil

02
Coire na Saobhaidh

88   **A**   **89**   **B**   **90**   **C**   **91**   **D**   **92**   **E**   **93**   **F**

A B C D E F

8

09

7

08

Memorial

Loch Morlich

Lochan nan Geadas

YHA

Glenmore Visitor Centre

Cairngorm Reindeer Centre

Glen More

Glenmore Lodge (National Outdoor Training Centre)

Allt Bàn

Allt na Ciste

Rothiemurchus Lodge

Airgiod-meall

Lochan Dubh a' Chadha

Coire Buidhe

PH22

Ford

Castle Hill

Allt Druidh

Creag a' Chalamain

Chalamain Gap

Allt Creag an Leth-choin

Allt Coire an t-Sneachda

Ford

Bathaich Fionndag

Chair Lift

An t-Aonach

Ski Tow

Ski Tow

Ski Centre

Base

Cairngorm Funicular Railway

Ski Tows

Shieling

Ski Tow

Ford

Coire Cas

Ski Tow

Ski Tows

Fiacaill a' Choire Chais

07

6

5

06

4

05

3

Rothiemurchus

Carn Odhar

Lochan Odhar

Lurcher's Crag/Creag an Leth-choin

Fiacaill Coire an t-Sneachda

Cairngorm Mountains

Coire an Lochain

04

2

Lairig Ghru

Miadan Creag an Leth-choin

Beanaidh Bheag

Coire Gorm

Cairn Lochan

Stob Coire an t-Sneachda

AB35

Coire Domhain

03

1

02

4 A 95 B 96 C 97 D 98 E 99 F

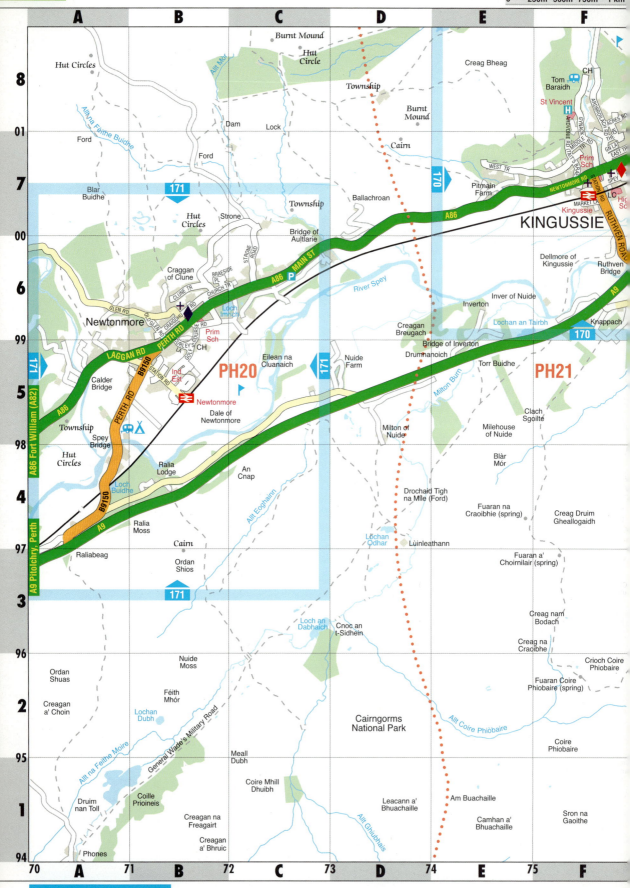

Scale: 1¾ inches to 1 mi

0   ¼   ½   mile
0 250m 500m 750m 1 km

Burnt Mound
Hut Circles
Hut Circle
Township
Creag Bheag
Tom Baraidh
CH
St Vincent
Dam
Lock
Ford
Cairn
Burnt Mound
Prim Sch
WEST TR
Ford
Blar Buidhe
171
170
Pitmain Farm
NEWTONMORE RD
A86
KINGUSSIE
Hut Circles
Strone
Township
Ballachroan
Kingussie
High Sch
SPEY
Bridge of Aultlarie
MAIN ST
Dellmore of Kingussie
Ruthven Bridge
Craggan of Clune
BRAESIDE PL
CLUNE TR
A86
P
River Spey
Inver of Nuide
A9
GLEN RD
CHURCH TR
Loch Imrich
Inverton
Lochan an Tairbh
Knappach
Newtonmore
CRAIGDHU
PERTH RD
Prim Sch
Craigdhu
Creagan Breugach
170
Bridge of Inverton
STATION RD
CH
GOLF COURSE
Eilean na Cluanaich
171
PH20
Nuide Farm
Drummnanoich
Torr Buidhe
PH21
171
B9150
Ind Est
Calder Bridge
PERTH RD
Newtonmore
Dale of Newtonmore
Milton Burn
Milton of Nuide
Clach Sgoilte
Milehouse of Nuide
Township
Spey Bridge
Ralia Lodge
An Cnap
Blàr Mór
Hut Circles
A86 Fort William (A82)
B9150
A9
Loch Buidhe
Ralia Moss
Allt Eoghainn
Drochaid Tigh na Mìle (Ford)
Fuaran na Craoibhie (spring)
Creag Druim Gheallogaidh
Raliabeag
Cairn
Lòchan Odhar
Lùinleathann
Fuaran a' Choirnilair (spring)
A9 Pitlochry, Perth
Ordan Shios
171
Loch an Dabhaich
Cnoc an t-Sidhein
Creag nam Bodach
Creag na Craoibhe
Nuide Moss
Crìoch Coire Phiobaire
Ordan Shuas
Féith Mhór
Fuaran Coire Phiobaire (spring)
Creagan a' Choin
Lochan Dubh
General Wade's Military Road
Cairngorms National Park
Allt Coire Phiòbaire
Coire Phiobaire
Allt na Fèithe Moire
Meall Dubh
Coire Mhill Dhuibh
Leacann a' Bhuachaille
Am Buachaille
Sron na Gaoithe
Druim nan Toll
Coille Prioineis
Creagan na Freagairt
Allt Ghiubhais
Camhan a' Bhuachaille
Phones
Creagan a' Bhruic

For full street detail of the highlighted area see pages 170 and 171.

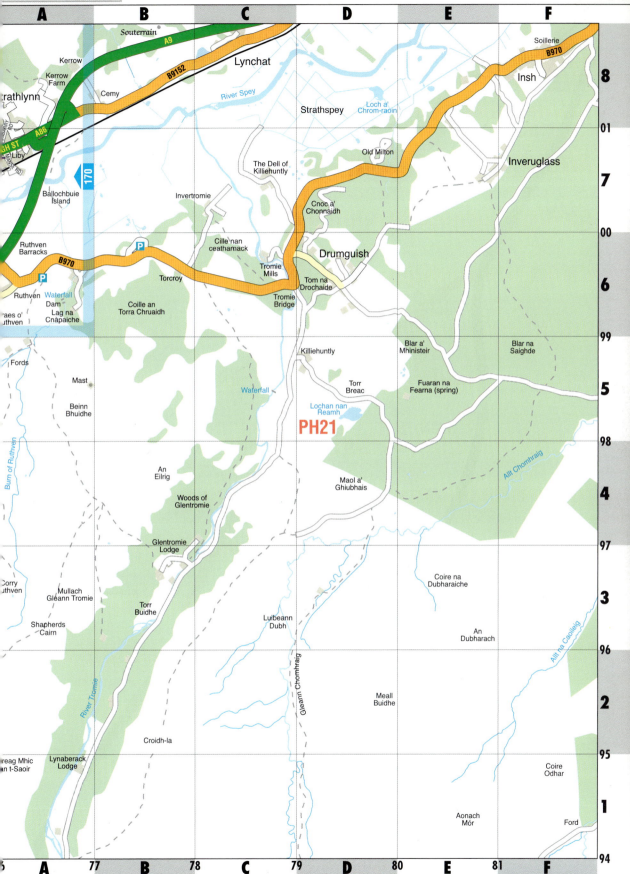

Scale: 1¾ inches to 1 mile

¼   ½   mile
250m 500m 750m 1 km

A B C D E F

8

01

7

00

6

99

5

98

4

97

3

96

2

95

1

94

Souterrain

A9

Kerrow

Kerrow Farm

Strathlynn

Cemy

B9152

Lynchat

River Spey

Strathspey

Loch a' Chrom-raoin

Soillerie

B970

Insh

Inveruglass

A86

QUARRY RD

HIGH ST

170

Liby

MANSE RD

Ballochbuie Island

The Dell of Killiehuntly

Old Milton

Invertromie

Cnoc a' Chonnaidh

Ruthven Barracks

B970

P

Cille nan ceatharnack

Drumguish

Torcroy

Tromie Mills

Tom na Drochaide

Ruthven

P

Waterfall

Dam

Lag na Cnàpaiche

Coille an Torra Chruaidh

Tromie Bridge

Braes o' Ruthven

Fords

Mast

Killiehuntly

Blar a' Mhinisteir

Blar na Saighde

Beinn Bhuidhe

Waterfall

Torr Breac

Fuaran na Fearna (spring)

Burn of Ruthven

Lochan nan Reamh

PH21

Allt Chomhraig

An Eilrig

Woods of Glentromie

Maol a' Ghiubhais

Glentromie Lodge

Coire na Dubharaiche

Corry Ruthven

Mullach Gleann Tromie

Torr Buidhe

Luibeann Dubh

An Dubharach

Allt na Caoileig

Shapherds Cairn

Gleann Chomhraig

River Tromie

Meall Buidhe

Croidh-la

Creag Mhic an t-Saoir

Lynaberack Lodge

Coire Odhar

Aonach Mór

Ford

A 77 B 78 C 79 D 80 E 81 F

For full street detail of the highlighted area see page 170.

Glenmorangie Distillery
Chy
Visitor Centre
Morangie

Dornoch Firth

St Mary's Well

A9

B9174

Superstore
Blarliath Industrial Estate
Hotel
Sewage Works
Football Gd
St Mary's Well
MORANGIE ROAD
MAYFIELD WYND
DITHAC WYND
CANMORE WAY
SPRINGFIELD GD
St Mary's Well
MURRAY ST
DUNCROSS
SHORE ROAD
ACADEMY ST
St Duthus Spec Sch
Tain Through Time
Tain
Plaids
St Duthus's Chapel
Tain Golf Club
CH

MOSS ROAD
MOSS ROAD
WELL ST
CHAPEL ST
STATION RD
CHAPEL RD
DUTHUS RD
St Duthus Cemetery
Kirksheaf
PROVOST GD
FERGUSON RD
MANSE CR
MURRAY PL
TOWER ST
HIGH ST
ROSE ST
1 CASTLE ST
2 BANK ST
3 CRAMMOND BRAE
4 MARKET ST
5 KING ST
6 SCOTSBURN CT

TAIN
STAGCRAFT PL
MANSE CR
VIEWHILL DR
GLEBE CR
QUEBEC
CRAIGHILL TERR
QUARRY
QUEEN ST
LAMINGTON ST
GEANIES ST
KIRKSHEAF ROAD
KIRKSHEAF ROAD

Craighill Prim Sch
CRAIGHILL TERRACE
ST ANDREWS RD
SCOTSBURN ROAD
CRAIGHILL TR
Liby
Knockbreck Prim Sch
Fendor Bridge

Tain Royal Academy
VICTORIA RD
UPPER KING ST
MARTFIELD
STAFFORD ST
CROMARTY RD
KNOCKBRECK CT
ANGERVILLE STREET
KNOCKBRECK ROAD
IV19

PH
QUARRY ROAD
BEN-Y-HW RD
VIEWFIELD RD
JUBILEE DR
CRAIG AVE
CRAIG CR
ST VINCENT
PLEASANT AVE
KINGSWAY
MAYFIELD ROAD
FOUNTAIN RD
BURGAGE DR
SUTHER CR
KNOCK AV
SUTHER CR
Knockbreck

Viewfield
VIEWFIELD PK
QUEBEC AV
CAMERON AV
CAMERON ROAD
ARGYLE CT
SEAFORTH RD
SEAFORTH GD
BURGAGE CT

St Vincent
ARTHURVILLE GD
CAMERON GD
HARTFIELD GD
SEAFORTH

Arthurville
B9174

Chimney
North Glastullich Farm
Hartfield
HARTFIELD ROAD
SCOTSBURN ROAD

Hilton

Tain Pottery & Aldie Mill

Aldie

Moor Farm

Hilton Bridge
A9

D4
1 SHANDWICK ST
2 KNOCKBRECK ST
3 PETLEY ST
4 PETLEY PL
5 DUKE ST
6 GOWER ST
7 CADBOLL PL

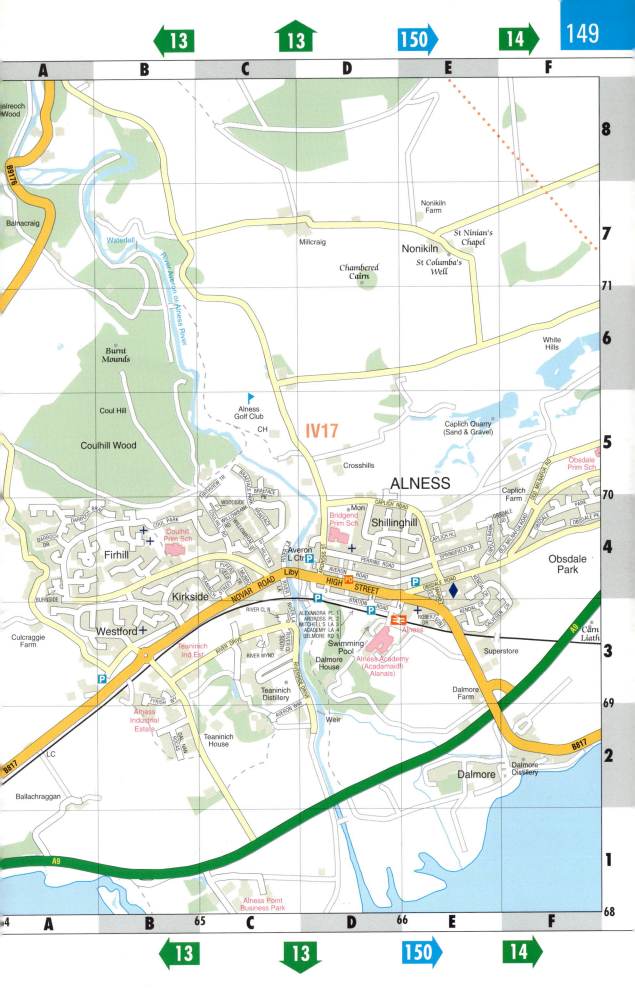

A B C D E F

8 Culcairn
Rosebank
Newmore Castle
Newmore Prim Sch
Rhicullen

7 Trout Fishery
Highfield
TOP STREET

71 Balnaguisich
Easter Kincraig

6 Mossfield
IV18
Kincraig House
A9

OLD MILNAFUA ROAD
Kincraig Farm

Achnagarron
Lower Kincraig

5 Milnafua
Achnagarron Farm
MILNAFUA
Obsdale Prim Sch
Achnagarron Burn

70 OBSDALE PK

4 A9
Auchintoul
Oak Wood

The House of Rosskeen

IV17
Rosskeen
Rosskeen Old Manse
CABERFEIDH DR

3 Church
Invergordon Golf Club
BIRCHWOOD
BIRCHWOOD
CH

Belle Port
Clach a' Mheirlich Symbol Stone
Rosskeen Bridge

69 B817
P
KING GEORGE STREET
SEAFORTH GR
QUEEN

Belleport Pier
P
P
P

2 P

1 Cromarty Firth

68 67 A 68 B C 69 D E F

14 15

A B C D E F

8

Northfield

A9

Broomhill

7

71

Tomich

6

Cromarty Firth
Industrial Park

IV18

Ord Farm

Ord

5

Saltburn

70

AULT-SALLAN ROAD

PO

B817

Inverbreakie
Industrial Estate

4

War
Meml

Invergordon
Mains

Inverbreakie

CROMARTY VIEW

Distillery

Bellfield
Strath
Avenue
Fraser
Rd
Mains
Av
Castle Pl
Castle Avenue
Davidson
Drive
Mackean Cr

County
H

INVERBREAKIE
DRIVE
ORD
JR
CADBOL RD
MURRAY RD
INGLIS RD
ELLIOT RD
GROSVENOR ST
BLACKPARK
GOLFVIEW TERRACE
WESTWOOD
WOODSIDE
OLD

Kilmuir
Macdonald
Strath
Ness Rd
Reid Rd
Reid Rd
Rosskeen Dr
Gordon
Terrace
Royal Oak Dr
Bermuda
Rd
Natal Pl

South Lodge
Prim Sch

Invergordon
Sports
Ctr

Chy
P

3

Invergordon
Academy

CASTLE AVENUE

ACADEMY RD

Oil
Depot

SEABANK RD

69

Park
Prim Sch

Agincourt
Cromlet Pk
Cromlet
Drive

CROMLET DR
CASTLE RD

Liby

P P

Albany
Rd

TOMICH RD
BANK ST
HIGH ST
JOSS ST
ESK CT
WYVIS CT
HIGH ST
MUNRO

SALTBURN ROAD

Pier

2

Invergordon

STATION
STREET

KING ST

2
3
4
5

OUTRAM ST

SHORE ROAD

Clyde St

P P
PO

Mon

B817

INVERGORDON

Cromarty Firth

1

P

MACKAY ST 1
NORMANS LA 2
MILL ST 3
HUGH MILLER ST 4
FERRY ROW 5

68

14 15

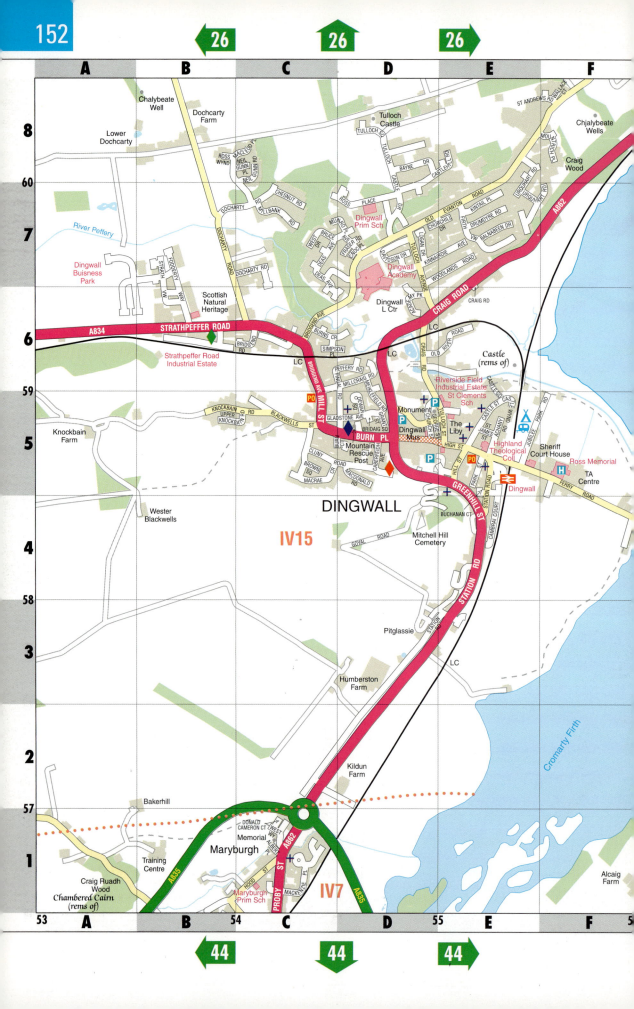

A   B   C   D   E   F

8

60

7

6

59

5

DINGWALL

IV15

4

58

3

2

57

Maryburgh

1

IV7

53   A   B   54   C   D   55   E   F   5

Chalybeate Well
Dochcarty Farm
Lower Dochcarty
Tulloch Castle
St Andrews Rd
Chjalybeate Wells
Craig Wood
ROSS WYND
MACLEOD PL
NEIL GUNN PL
NEIL GUNN RD
DOCHARTY
CHESNUT RD
MILLBANK RD
TULLOCH SQ
TULLOCH RD
CASTLE LEY RD
BAYNE DR
CASTLEY RD
MOU
RICHARDSON
A862
River Peffery
Dingwall Buisness Park
FOODERTY WAY
STRATH
VW
DOCHARTY ROAD
DOCHARTY RD
ROSS PLACE
WEST BRUCE DR
DEAS AVE
FRASER RD
MUNRO CR
ALVER RD
CADCH
Dingwall Prim Sch
OLD EVANTON RD
CHURCHILL DR
EVANTON ROAD
KINTAIL PL
FIRTH
DRUMOYNE RD
URQUHART RD
CRAIG ROAD
CRAIG RD
Scottish Natural Heritage
DEAS AVE
DAVIDSON DR
LOGAN RD
TULLOCH
KINNAIRDIE AVE
Dingwall Academy
WOODLANDS ROAD
BALNABEEN DR
VW
A834
STRATHPEFFER ROAD
BRIDGEND AVE
BURNS CR
SIMPSON PL
Dingwall L Ctr
MY PK
Castle (rems of)
Strathpeffer Road Industrial Estate
BRIDGE RD
LC
PEFFERY RD
FINGAL RD
MILLCRAIG RD
MCENFIELD RD
LC
CRAIG
OLD RIVER RD
ROAD
LC
Riverside Field Industrial Estate
St Clements Sch
CASTLE ST
ORAM
Knockbain Farm
UPPER KNOCKBAIN
KNOCKBAIN RD
BLACKWELLS
MILL ST
DEWAR RD
GLADSTONE AVE
BRIDAIG SQ
GRANT
Monument
P
P
The Liby
CASTLE ST CAS
ACHANY RD
JAMES ST
JUBILEE PARK RD
BURN PL
BURN ST
Dingwall Mus
GEORGE ST
CHURCH ST
HIGH ST
Highland Theological Coll
Sheriff Court House
Ross Memorial
Wester Blackwells
CLUNY CR
BROWN SQ
MACRAE
MOUNTAIN RESCUE POST
Mountain Rescue Post
CABERFEIDH AVE
MACDONALD RD
P
PO
HILL ST
PARK
H
Dingwall
TA Centre
FERRY ROAD
Knockbain Farm
DINGWALL
GOYAL ROAD
Buchanan Ct
GREENHILL ST
CAMBRAI COURT
Mitchell Hill Cemetery
IV15
STATION RD
Pitglassie
STATION RD
CAMBRAI ROAD
LC
Humberston Farm
Cromarty Firth
Kildun Farm
Bakerhill
A862
Donald Cameron Ct
WEST VW
ALBER
Training Centre
Memorial
Maryburgh
A835
PROBY ST
HOOD
MACKENZIE PL
Maryburgh Prim Sch
IV7
A835
Alcaig Farm
Craig Ruadh Wood
Chambered Cairn (rems of)

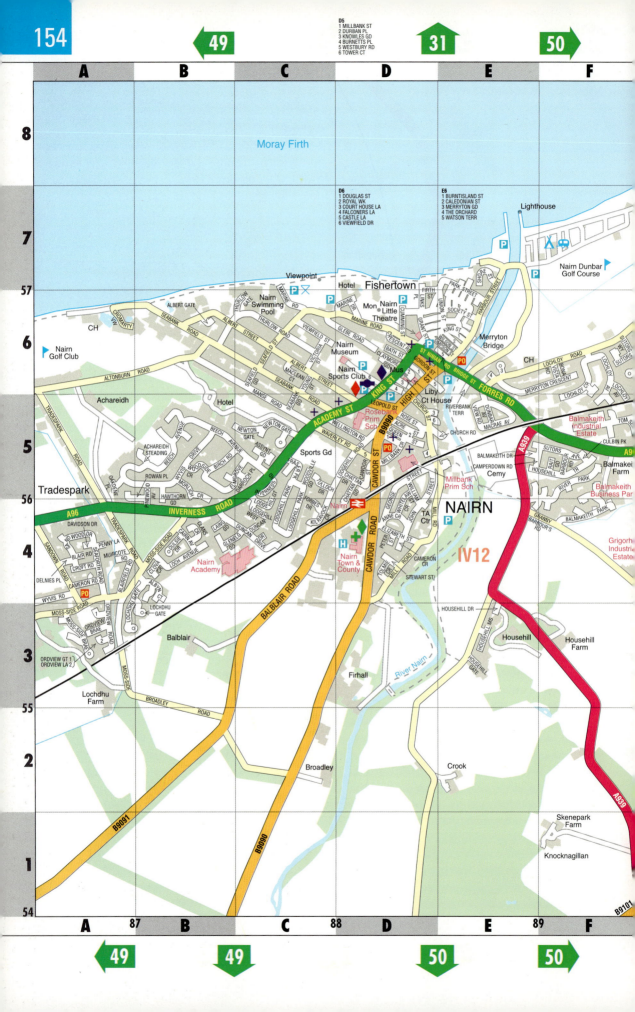

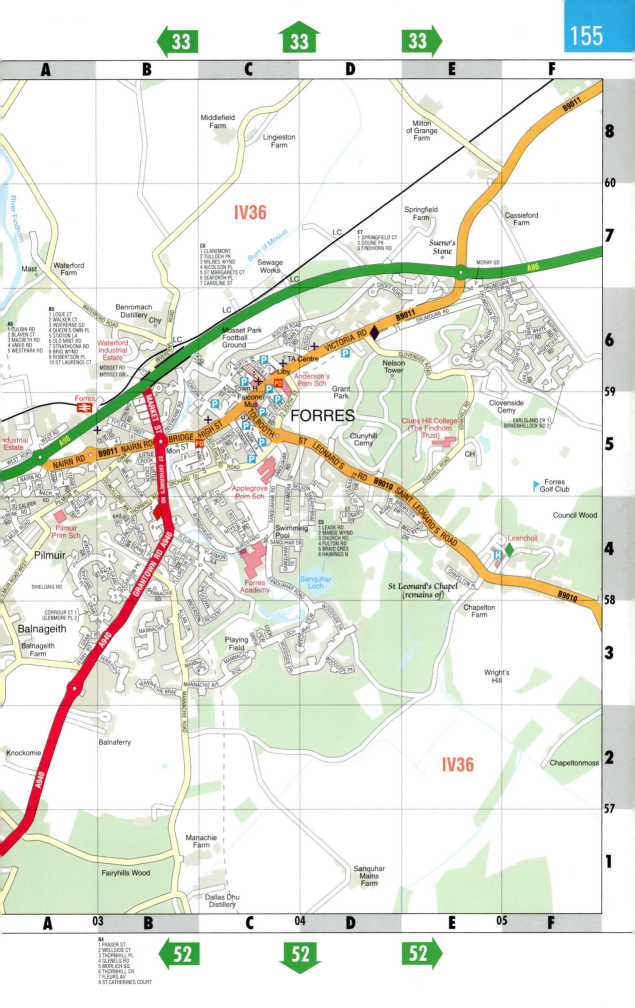

LOSSIEMOUTH

IV31

Branderburgh

Seatown

Stotfield

Moray Golf Course

Stotfield Links

RAF Lossiemouth

Kineddar Farm

Oakenhead Wood

Easter Greens

Cemetery

The Lossiemouth Fisheries & Comm Museum

Scarf Craig

Grant Park (Lossiemouth FC)

Bishops Palace (remains of)

Cross (remains of)

Coulardbank Ind Est

Muirton

Muirton CT

B9040
B9135
B9103
A941

QUEEN STREET
STOTFIELD ROAD
CLIFTON ROAD A941
SEATOWN RD
PITGAVENY ST
ELGIN ROAD
SCHOOL BRAE
INCHBROOM ROAD

F7
1 MITCHELL ST
2 BAKER ST
3 PITGAVENY ST

E6
1 PROSPECT VW

F6
1 PROSPECT CT
2 LESMURDIE PL
3 HILL ST

E5
1 CHAPEL LA
2 ROSE LA
3 OGSTON LA

D5
1 HYTHEHILL PL
2 COULARD BANK CT

C5
1 SMITHFIELD PL

St Gerardine's Prim Sch
Hythehill Prim Sch
Lossiemouth High Sch

Recreation Gd
Town Hall
Lby
PO

Muirton CR
Balormie PL
Macroberts Reply
Coulardbank CR

Paradise Row

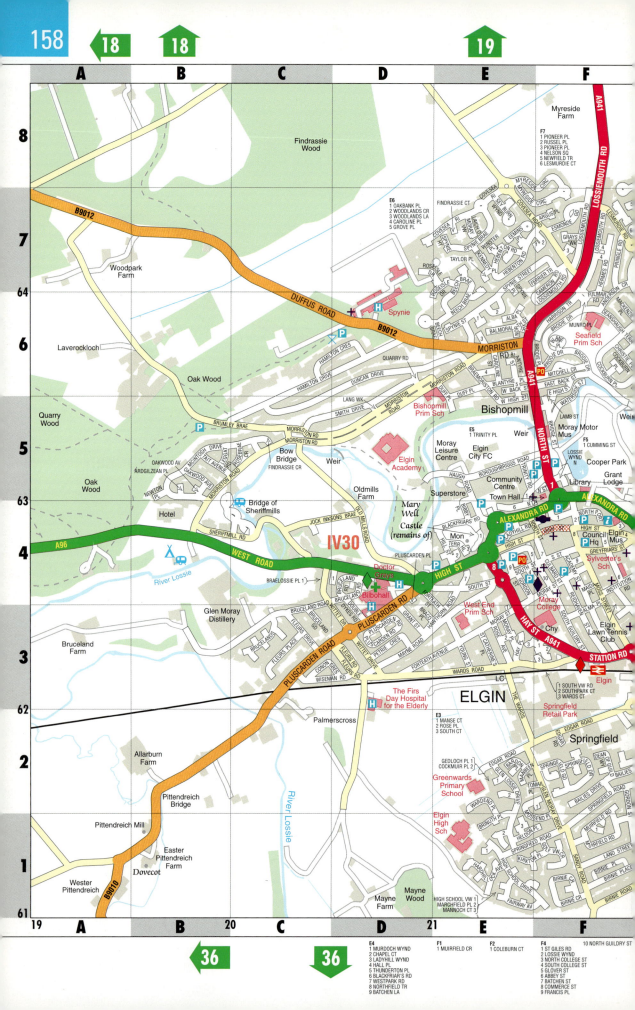

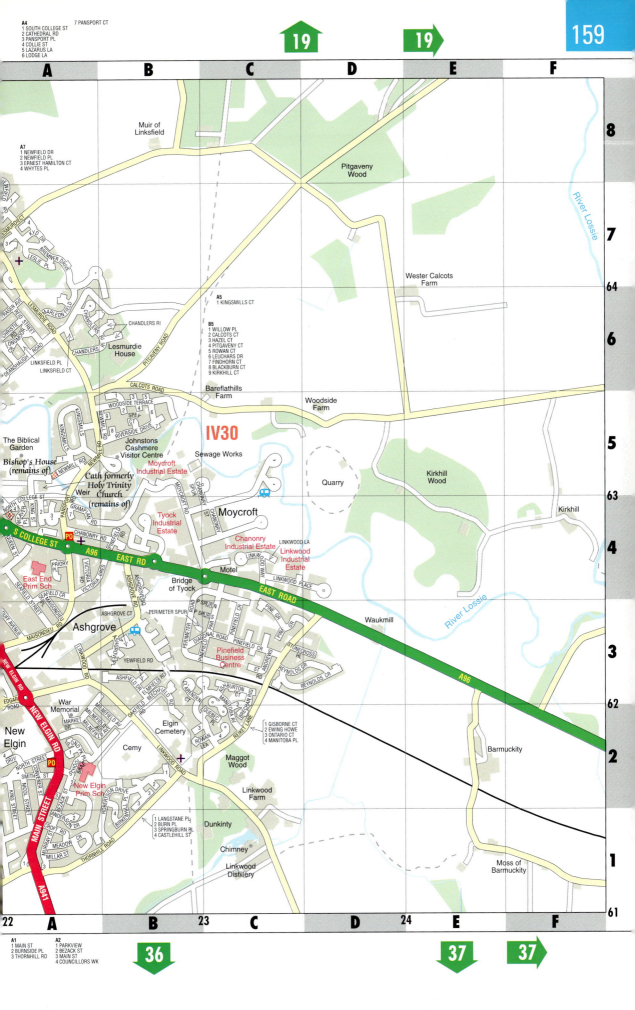

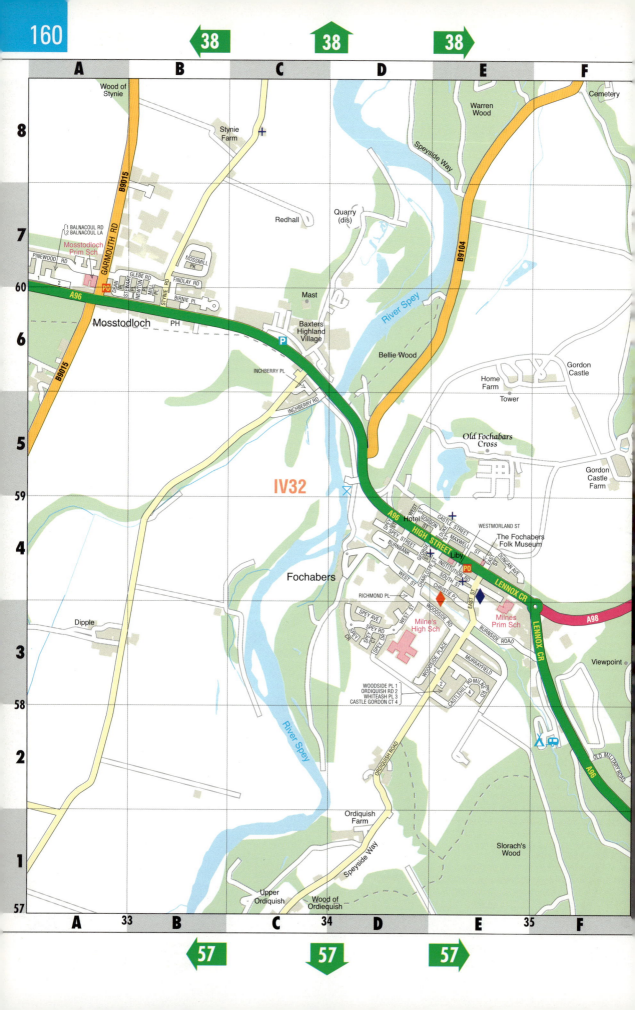

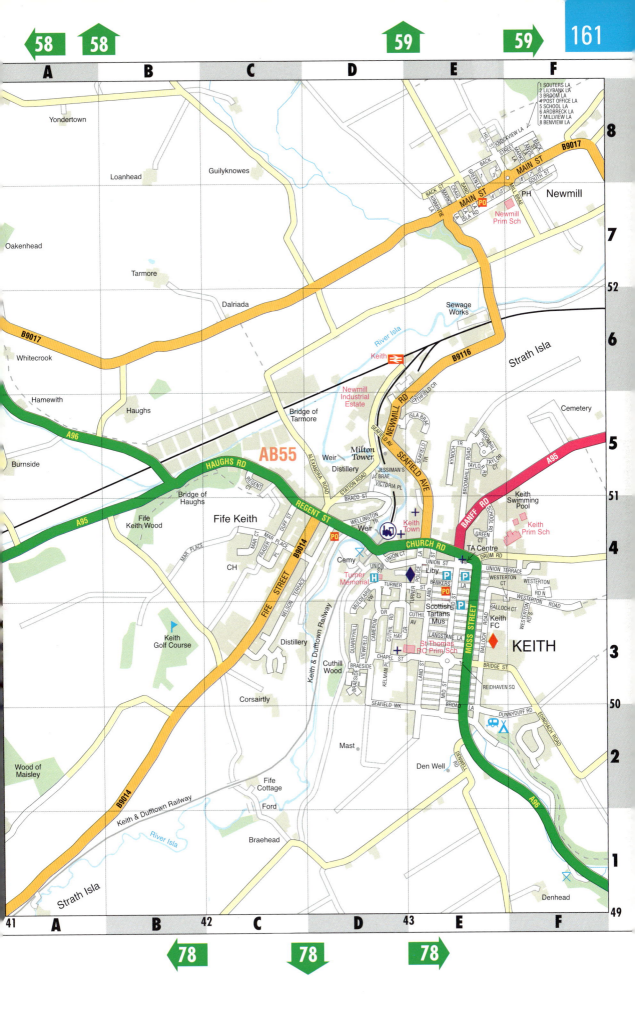

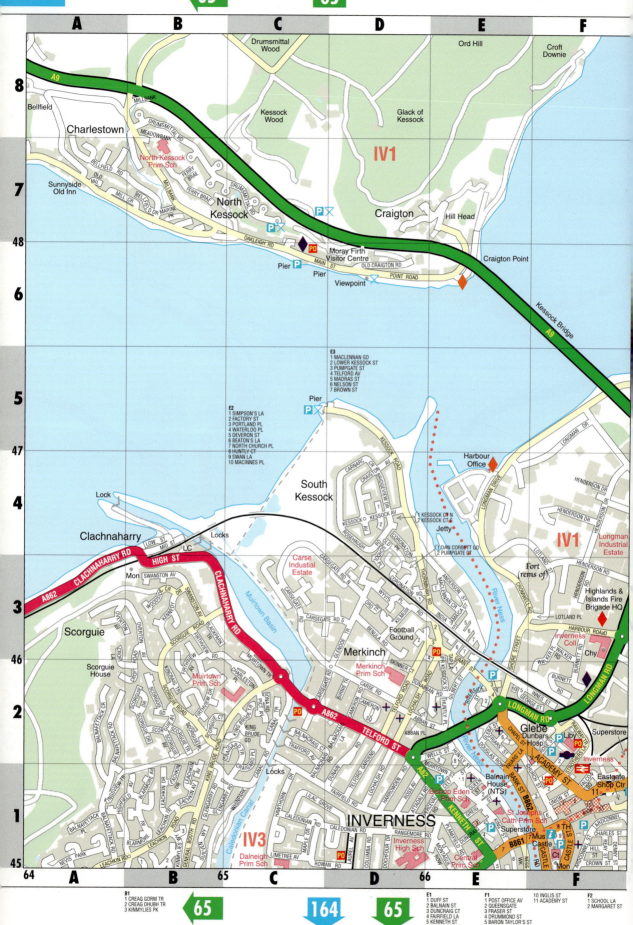

A B C D E F

8

Moray

Firth

7

48

6

Longman
Point

Caledonian Stadium
(Inverness Caledonian
Thistle FC)

5

47

IV1

4

LONGMAN RD B82

Seafield RD

Seafield RD

Government
Offices

HARBOUR RD

HARBOUR RD

HARBOUR ROAD

3

Seafield

A96

46

2

LC

Motel

Hotel

MILLBURN RD

MILLBURN RD

Chy

Hotel

Inverness Business
Park

EASTFIELD WAY

Aqueduct

Inverness
Retail Park

B865

AULDCASTLE RD

DIRIEBUGHT RD

VICTORIA LA

VICTORIA TR

Milburn

MILLBURN CT

Barracks

B865

B9006

KING DUNCAN'S RD

MACKINTOSH RD

MACKINTOSH RD

CHATTAN AV

ASHTON RD

OLD PERTH RD

CROWN AV

ABERTARFF RD

CROWN RD

BEAUFORT RD

LOVAT RD

CANDOR RD

DIRIEBUGHT

VICTORIA DR

Millburn
Academy

SICILY RD

WINDMILL WY

MAYFIELD RD

PLANTN

SOMME PL

RHIME CT

ANZIO DR

BEECHWOOD

ASHTON CRES

BEECHWD CT

ASHTON

STRATTON RD

Raigmore
Prim Sch

BURMA CT

CHURCHILL RD

Raigmore

BALMORAL TR

QSIDE

IV2

Coll

Crown

CROWN

MIDMILLS RD

HILL ST

KINGSMILLS RD

Crown
Prim Sch

UNION RD

BROADSTONE PARK

MACKENZIE PL

BROADSTONE RD

MARYFIELD GD

Cairn

A9

1

45

67 A 68 B 68 C D 69 E F

A1
1 STEPHEN'S ST
2 SOUTHSIDE RD
3 BROADSTONE AV
4 STEPHEN'S BRAE

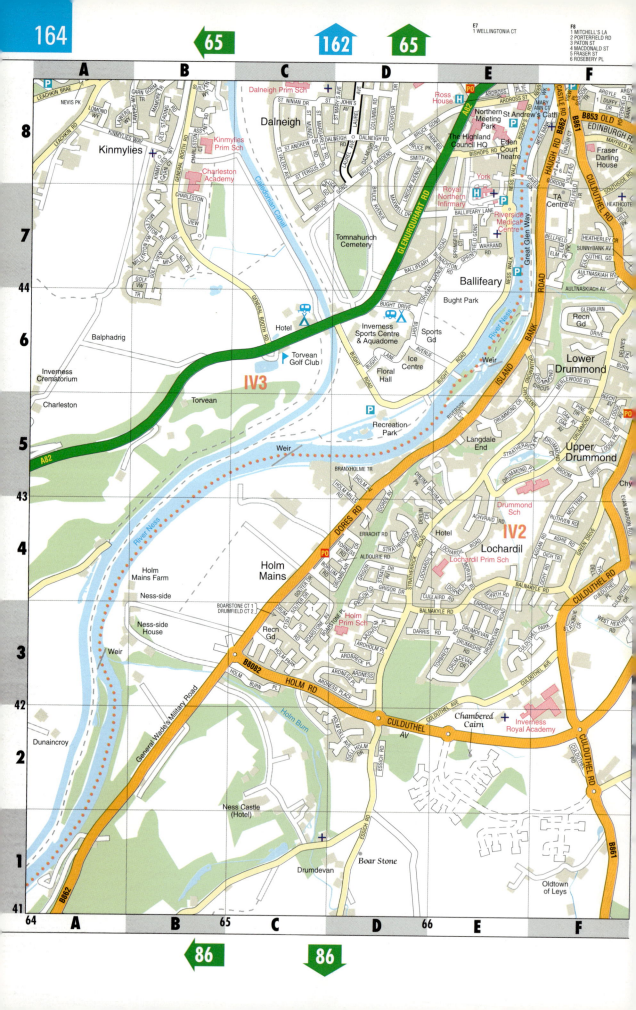

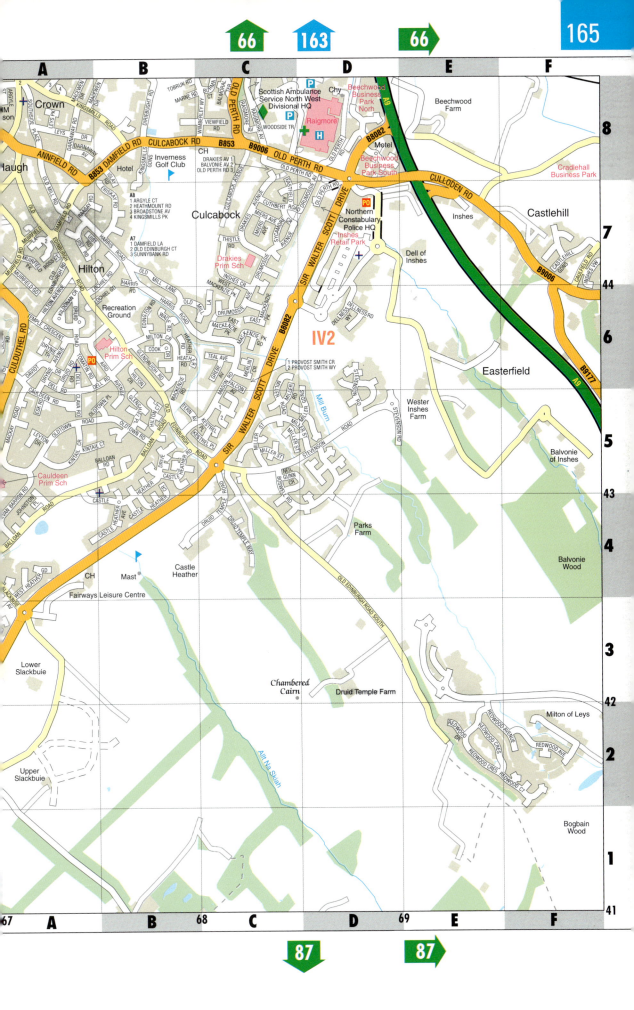

66
163
66
87
87

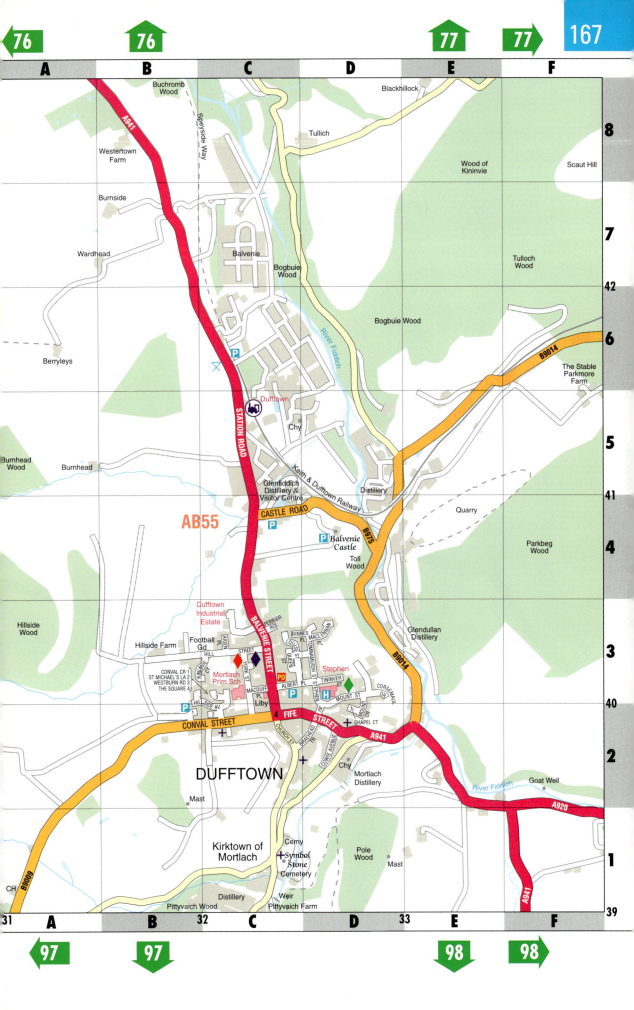

Coachass End

Burnside
Farm

1 BURNSIDE AV
2 BURNSIDE PL
3 MUIRTON

Dalfaber
Ind Est

CRAIGGOWRIE PL

Milton

CROFTSIDE

BRAERIACH

ELLACHIE
CR

DALFABER DRIVE

Cairngorm Technology
Park

Ind
Est

LC

Dalfaber
Farm

8

Ring
Cairn

BURNSIDE AV

Ind
Est

CH

Milton
Park

KINVEACHY
GDNS

Football
Ground

Dalfaber

Dalfaber Golf
& Country Club

River Spey

Loch
Pityoulish

7

Aviemore
Prim Sch

Aviemore

The Strathspey Railway

CAIRN
AV

1 CAIRN AVIE
2 CAIRN MORE
3 BEN GOOLABIN
4 CAIRN SLOWNE
5 MILL BUIE
6 CAIRN JERRIG

Callart
Hill

13

Chy

PO
P

Myrtlefield
Industrial
Estate

6

P

P

Cambusmore

12

Lib

Aviemore

PH22

B970

Guislich
Farm

5

GRAMPIAN RD

Loch
Puladdern

Hotel

GRAMPIAN
CT

Ford

4

i

YH

Fish
Farm

B970

B9152

Dell of Rothiemurchus

3

PH

DALFABER RD

Corrour House
(Hotel)

Aber Druie
West Wood

Cairngorm Mountain
Rescue Post

Rothiemurchus
Estate

River Druie

11

P

P

Inverdruie

Coylum
Bridge

2

DELL MOR

Rothiemurchus
Visitor Centre

Hotel

The Fun
House

Coylumbridge

River Spey

B970

Gravel
Pit

1

89 A B 90 C D 91 E F 10

A B C D E F

8

7

02

6

Loch
Gynack

Pitmain
Lodge

Glen
Gynack

Dam

Township

Alll Cealgach

Kingussie
Golf Club

Creag
Bheag

CH

Tom
Baraidh

Gynack Burn

Kerrow
Farm

A9

5

St Vincent

H

ARDVONIE RD

Strathlynn

Craig-an-
Darach

B9152

Monument

ACRES RD

KERROW DR

DUNBARRY TR

CAMPBELL RD

CROILA RD

HILLSIDE

01

Pitmain Burn

BOA VISTA
RD

THE CR ORCHARD
CT

CLUNY
TR

JAMES CT

HILLSIDE
AV

A86

River Spey

4

KINGUSSIE

PH21

OLD DISTILLERY ROAD

MIDDLE TR

GYNACK ROAD

MILL RD

GREEN LA

JONATHAN'S BRAE

EAST TR

MANSE
RD

E4
1 GLEBE CT
2 THE GLEBE
3 COLUMBA TER
4 RUTHVEN CT
5 GARRALINE TER

HIGH STREET

P

Hotel

PO

Library

NEWTONMORE RD

WEST TERRACE

STATION RD

SPEY ST

KING ST

DUKE ST

Highland
Folk Mus

MANSE
RD

P

Kingussie
Prim Sch

Kingussie

GYNACK

LC

Pitmain
Farm

A86

B970

RUTHVEN ROAD

MARKET LA

Kingussie
High Sch

Ballochbuie
Island

3

Cairn

00

2

Dellmore of
Kingussie

River Spey

Ruthven
Bridge

Ruthven

Remains of
Ruthven
Barracks

B970

P

1

Inver of Nuide

Inverton

Burn of Inverton

Lochan
an Tairbh

A9

Knappach

Braes o' Ruthven

Waterfalls

Dam

99

74 A B 75 C D 76 E F

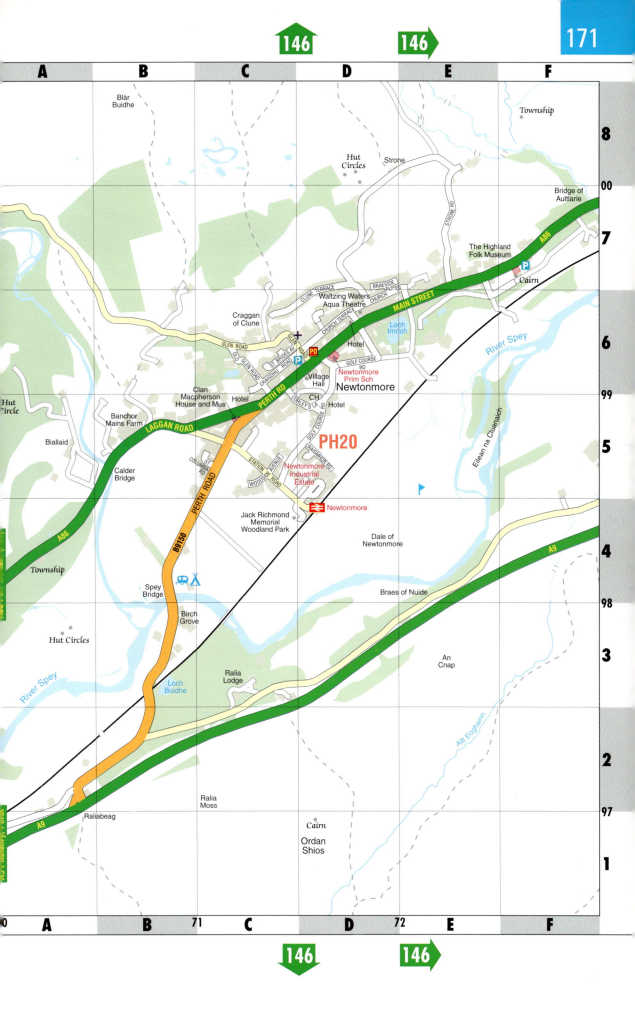

A B C D E F

8

7

10

6

5

09

4

3

08

2

1

07

36 A B 37 C D 38 E F

Great Glen Way

A82

Cherry Island
Crannog

Hotel

Old Pier

Loch Ness

Creag an-
Iarlain

Balantou Burn

Old Military Road

Blairconard

Jenkins
Park

Bunoich

BUNDICH BRAE

P

Inveroich
House

CHURCH RD

Hotel

THE RIGGS

Lighthouse

Fort Augustus

Caledonian Canal Mus

CANAL SIDE

OICH RD

Fort Augustus
Highlands &
Rare Breeds Croft

Forestry
Office

Locks

CANAL SIDE

Swing
Bridge

Sports
Gd

Fort Augustus
Abbey

Cemetery

P

PO

GLENDOE RD

Kilchuimen
Academy

2

1

Kilchuimen
Prim Sch

PH32

Hotel

1 STATION RD
2 LOVAT TER

Bridge of
Tarff

Sports
Ground

River Tarff

B862

ABERTARFF
PL

River Olch

Fort Augustus
Golf Club

CH

P

Borlum

Caledonian Canal

Burial
Ground

Tomamhoid

Eilean
Fioda

Tom na
Croiche

Torr a' Choiltreich

Ardachy
Lodge

Tom a' Mhoid

Great Glen Way

Coille Faileige

A82

Ardachy
Bridge

Ardachy
Wood

Loch
Uanagan

Index

Church Rd `6` Beckenham BR2..........**53** C6

Place name	**Location number**	**Locality, town or village**	**Postcode district**	**Page and grid squa**
May be abbreviated on the map	Present when a number indicates the place's position in a crowded area of mapping	Shown when more than one place has the same name	District for the indexed place	Page number and gr reference for the standard mapping

Public and commercial buildings are highlighted in magenta   **Places of interest** are highlighted in blue with a star ★

Abbreviations used in the index

Acad	**Academy**	Comm	**Common**	Gd	**Ground**	L	**Leisure**	Prom	**Prom**
App	**Approach**	Cott	**Cottage**	Gdn	**Garden**	La	**Lane**	Rd	**Road**
Arc	**Arcade**	Cres	**Crescent**	Gn	**Green**	Liby	**Library**	Recn	**Recreation**
Ave	**Avenue**	Cswy	**Causeway**	Gr	**Grove**	Mdw	**Meadow**	Ret	**Retail**
Bglw	**Bungalow**	Ct	**Court**	H	**Hall**	Meml	**Memorial**	Sh	**Shopping**
Bldg	**Building**	Ctr	**Centre**	Ho	**House**	Mkt	**Market**	Sq	**Square**
Bsns, Bus	**Business**	Ctry	**Country**	Hospl	**Hospital**	Mus	**Museum**	St	**Street**
Bvd	**Boulevard**	Cty	**County**	HQ	**Headquarters**	Orch	**Orchard**	Sta	**Station**
Cath	**Cathedral**	Dr	**Drive**	Hts	**Heights**	Pal	**Palace**	Terr	**Terrace**
Cir	**Circus**	Dro	**Drove**	Ind	**Industrial**	Par	**Parade**	TH	**Town Hall**
Cl	**Close**	Ed	**Education**	Inst	**Institute**	Pas	**Passage**	Univ	**University**
Cnr	**Corner**	Emb	**Embankment**	Int	**International**	Pk	**Park**	Wk, Wlk	**Walk**
Coll	**College**	Est	**Estate**	Intc	**Interchange**	Pl	**Place**	Wr	**Water**
Com	**Community**	Ex	**Exhibition**	Junc	**Junction**	Prec	**Precinct**	Yd	**Yard**

A

Abban Pl IV3 162 D2
Abban St IV3 162 D2
Abbey Cres IV36 34 B4
Abbey St 6 IV30 158 F4
Abbeylands Rd IV30 54 C8
Abbotshaven IV20 11 B2
Aberlour House (Prep School) AB38 166 E5
Aberlour Prim Sch AB38 166 C3
Abernethy Forest Nature Reserve★ PH25 129 B1
Abernethy Prim Sch PH25 129 E4
Abertarff Pl PH32 172 D4
Abertarff Rd IV2 163 A1
Aboyne St AB56 157 E7
Abrach Rd PH33 173 D5
Acadamaidh Alanais / Alness Acad IV17 149 D3
Academy La IV17 149 D4
Academy Pk IV15 152 D6
Academy Rd IV18 151 B2
Academy St Elgin IV30 158 F4
Fortrose IV10 47 C7
Inverness IV1 162 F2
11 Inverness IV1 162 F1
Nairn IV12 154 C5
Tain IV19 148 C5
Achany Rd IV15 152 E5
Achareidh Steading IV12 154 B5
Achintore Rd PH33 173 A2
Achnagonlin Ind Est PH26 168 C4
Achonochy Rd IV6 43 B4
Achvraid Rd IV2 164 E4
Acre St IV12 154 D5
Acres Rd PH21 170 D5
Adam Dr IV36 155 D4
Adams Rd IV2 48 B8
Addison St 1 AB56 22 B5
Admiralty St
2 Buckie AB56 157 C6
Portknockie AB56 22 B5
Agincourt IV18 151 A2
Aigen Pl AB55 167 C3
Aird Ave IV2 165 B6
Aird Rd IV4 63 D4
Airfield Rd IV16 13 B2
Alamein Dr IV2 163 B1
Alba Pl IV30 158 E6
Albany Pl IV5 64 A4
Albany Rd IV18 151 B2
Albert Gate IV12 154 B6
Albert Pl
Conon Bridge IV7 152 C1
Dufftown AB55 167 C3
Albert St Forres IV36 155 B4
Nairn IV12 154 B6
Albert Terr AB56 22 D4
Albyn Ct IV12 154 B4
Alder Pl 3 IV2 66 E5
Aldourie Prim Sch IV2 85 F3
Aldourie Rd IV2 164 D4
Alexander Ct 2 IV10 47 C7
Alexander Pl 6 IV3 162 E1
Alexander St
8 Avoch IV9 47 A6
2 Buckie AB56 157 B5
Alexandra Pl IV17 149 D4
Alexandra Rd
Elgin IV30 158 E4
Keith AB55 161 D5
Alexandra Terr IV36 155 C4
Allachie Dr AB38 166 D3
Allachy Terr AB38 166 C3
Allan Dr IV36 155 B3
Allan La IV31 156 E5
Allan Rd IV2 48 B8
Allan Sq 9 IV11 15 F2
Allarburn Pk 1 IV4 84 B8
Allarburn Pl 3 IV4 84 B8
Allardyce Cres AB38 166 C3
Alltan Pl 11 IV2 66 E5
Alma Pl IV30 158 F3
Alma Rd PH33 173 C3
Alnath Pl 1 AB56 157 B4
Alness Acad / Acadamaidh Alanais IV17 149 D3
Alness Ind Est IV17 149 B2
Alness Point Bsns Pk IV17 149 C1
Alness Sta IV17 149 E3
Altgowrie IV30 55 F7
Altonburn Rd IV12 154 A6
Alves Prim Sch IV30 35 A5
Alvie Prim Sch PH21 143 B5
Anagach Hill PH26 168 D4
Anderson Cres
Elgin IV30 158 F6
Forres IV36 155 B4
Anderson Dr Avoch IV9 28 D1
Elgin IV30 159 A1
8 Fortrose IV10 47 C7
Huntly AB54 80 D6
Anderson St IV3 162 E3
Anderson's Prim Sch IV36 155 D6
Angus Cres PH33 173 B1
Ankerville St IV19 148 D4
Anne Cres IV12 154 D4
Annfield Rd IV2 165 A8
Anson Way AB56 157 E5
Anton St AB56 157 B5
Anvil La AB55 161 F8
Anzio Rd IV2 163 C1
Apkaig Cres 1 PH33 173 C8
Applegrove Prim Sch IV36 155 C5
Archibald Gr AB56 157 E4
Ardbreck La AB55 161 F8
Ardbreck Pl IV2 164 D3
Ardbroilach Rd PH21 170 D5
Ardconnel St IV2 162 F1
Ardconnel Terr IV2 162 F1
Ardcroy Rd IV2 68 A8
Ardersier Prim Sch IV2 48 B5
Ardgilzean Pl IV30 158 B5
Ardholm Pl IV2 164 D3
Ardivot Pl IV31 156 C5
Ardness Pl IV2 164 D3
Ardnevis Rd PH33 173 D4
Ardross Pl Alness IV17 149 D4
Inverness IV3 164 E8
Ardross Prim Sch IV17 13 D8
Ardross St Alness IV17 149 D4
Inverness IV3 164 E8
Ardvonie Rd PH21 170 C4
Argentier Rd IV36 155 F6
Argus Pl IV30 158 F7
Argyle Ct
1 Inverness IV2 165 A8
Tain IV19 148 C3
Argyle St Inverness IV2 164 F8
Lossiemouth IV31 156 E6
Argyle Terr IV2 164 F8
Argyll Rd PH33 173 B3
Argyll Terr PH33 173 A2
Arthurville Gdns IV19 148 B3
Ash Hill IV16 12 E1
Ashburn La PH33 173 A2
Ashburton Ct IV30 159 C3
Ashfield Dr IV30 159 B3
Ashgrove Ct IV30 159 B3
Ashgrove Pl IV30 159 B3
Ashgrove Rd IV30 159 B4
Ashgrove Sq IV30 159 B4
Ashie Rd IV2 164 F4
Ashton Cres IV2 163 C1
Ashton Rd IV2 163 D1
Ashville Ct 2 AB38 76 B8
Aspen Pl 4 IV2 66 E5
Assynt Gdns IV12 154 C5
Assynt Rd IV3 164 B8
Assynt St IV16 12 F1
Attadale Rd IV3 162 E1
Auchindoun Castle★ AB55 98 C4
Auldcastle Rd IV2 163 A2
Aultnaskiach Ave IV2 164 F7
Aultnaskiah Rd IV2 164 F7
Ault-sallan Rd IV18 151 E4
Averon Leisure Ctr IV17 149 D3
Averon Rd IV17 149 D4
Averon Way IV17 149 C2
Aviemore Prim Sch PH22 169 A7
Aviemore Sta PH22 169 B5
Avoch Prim Sch IV9 46 F6
Avon Way IV7 44 C6
Ayr Pl PH33 173 A1

B

Back St Balintore IV20 11 C3
Burghead IV30 17 E6
Keith AB55 161 E7
Baddon Dr 1 IV6 43 C4
Bailey Pl IV31 156 D4
Bailies Dr IV30 158 F2
Bailies Rd IV36 155 B4
Baker St 2 IV31 156 F7
Bakers La 10 IV30 17 F6
Balblair Rd IV12 154 C3
Balconie Pk 6 IV16 12 F1
Balconie St
Dingwall IV16 27 C8
Evanton IV16 12 F1
Balgate Dr 4 IV4 84 B8
Balintore Pk IV20 11 A2
Balifeary La IV3 164 E7
Ballifeary Rd IV3 164 D7
Ballindalloch Castle & Gdns★ AB37 95 C3
Balloan Rd
Inverness IV2 165 A4
Muir of Ord IV6 43 C4
Balloch Ct AB55 161 E3
Balloch Prim Sch IV2 66 F6
Balloch Rd AB55 161 E3
Ballone Castle★ IV20 6 B2
Balmacaan Rd IV63 104 B3
Balmakeith Bsns Pk IV12 154 F5
Balmakeith Dr IV12 154 E5
Balmakeith Ind Est IV12 154 F5
Balmakeith Pk IV12 154 F4
Balmenach Rd PH26 113 E1
Balmoral Terr
Elgin IV30 158 E6
Inverness IV2 163 C1
Balnabeen Dr IV15 152 E7
Balnacoul La IV32 160 A7
Balnacoul Rd IV32 160 A7
Balnacraig Ct IV3 162 C2
Balnacraig La IV3 162 D2
Balnacraig Rd IV3 162 C1
Balnafettack Cres IV3 162 A2
Balnafettack Pl IV3 162 A1
Balnafettack Rd IV3 162 A1
Balnain House (NTS)★ IV3 162 E1
Balnain Prim Sch IV63 103 B5
Balnain St 2 IV3 162 E1
Balnakyle Rd IV2 164 D3
Balnatua IV7 27 B1
Balormie Pl IV31 156 C5
Balvaird Rd IV6 153 C5
Balvaird Terr IV6 153 C6
Balvenie Castle★ AB55 167 D4
Balvenie St AB55 167 C3
Balvonie Ave IV2 165 D7
Banavie Rd PH33 173 D8
Banff Cres PH33 173 B1
Banff Rd AB55 161 E4
Banff St 8 AB56 157 C6
Bank La Forres IV36 155 C5
6 Inverness IV1 162 F1
Bank St Balintore IV20 11 B2
Buckie AB56 157 C6
Conon Bridge IV7 44 C6
Cromarty IV11 15 F2
Fort William PH33 173 B4
Invergordon IV18 151 B2
Inverness IV1 162 E1
Tain IV19 148 D5
Bankers La AB55 161 E4
Barbour Rd IV12 154 F5
Bardon Pl IV30 158 E2
Barfield Rd AB56 157 B4
Barhill Rd AB56 157 A4
Barkly St 3 IV11 15 F2
Baron St AB56 157 C6
Baron Taylor's St 5 IV1 162 F1
Barwell Rd IV36 155 F6
Base Sta PH22 145 F5
Batchen La 9 IV30 158 E4
Batchen St 7 Elgin IV30 158 F4
Forres IV36 155 C6
Bath St 1 Burghead IV30 17 B6
Nairn IV12 154 D6
Battle Hill IV12 50 D6
Baxter Pl 7 IV30 37 D4
Bayne Dr IV15 152 D8
Bayview 2 IV30 17 D5
Bayview Cres IV11 15 F2
Bayview Rd 15 AB56 22 D4
Beach Rd Dornoch IV25 4 B8
Fochabers IV32 38 D8
Beachen Ct PH26 168 B6
Beaton's La 6 IV1 162 E2
Beaufighter Rd IV32 39 A6
Beaufort Gdns IV4 63 D4
Beaufort Rd IV2 163 A1
Beauly Prim Sch IV4 63 D5
Beauly Sta IV4 63 D4
Bede Rd AB56 21 C2
Beech Ave Forres IV36 52 A7
Inverness IV2 164 F5
Nairn IV12 154 B5
Beech Brae IV30 158 E6
Beeches The IV63 104 B3
Beechfield Rd IV30 159 B3
Beechway IV36 155 D3
Beechwood Bsns Pk N IV2 165 D8
Beechwood Bsns Pk S IV2 165 D8
Beechwood Ct IV2 163 C1
Beechwood Rd IV2 163 C1
Beils Brae IV30 37 E5
Beinn View IV7 44 C5
Belford Hospl PH33 173 C4
Belford Rd PH33 173 B4
Bellfield IV18 151 A3
Bellfield Dr IV1 162 B7
Bellfield Pk IV2 164 F7
Bellfield Rd IV1 162 A7
Bellfield Terr IV2 164 F7
Ben Goolabin PH22 169 C7
Ben View Rd IV19 148 B4
Benromach Distillery★ IV36 155 B6
Benula Rd IV3 162 D3
Benview La AB55 161 F8
Bermuda Rd IV18 151 A2
Bezack St 2 IV30 159 A2
Bibby Pl IV30 158 E4
Biblical Gdn The★ IV30 159 A5
Big Vennel 1 IV11 16 A2
Bilbohall Hospl IV30 158 D4
Bin Ave AB54 79 D3
Binview Rd 3 AB56 22 D3
Birch Brae Dr IV5 64 A4
Birch Brae Terr IV5 64 A4
Birch Dr IV7 44 B6
Birch Gr PH24 128 D2
Birch Pl 1 IV2 66 E5
Birch Rd
Aviemore PH22 169 B7
Nairn IV12 154 B5
Birchview Terr PH26 168 C6
Birchwood IV18 150 F3
Birchwood Brae IV2 66 D2
Birchwood La IV2 66 D2
Birchwood Pl IV2 66 D2
Birchwood Rd IV2 66 D2
Birchwood Terr IV2 66 D2
Birkenhill Pl IV30 159 B1
Birkenhillock Rd IV36 155 F6
Birnie Cres IV30 158 F1
Birnie Pl Elgin IV30 158 F1
Birnie Pl *continued*
Fochabers IV32 160 B6
Birnie Rd IV30 158 F1
Birnie Terr IV3 162 D2
Bishop Eden Prim Sch IV3 162 E1
Bishopfield Rd 15 IV25 4 A8
Bishopmill Prim Sch IV30 158 D5
Bishops Ct IV31 156 C4
Bishops Rd
Fortrose IV10 47 C7
Inverness IV3 164 E8
Bishop's Rd IV3 164 E8
Black Isle Rd IV6 153 D4
Blackburn Ct 8 IV30 159 B5
Blackfriars' Rd 6 IV30 158 E4
Blackmuir Wood IV14 43 C8
Blackpark Ave IV18 151 D4
Blackpark Terr IV3 162 B3
Blackthorn Rd IV2 66 E5
Blackwell Ave 6 IV2 66 F5
Blackwell Ct 8 IV2 66 F5
Blackwell Rd 7 IV2 66 F5
Blackwells St IV15 152 C5
Blair Rd IV12 154 A4
Blairdaff St AB56 157 C5
Blairfield Rd IV12 154 A4
Blane Pl IV30 158 F6
Blantyre Pl IV30 158 E6
Blantyre St Cullen AB56 22 D4
Elgin IV30 158 E6
Blantyre Terr
Buckie AB56 157 E7
8 Findochty AB56 21 E5
Blar Mhor Ind Est PH33 173 E8
Blar Mhor Rd PH33 173 C8
Blarliath Ind Est IV19 148 C6
Blarmore Ave IV3 162 B1
Blaven Ct 2 IV36 155 A5
Boa Vista Rd PH21 170 D5
Boarstone Ave IV2 164 C3
Boarstone Ct IV2 164 C3
Boarstone Pl IV2 164 C3
Boat of Garten Sta PH24 128 D1
Boath Rd IV12 50 D6
Bogmoor Rd IV32 38 F6
Bogton Rd IV36 155 C6
Boharm Sch AB55 57 F1
Bona Vista Rd IV12 154 F6
Borlum Rd IV2 164 C4
Borough Briggs (Elgin City FC) IV30 158 E5
Boroughbriggs Rd IV30 158 E5
Boswell Rd IV2 165 C5
Botriphnie Prim Sch AB55 77 F3
Bow The AB56 157 B4
Bowie's La AB56 157 B6
Boyd Anderson Dr IV31 156 D4
Bracany Gdns IV30 55 F8
Bracany Pk IV30 55 F7
Braco Pl IV30 158 D3
Braco St AB55 161 D4
Brae Foot IV20 11 C3
Brae Pk IV8 46 A4
Brae Terr IV8 46 A4
Brae The
Kingussie PH21 143 B4
2 Muir of Ord IV6 43 C4
Braeface IV17 149 C4
Braeface Pk IV17 149 C5
Braehead Avoch IV9 47 A6
Cromarty IV11 15 F2
Braehead Terr AB55 167 C2
Braelossie Pl IV30 158 D4
Braemoray Ave PH26 168 B5
Braemore Pl PH33 173 C3
Braemoriston Rd IV30 158 E6
Braeriach Ct PH22 169 B8
Braeriach Rd PH21 143 B4
Braes of Allachie AB38 166 D3
Braes of Conon IV6 44 C5
Braeside AB55 161 D3
Braeside Pk IV2 67 A6
Braeside Pl PH20 171 D7
Braeview Pk IV4 63 D5
Braeview Rd AB56 157 B4
Brahan View IV7 44 C5
Braid Cres 5 IV36 155 C5
Brander St
6 Burghead IV30 17 C6
Lossiemouth IV31 156 E7
Brannen Terr 17 IV25 4 A8
Branxholme Terr IV2 164 D5
Brechan Rig IV30 159 A7
Breich St AB38 76 A8
Bremner Dr IV30 159 A7
Brewster Dr IV36 155 D4
Brickfield Rd AB38 76 C3
Bridaig Sq IV15 152 D5
Bridge End AB56 157 B6
Bridge Pl AB56 157 B6
Bridge St Avoch IV9 46 F6
6 Burghead IV30 17 C5
18 Dornoch IV25 4 A8
Elgin IV30 158 F5
Forres IV36 155 B5
Fortrose IV10 47 D8
8 Inverness IV2 162 F1
Keith AB55 161 E3
Nairn IV12 154 E6
7 Portknockie AB56 22 B5
Bridge View IV7 44 C6
Bridgend Ave IV15 152 C6
Bridgend Prim Sch IV17 149 D4
Bridgend Rd IV15 152
Bridgeview Dr IV3 162
Brig Wynd 8 IV36 155
Brinkman Terr IV2 66
Brinuth Pl IV30 158
Broad La AB55 161
Broadstone Ave 3 IV2 165
Broadstone Pk IV2 163
Brodie Ave AB56 157
Brodie Dr IV30 158
Brodie Pl Elgin IV30 158
Forres IV36 155
Brookfield IV2 67
Broom Dr
Fort William PH33 173
Inverness IV2 164
Broom La AB55 161
Broom Wlk IV36 33
Broomhill Ct AB55 161
Broomhill Rd AB55 161
Broomhill Sta PH26 129
Brown Sq IV15 152
Brown St 7 IV3 162
Bruce Ave Buckie AB56 157
Dingwall IV15 152
Inverness IV3 164
Bruce Gdns IV3 164
Bruce Pk IV3 164
Bruce Pl
Fort William PH33 173
9 Portknockie AB56 22
Bruce St 8 IV30 17
Bruceland Gdns IV30 158
Bruceland Rd IV30 158
Brucelands IV30 158
Brumley Brae IV30 158
Bryson Cres AB56 157
Buchanan Ct IV15 152
Buckie District Fishing Heritage Mus★ AB56 157
Buckie Drifter Maritime Heritage Ctr The★ AB56 157
Buckie High Sch AB56 157
Bught Ave IV3 164
Bught Dr IV3 164
Bught La IV3 164
Bught Rd IV3 164
Bunoich Brae PH32 172
Burdshaugh IV36 155
Burdsyard Rd IV36 155
Burgage Ct IV19 148
Burgage Dr IV19 148
Burgh Gdns 7 IV25 4
Burghead Prim Sch IV30 17
Burghead Rd IV30 35
Burma Ct IV2 163
Burn Brae IV2 66
Burn Brae Ave IV2 66
Burn Brae Cres IV2 66
Burn Brae Pl 9 IV2 66
Burn Brae Terr IV2 66
Burn Ct IV15 152
Burn Pl Dingwall IV15 152
Elgin IV30 159
Munlochy IV8 46
Burn Rd IV2 164
Burnbank Buckie AB56 157
Fochabers IV32 160
Burnett Rd IV1 162
Burnetts Pl 4 IV12 154
Burnfield Ave PH26 168
Burns Ave IV6 153
Burns Cres IV15 152
Burns Rd 6 IV30 37
Burnside AB56 22
Burnside Ave PH22 169
Burnside La 3 IV7 44
Burnside Pl
Aviemore PH22 169
2 Elgin IV30 159
Burnside Rd
Aviemore PH22 169
Duffus IV30 18
Fochabers IV32 160
Lhanbryde IV30 37
Burnside St AB38 76
Burntisland St 1 IV12 154
Bute Pl 2 PH33 173
Bynack Pl Forres IV36 155
1 Nethy Bridge PH25 129

C

Caberfeidh Ave IV15 152 C
Caberfeidh Dr IV18 150 F
Cabrach Prim Sch AB54 118
Cadboll Ind Est IV20 11
Cadboll Pl 7 IV19 148 D
Cadboll Rd IV18 151 D
Cadgers Rd IV32 38 D
Cairn Ave IV12 154 E
Cairn Avie PH22 169 C
Cairn Ct IV3 164 E
Cairn Jerrig PH22 169 C
Cairn More PH22 169 C
Cairn Slowne PH22 169 C
Cairney Prim Sch AB54 79 D
Cairnfield Cres AB56 157 B
Cairngorm Ave
Aviemore PH22 169 B
Grantown-on-Spey PH26 168 B
Cairngorm Funicular Rly★ PH22 145 F
Cairngorm Reindeer Ctr★ PH22 145 E

Drumduan Rd IV36 ...155 E6
Drumdyre Rd IV15 ...152 E7
Drumfield Ct IV2 ...164 C3
Drumfield Rd IV2 ...164 C3
Drumin Castle★ AB37 ...115 D5
Drumine Rd IV36 ...155 A4
Drummond Cir IV2 ...164 F6
Drummond Cres IV2 ...164 E5
Drummond Ct IV2 ...164 F5
Drummond Pl IV2 ...164 E5
Drummond Rd
Dingwall IV16 ...27 C8
Inverness IV2 ...164 F5
Drummond Sch IV2 ...164 E4
Drummond St 4 IV1 ...162 F1
Drummuir St IV30 ...17 F6
Drummuir Sta AB55 ...77 E3
Drumossie Ave IV2 ...165 C6
Drumsmittal Rd IV1 ...162 B8
Drynie Ave IV2 ...165 A6
Drynie Terr IV2 ...165 A6
Dubh Macdonald Rd PH33 ...173 D5
Duff Ave IV30 ...159 A3
Duff Pl IV30 ...158 E6
Duff St 1 Inverness IV3 ...162 E1
Keith AB55 ...161 C4
Dufftown Ind Est AB55 ...167 C3
Dufftown Sta AB55 ...167 C5
Duffus Castle★ IV30 ...18 E4
Duffus House (Gordonstoun Sch) IV30 ...18 C5
Duffus Rd IV30 ...158 C6
Duffy Dr IV2 ...164 F8
Duguid St AB56 ...157 C5
Duke St Buckie AB56 ...39 D7
2 Cromarty IV11 ...15 F2
Findochty AB56 ...21 E5
Fochabers IV32 ...160 E4
Kingussie PH21 ...170 D4
5 Tain IV19 ...148 D4
Dulaig Ct PH26 ...168 B6
Dulsie Dr IV12 ...154 B4
Dunabban Rd IV3 ...162 D2
Dunachton Rd
Inverness IV3 ...164 E7
Kingussie PH21 ...143 A4
Dunain Rd IV3 ...162 D1
Dunbar Ave IV12 ...154 E5
Dunbar Ct IV31 ...156 E6
Dunbar La
2 Burghead IV30 ...17 C6
Lossiemouth IV30 ...18 B5
Dunbar St Buckie AB56 ...157 B4
Burghead IV30 ...17 F6
Lossiemouth IV31 ...156 D5
Dunbarry Rd PH21 ...170 E4
Dunbarry Terr PH21 ...170 E5
Dunbarton Rd PH33 ...173 A2
Duncan Ave IV32 ...160 E4
Duncan Dr Elgin IV30 ...158 D6
Nairn IV12 ...154 C4
Duncan Forbes Prim Sch IV2 ...66 F5
Duncraig Ct 3 IV3 ...162 E1
Duncraig St IV3 ...162 E1
Dunglass Rd IV7 ...44 B6
Dunkirk Rd IV32 ...38 D7
Dunnstaffnage Brae PH26 ...168 C5
Dunnyduff Rd AB55 ...161 E2
Dunrobin St IV19 ...148 C5
Durban Pl 2 IV12 ...154 D5
Duthac Wynd IV19 ...148 B5
Duthie Pl AB56 ...157 E4
Dyce Cres 12 AB56 ...21 E4
Dyke Prim Sch IV36 ...32 E1

E

Eaglefield Rd 3 IV25 ...4 A8
Earl of Inverness Rd PH33 ...173 D5
Earl St AB56 ...39 D7
Earlsland Cres IV36 ...155 F6
East Back St IV30 ...158 F6
East Carlton Terr 7 AB56 ...157 C6
East Cathcart St AB56 ...157 D5
East Church St AB56 ...157 E5
East End Prim Sch IV30 159 A4
East High St
8 Buckie AB56 ...39 D7
Elgin IV30 ...158 F6
East Mackenzie Pk IV2 ...165 C6
East Rd IV30 ...159 C4
East Rosehaugh Dr 2 IV9 ...46 F6
East St Balintore IV20 ...11 B2
Fochabers IV32 ...160 E3
East Terr PH21 ...170 D4
East Watergate 10 IV10 ...47 C7
Easter Greengate IV10 ...47 C7
Easter Rd IV36 ...34 B4
Eastfield Ave IV2 ...165 C8
Eastfield Way IV2 ...163 E2
Eastgate Sh Ctr IV1 ...162 F1
Edderton Prim Sch IV19 ...2 D3
Eden Ct Theatre★ IV3 ...164 E8
Edgar Rd IV30 ...158 E2
Edgehill Rd IV36 ...155 E5
Edgemoor Pk IV2 ...67 A5
Edindiach Rd AB55 ...161 F2
Edington Rd IV2 ...165 B6
Edithfield Cres AB55 ...161 E5
Edward Ave AB38 ...76 B3
Edward Rd IV36 ...155 B5
Eemins Pl IV30 ...158 E7
Elchies Rd AB38 ...166 B3
Elgin Acad IV30 ...158 D5
Elgin City FC (Borough Briggs) IV30 ...158 E5
Elgin High Sch IV30 ...158 E1
Elgin Mus★ IV30 ...158 F4
Elgin Rd IV31 ...156 E4
Elgin Sta IV30 ...158 F3
Elizabeth Cres IV25 ...4 B8
Elizabeth Ct 2 IV25 ...4 B8
Elizabeth Gdns 1 IV25 ...4 B8
Elizabeth St IV12 ...154 D4
Ellanwood Rd 4 PH23 ...127 F5
Ellington Pk 8 IV36 ...34 A4
Elliot Rd IV18 ...151 D3
Ellis Pk IV7 ...44 C6
Elm Pk IV2 ...164 F7
Elmfield Rd IV30 ...159 B3
Elmgrove IV12 ...154 B5
Elsher Cl 1 IV30 ...37 E4
Elsher Rd IV30 ...37 D4
Elsley Pl 6 AB56 ...157 B5
Elvin Pl IV36 ...33 E7
Enrick Cres IV63 ...104 C4
Eriskay Rd IV2 ...165 B7
Ernest Hamilton Ct 3 IV30 ...159 A7
Erracht Dr PH33 ...173 C8
Erracht Rd IV2 ...164 D4
Erracht Terr PH33 ...173 C7
Errogie Rd IV2 ...164 E3
Esk La IV18 ...151 B2
Esk Rd IV2 ...165 A5
Esmonde Gdns IV30 ...158 F7
Essich Rd IV2 ...164 D1
Evan Barron Rd IV2 ...164 F5
Evelix Rd IV25 ...3 F8
Ewing Howe IV30 ...159 C2

F

Factory La 4 IV9 ...47 A5
Factory St 2 IV1 ...162 E2
Fairburn Twr★ IV6 ...43 A3
Fairfield La 4 IV3 ...162 E1
Fairfield Rd IV3 ...162 D1
Fairisle Pl IV31 ...156 D4
Fairmuir Rd IV6 ...153 C5
Fairway Ave IV30 ...158 E1
Fairways Leisure Ctr IV2 ...165 A4
Falcon Ave IV2 ...165 C6
Falcon Sq IV1 ...162 F1
Falconer Mus★ IV36 ...155 C5
Falconers La 4 IV12 ...154 D6
Farm Cl AB38 ...166 D4
Faroes Ct IV31 ...156 D4
Farquhar St 2 IV30 ...17 F6
Farquhar's La 1 AB56 ...157 D5
Farr Prim Sch IV2 ...107 B8
Fassifern Rd PH33 ...173 B3
Fastnet Pl IV31 ...156 D4
Fearn Sta IV20 ...10 C5
Ferintosh Prim Sch IV6 ...44 F6
Fern Pl IV2 ...66 F5
Ferntower Ave IV2 ...66 F4
Ferntower Ct 13 IV2 ...66 E5
Ferntower Pl 9 IV2 ...66 F5
Ferrier Rd AB55 ...167 C3
Ferrier Terr IV30 ...158 E7
Ferry Brae IV1 ...162 B7
Ferry La IV4 ...63 D5
Ferry Rd Beauly IV4 ...63 D5
Dingwall IV15 ...152 F5
Forres IV36 ...155 A3
Ferry Row IV18 ...151 B1
Ferryhill IV36 ...155 B3
Fettes Rd IV2 ...48 C5
Fiery Hillock 2 IV10 ...47 D7
Fife Pl PH33 ...173 B1
Fife St Aberlour AB38 ...76 B3
Dufftown AB55 ...167 D2
Keith AB55 ...161 C3
Findhorn Ct 7 IV30 ...159 B5
Findhorn Her Ctr★ IV36 ...33 D7
Findhorn Rd 3 IV36 ...155 E7
Findlater Ave 20 AB56 ...22 A5
Findlater Dr AB56 ...22 D3
Findlater St 1 AB56 ...21 C3
Findlay Rd IV32 ...160 B7
Findochty Prim Sch AB56 ...21 E4
Findrassie Cres IV30 ...158 C5
Findrassie Ct IV30 ...158 E7
Fingal Rd IV15 ...152 C6
Fingask Dr IV5 ...64 A4
Finlayson Ct IV6 ...153 D5
Finlayson St IV20 ...10 E4
Firs Day Hospl for the Elderly The IV30 ...158 D3
Firth St IV12 ...154 D6
Firth View
7 Burghead IV30 ...17 C5
Dingwall IV15 ...152 E7
Firthview 6 AB56 ...22 A5
Firthview Ave IV3 ...162 B2
Firthview Dr IV3 ...162 B2
Firthview Rd IV3 ...162 B3
Firthview Terr IV17 ...149 C4
Fisher Pl IV31 ...156 D4
Fleming Cottage Hospl AB38 ...166 C3
Fletcher Gdns 4 IV9 ...46 F6
Fleurs Ave 7 IV36 ...155 B4
Fleurs Cres IV36 ...155 B4
Fleurs Dr Elgin IV30 ...158 C3
Forres IV36 ...155 B4
Fleurs Pl Elgin IV30 ...158 C3
Forres IV36 ...155 B4
Fleurs Rd Elgin IV30 ...158 D3
Forres IV36 ...155 B4
Floral Hall IV3 ...164 D6
Fochabers Folk Mus The★ IV32 ...160 E4
Fodderty Way IV15 ...152 B7
Forbes Dr IV12 ...154 C4
Forbes Hill IV36 ...155 F6
Forbes Pl 4 IV2 ...66 E4
Forbes Rd IV36 ...155 A5
Forde Way IV32 ...39 A6
Forest Dr Burghead IV30 ...17 C5
9 Culloden IV2 ...67 A5
Forest Rd
10 Burghead IV30 ...17 C5
Grantown-on-Spey PH26 ...168 C6
Forgue Prim Sch AB54 ...81 E3
Forres Acad IV36 ...155 C4
Forres Ent Pk IV36 ...34 A2
Forres Mechanics FC (Mosset Pk Football Gd) IV36 ...155 C6
Forres Rd IV12 ...154 E6
Forres Sta IV36 ...155 A5
Forsyth Ave 3 AB38 ...76 B8
Forsyth Pl 5 IV11 ...15 F2
Forsyth St IV30 ...17 F6
Fort Augustus Highlands & Rare Breeds Croft★ PH32 ...172 E5
Fort William FC PH33 ...173 F4
Fort William Prim Sch PH33 ...173 A3
Fort William RC Prim Sch PH33 ...173 C4
Fort William Sta PH33 ...173 C4
Forteath Ave IV30 ...158 D3
Forteath St
Burghead IV30 ...17 C6
Elgin IV30 ...158 D4
Forth Pl IV31 ...156 D4
Forties Pl IV31 ...156 D4
Fortrose Acad IV10 ...47 C7
Fountain Rd IV19 ...148 D4
Foyers Prim Sch IV2 ...122 B4
Francis Pl 9 IV30 ...158 F4
Fraser Ave IV30 ...159 A6
Fraser Ct 8 IV2 ...66 E5
Fraser Pk IV12 ...154 C5
Fraser Pl AB55 ...161 C4
Fraser Rd
Burghead IV30 ...17 D5
Dingwall IV15 ...152 D7
Invergordon IV18 ...151 A3
Fraser Sq 1 PH33 ...173 B3
Fraser St Beauly IV4 ...63 D5
Conon Bridge IV7 ...44 C6
1 Forres IV36 ...155 B4
3 Inverness IV1 ...162 F1
5 Inverness IV2 ...164 F8
Freeman Way IV31 ...156 D5
Freuchny La AB56 ...157 D5
Freuchny Rd AB56 ...157 E7
Friars' La IV1 ...162 E1
Friars' St IV1 ...162 E2
Front St 2 IV20 ...5 B1
Fuaran 1 IV20 ...5 B1
Fulmar Cres IV2 ...48 C6
Fulmar Rd Elgin IV30 ...158 F6
Lossiemouth IV31 ...156 C5
Fulton Rd IV36 ...155 C5
Fun House The★ PH22 ...169 E2
Fyrish Cres IV16 ...13 A1
Fyrish Ct 7 IV16 ...12 F1
Fyrish Rd IV36 ...33 E7
Fyrish Way IV17 ...149 B3

G

Gairloch Cres 10 IV7 ...44 C6
Gairs Croft 9 IV7 ...44 C6
Galloway Dr IV2 ...66 E5
Garden La AB56 ...157 D5
Garden Pl IV4 ...63 D5
Garlichill Ct IV12 ...50 D6
Garmouth Rd
Fochabers IV32 ...160 A7
Lhanbryde IV30 ...37 D4
Garraline Terr 5 PH21 ...170 E4
Garrie View IV7 ...44 C6
Garth Rd IV2 ...164 E4
Garve Sta IV23 ...23 F4
Gas Rd AB38 ...166 C4
Geanies St IV19 ...148 D4
Geddes Ave AB56 ...22 B5
Gedloch Pl IV30 ...158 E2
General Booth Rd IV3 ...162 B1
George St 4 Avoch IV9 ...47 A6
5 Buckie AB56 ...21 C3
1 Cromarty IV11 ...15 F2
Dingwall IV15 ...152 D5
Fochabers IV32 ...160 D4
Inverness IV1 ...162 E2
Nairn IV12 ...154 D4
George Wilson Rd IV12 ...50 E6
Gibb's La 1 AB56 ...157 B5
Gilbert St IV3 ...162 E2
Gilchrist Sq 11 IV25 ...4 A8
Gilliebog Pl 13 IV30 ...37 D4
Gilmour Cres IV31 ...156 E4
Gisborne Ct IV30 ...159 C3
Gladstone Ave IV15 ...152 C5
Glasdrum Ct PH33 ...173 B2
Glasdrum Gr PH33 ...173 B2
Glasdrum Mews PH33 ...173 B3
Glasdrum Rd PH33 ...173 B2
Glass Prim Sch AB54 ...99 D6
Glebe Cres
2 Kinloss IV36 ...34 A4
Tain IV19 ...148 C5
Glebe Ct 1 PH21 ...170 E4
Glebe Pk IV36 ...32 E1
Glebe Pk Cres 4 AB56 ...22 D3
Glebe Rd
Fochabers IV32 ...160 B7
3 Kinloss IV36 ...34 A4
Nairn IV12 ...154 D6
Glebe St IV1 ...162 E2
Glebe The 2 PH21 ...170 E4
Glen Elgin Rd IV30 ...55 F8
Glen Grant Distillery & Gdn★ AB38 ...76 A8
Glen Lossie Dr IV30 ...158 E2
Glen Moray Distillery★ IV30 ...158 B3
Glen Moray Dr IV30 ...158 F2
Glen More Forest Pk★ PH22 ...141 F1
Glen Nevis Bsns Pk PH33 ...173 F5
Glen Nevis Pl PH33 ...173 D4
Glen Nevis Rd PH33 ...173 C8
Glen Ord Distillery★ IV6 ...153 A6
Glen Rd PH20 ...171 C6
Glen Urquhart Prim Sch IV63 ...104 B4
Glenburn Dr IV2 ...164 F6
Glendessary St PH33 ...173 C7
Glendessary Terr 2 PH33 ...173 C7
Glendoe Rd PH32 ...172 D5
Glendoe Terr IV3 ...162 D3
Glendronach Distillery★ AB54 ...81 F3
Glendruidh Rd IV2 ...165 B6
Glenelg Gdns IV12 ...154 B4
Glenelg Rd 4 IV36 ...155 B4
Glenesk Rd IV30 ...37 D4
Glenfarclas Distillery★ AB37 ...96 A5
Glenfiddich Distillery & Visitor Ctr★ AB55 ...167 C5
Glengarry Rd IV3 ...162 B1
Glenglass Rd 2 IV16 ...12 F1
Glenkingie St PH33 ...173 B8
Glenkingie Tr PH33 ...173 C8
Glenlivet Distillery The★ AB37 ...115 E4
Glenlivet Prim Sch AB37 ...115 E4
Glenlossie Rd IV30 ...55 D8
Glenloy St PH33 ...173 C8
Glenmallie Rd PH33 ...173 C7
Glenmallie Terr 3 PH33 ...173 C7
Glenmhor Terr PH33 ...173 F6
Glenmorangie Distillery★ IV19 ...148 A8
Glenmore Lodge (National Outdoor Training Ctr)★ PH22 ...145 E8
Glenmore Pl IV36 ...155 B3
Glenmore Visitor Ctr★ PH22 ...145 E8
Glenpane St 1 PH33 ...173 C7
Glenshiel Pl IV2 ...165 B5
Glenurquhart Rd IV3 ...164 D7
Glover St 5 IV30 ...158 F4
Golf Course Rd
Grantown-on-Spey PH26 ...168 D7
Newtonmore PH20 ...171 D5
Golf Cres 11 IV30 ...17 F6
Golf Cresent IV30 ...18 A6
Golf Rd Burghead IV30 ...18 A6
Dornoch IV25 ...4 A8
Golf Terr IV6 ...153 C4
Golf View IV30 ...18 A6
Golf View Cres IV30 ...158 F1
Golf View Dr AB56 ...157 A4
Golf View Rd IV3 ...164 B7
Golf View Terr IV3 ...164 B7
Golfview Terr IV18 ...151 D3
Gollanhead Ave IV10 ...47 D8
Gordon Pl
Invergordon IV18 ...151 A2
Tain IV20 ...10 E4
Gordon Sq PH33 ...173 B3
Gordon St Buckie AB56 ...157 C6
3 Burghead IV30 ...17 F6
Elgin IV30 ...158 E4
Fochabers IV32 ...160 D4
Forres IV36 ...155 B6
Nairn IV12 ...154 D6
11 Portknockie AB56 ...22 A5
Gordon Terr
Invergordon IV18 ...151 A2
Inverness IV2 ...164 F8
Tain IV20 ...10 E5
Gordon's La 8 IV11 ...15 F2
Gordonstoun Rd IV30 ...18 C5
Gordonstoun Sch IV30 ...18 D5
Gordonville Rd IV2 ...164 F8
Gowan Bank Pl IV20 ...11 B3
Gowanbrae Cres 4 IV10 47 D8
Gower St 6 IV19 ...148 D4
Goyal Rd IV15 ...152 D4
Grampian Cres 1 PH24 128 C2
Grampian Ct PH22 ...169 A5
Grampian Rd
Aviemore PH22 ...169
Elgin IV30 ...159
Grampian View PH22 ...169
Granary La 3 IV30 ...17
Granary Pk IV36 ...53
Granary St IV30 ...17
Grange Rd Dornoch IV25 ...4
Forres IV36 ...34
Fort William PH33 ...173
Grange Terr PH33 ...173
Granny Barbour's Rd IV12 ...154
Grant Cres IV7 ...44
Grant Dr IV36 ...155
Grant La 7 Burghead IV30 17
Lossiemouth IV31 ...156
Grant Pl Forres IV36 ...155
Fort William PH33 ...173
Grant Rd 3 Culloden IV2 ...67
Forres IV36 ...155
Grantown-on-Spey PH26 ...168
Grant St Buckie AB56 ...157
8 Cullen AB56 ...22
Dingwall IV15 ...152
Elgin IV30 ...158
Inverness IV3 ...162
Nairn IV12 ...154
Grantown Gram Sch PH26 ...168
Grantown Mus★ PH26 ...168
Grantown Prim Sch PH26 ...168
Grantown Rd IV36 ...155
Grays Pk IV2 ...122
Grays Wlk IV30 ...158
Great Eastern Rd AB56 ...21
Great Western Ct AB56 ...157
Great Western Rd AB56 157
Grebe Ave IV2 ...165
Green Acres IV36 ...52
Green Ct AB55 ...161
Green Dr IV2 ...164
Green La Fochabers IV32 ...38
Keith AB55 ...161
Kingussie PH21 ...170
Green Rd
2 Fochabers IV32 ...38
Forres IV36 ...155
Green St AB38 ...76
Greenbank Ct 3 AB56 ...157
Greenfield Rd 4 IV8 ...46
Greengates Pl 1 IV10 ...47
Greenhill St IV15 ...152
Greenside Ave IV10 ...47
Greenwards Prim Sch IV30 ...158
Gregory Pl IV31 ...156
Greig St IV3 ...162
Greshop Rd IV36 ...33
Greyfriars' St IV30 ...158
Grigor Dr IV2 ...164
Grigor Gdns IV2 ...164
Grigorhill Ind Est IV12 ...154
Groam Cres IV5 ...64
Groam Ct IV5 ...64
Groam House Mus★ IV10 ...47
Grosvenor St IV18 ...151
Grove Pl 5 IV30 ...158
Gynack Rd PH21 ...170
Gynack St PH21 ...170

H

Haig Pl 21 AB56 ...22
Haig St AB56 ...22
Hainings N 6 IV36 ...155
Hainings Rd IV36 ...155
Hall Pl 4 Elgin IV30 ...158
Lossiemouth IV30 ...18
Hall St Buckie AB56 ...157
6 Findochty AB56 ...21
Halliman Way IV31 ...156
Hallowood Rd IV30 ...37
Hamilton Cres IV30 ...158
Hamilton Dr IV30 ...158
Hamilton Path AB56 ...157
Hanover Ct 3 AB56 ...157
Harbour Head 1 AB56 ...39
Harbour House La 2 AB56 ...157
Harbour Rd
Fortrose IV10 ...47
Inverness IV1 ...162
2 Portknockie AB56 ...22
Harbour St
Buckie AB56 ...157
Burghead IV30 ...17
Nairn IV12 ...154
Tain IV20 ...6
Harbour Terr 9 AB56 ...22
Harbour View 2 IV20 ...11
Hardhillock Ave IV30 ...158
Harris Rd IV2 ...165
Harris St 5 IV36 ...34
Harrison Terr IV30 ...158
Harrowden Rd IV3 ...162
Hartfield Gdns IV19 ...148
Hartfield Rd IV19 ...148
Hartfield St IV19 ...148
Hatton Way IV36 ...34
Haugh Ct IV2 ...164
Haugh Rd Elgin IV30 ...158
Inverness IV2 ...164
Haughs Rd AB55 ...161
Hawkhill Rd 3 IV10 ...47

Maclean Ct
9 Culloden IV2 66 E5
Nairn IV12 154 C6
Maclennan Cres IV3 162 E3
Maclennan Gdns 1 IV3 162 E3
Maclennan Pl AB55 167 D3
Macleod Dr 7 IV7 44 C6
Macleod Organics Visitor Ctr★ IV2 48 C6
Macleod Pl IV15 152 B8
Macleod Rd 4 IV2 67 A5
Macmillan Pl 2 PH33 173 C8
Macpherson St 7 IV30 17 F6
Macquarrie Ct PH33 173 D8
Macrae Ave IV12 154 E5
Macrae Cres
Dingwall IV15 152 C5
Kingussie PH21 143 B5
Macroberts Reply IV31 156 C5
Madras St 5 IV3 162 E3
Maida Pl IV30 158 F4
Main Rd Buckie AB56 21 C2
Elgin IV30 35 B4
Tain IV20 10 D5
Main St Balintore IV20 11 B2
Ballindalloch AB37 132 B1
Buckie AB56 157 B5
1 Elgin IV30 159 A1
6 Findochty AB56 21 E5
Inverness IV1 162 C6
Keith AB55 161 E7
Tain IV20 5 B1
Mains Ave IV18 151 A3
Mairs St 2 AB56 22 B5
Maisondieu Pl IV30 159 A4
Maisondieu Rd IV30 159 A3
Malin Pl IV31 156 D4
Mamore Cres PH33 173 C3
Mamore Terr IV3 164 B8
Manar St AB56 157 F7
Manbeen Pl IV30 158 E2
Manitoba Ave IV30 159 C3
Manitoba Pl IV30 159 C2
Mannachie Ave IV36 155 B3
Mannachie Brae IV36 155 B3
Mannachie Gdns IV36 155 B4
Mannachie Gr IV36 155 B3
Mannachie Rd IV36 155 B3
Mannachie Rise IV36 155 C3
Mannachie Terr IV36 155 B3
Mannfield Pl 2 PH23 127 F5
Mannoch Ct IV30 158 E1
Mannoch Rd IV30 55 D1
Mannochmore IV30 55 D8
Manse Brae IV10 47 D8
Manse Cres IV19 148 C5
Manse Ct 1 IV30 158 E3
Manse Gdns
1 Conon Bridge IV7 44 C6
Tain IV19 148 B5
Manse La AB38 76 A8
Manse Rd Ardersier IV2 48 C5
Elgin IV30 17 F6
Kingussie PH21 170 E4
1 Kinloss IV36 34 A4
Nairn IV12 154 C6
Manse St IV19 148 C5
Manse Wynd IV36 155 C5
Manson Terr IV31 156 E5
Maple Dr IV3 162 C1
Maple Vale 3 IV4 63 D4
Mar Ct AB55 161 C4
Mar Pl AB55 161 B4
March La AB56 157 F6
March Rd AB56 157 F6
March Rd E AB56 157 F6
March Rd Ind Est AB56 157 F6
March Rd W AB56 157 F6
March St AB56 157 E7
Marchfield Pl IV30 158 E1
Marchmont Cres AB56 157 E6
Margaret St 5 Avoch IV9 47 A5
2 Inverness IV1 162 F2
Margarets Dr IV6 153 C5
Marine Ct IV31 156 E6
Marine Dr IV12 154 D6
Marine Pk IV1 162 B7
Marine Pl AB56 157 D6
Marine Rd IV12 154 C7
Marine Terr
Cromarty IV11 15 F2
Fortrose IV10 47 D8
Market Dr IV30 159 A2
Market La Keith AB55 161 F8
Kingussie PH21 170 D3
Market Rd PH26 168 C7
Market St Alness IV17 149 E4
Forres IV36 155 B4
Tain IV19 148 D5
Marks La AB55 161 E7
Marleon Field IV30 159 A6
Marne Rd IV2 165 B8
Mary Ann Ct IV3 164 F8
Mary Ave AB38 166 C3
Mary Croft IV36 53 A6
Mary St PH33 173 C4
Marybank Prim Sch IV6 43 B4
Maryburgh Prim Sch IV7 152 C1
Maryfield Gdns IV2 163 B1
Mason Rd IV2 165 C5
Matheson Rd IV23 23 F4
Maud View AB56 157 E4
Maxwell Dr IV3 164 D7
Maxwell St IV32 160 E4
Mayfield Rd IV2 164 F8
Mayfield Wynd IV19 148 C6
Mayne Rd IV30 158 D3
McAlpine Pl PH33 173 E7
McInnes Pl PH22 169 C8
McIntosh Dr IV30 158 B5
McKenzie Pl 11 IV30 17 C5
McKenzie Rd AB56 157 B5
McNaughton Ave AB56 157 D4
McWilliam Cres AB56 157 D5
Meadow Cres IV30 159 A1
Meadow Gdns IV30 18 A6
Meadow Rd IV2 67 A6
Meadow View IV30 18 A6
Meadowbank IV1 162 B8
Meadows The
Buckie AB56 157 C4
Dornoch IV25 4 A8
Muir of Ord IV6 153 B6
Meft Rd IV30 37 E5
Meikle Crook IV36 155 B5
Meiklefield Rd IV15 152 D6
Melantee PH33 173 E4
Merkinch Prim Sch IV3 162 D2
Merlewood Rd IV2 164 F6
Merlin Cres IV2 165 C6
Merryton Cres IV12 154 E5
Merryton Gdns 3 IV12 154 E6
Merson St AB56 157 A5
Mid St Beauly IV4 63 D5
Buckie AB56 157 C6
Burghead IV30 17 F6
Fochabers IV32 38 D8
Inverness IV3 162 B4
Keith AB55 161 E3
14 Portknockie AB56 22 A5
Middle St PH33 173 B3
Middle Terr PH21 170 C4
Midmar St AB56 157 D5
Midmills Rd IV2 163 A1
Miers Ave IV2 165 C7
Mile End Pl IV3 164 B7
Mill Brae AB55 161 F7
Mill Buie PH22 169 C7
Mill Cres Buckie AB56 157 D5
North Kessock IV1 162 A7
Mill Croft Rd IV12 50 D6
Mill La PH25 129 D3
Mill Pl IV32 160 B6
Mill Rd 1 Fortrose IV10 47 D8
Kingussie PH21 170 D4
Nairn IV12 154 D4
Mill St Dingwall IV15 152 C5
Invergordon IV18 151 B2
Millar St IV30 159 A1
Millbank IV1 162 B7
Millbank Cres IV12 154 D5
Millbank Prim Sch
Buckie AB56 157 E5
Nairn IV12 154 E5
Millbank Rd
Dingwall IV15 152 C7
Munlochy IV8 46 A4
Millbank St 1 IV12 154 D5
Millbank Terr AB56 157 D5
Millburn Acad IV2 163 B1
Millburn Ct IV2 163 B2
Millburn Rd IV2 163 A2
Millcraig Rd IV15 152 D6
Miller Gdns IV2 165 D5
Miller Rd Cromarty IV11 16 A2
Inverness IV2 165 C5
Miller St IV2 165 C5
Millerton Ave IV3 164 B7
Millerton View IV3 164 B7
Millfield Dr IV30 18 A6
Millview La AB55 161 F8
Milnafua IV17 150 A5
Milne La IV30 18 B5
Milne Rd IV32 160 E3
Milnefield Ave IV30 159 A2
Milne's High Sch IV32 160 D3
Milnes Prim Sch IV32 160 E3
Milnes Wynd IV36 155 C6
Milton Cres IV2 165 B6
Milton Dr AB56 157 E5
Milton Pk PH22 169 B7
Milton Prim Sch IV18 9 D1
Miltonduff Distillery★ IV30 36 A3
Mitchell Cres IV30 158 F6
Mitchell St 1 IV31 156 F7
Mitchell's La
Alness IV17 149 D4
1 Inverness IV2 164 F8
Moir St 1 IV30 35 B5
Montague Row IV3 162 E1
Montrose Ave PH33 173 D5
Monzie Sq PH33 173 B3
Moor Rd PH33 173 D8
Morangie Rd IV19 148 B6
Moray Ave 2 IV30 35 B5
Moray Coll IV30 158 F4
Moray Dr IV2 67 A5
Moray Firth Visitor Ctr★ IV1 162 D6
Moray Firth Wildlife Ctr★ IV32 38 F8
Moray Gdns IV36 155 E7
Moray La 5 Buckie AB56 157 C6
Lossiemouth IV31 156 E5
Moray Leisure Ctr IV30 158 E5
Moray Motor Mus★ IV30 158 F5
Moray Pk Ave IV2 66 F5
Moray Pk Cres 3 IV2 66 F5
Moray Pk Pl 2 IV2 66 F5
Moray Pk Terr IV2 66 F5
Moray Pk Wynd 4 IV2 66 F5
Moray Pl Elgin IV30 158 E3
Fort William PH33 173 A2
Moray St
1 Burghead IV30 17 F6
Elgin IV30 158 E3
Forres IV36 155 A4
Lossiemouth IV31 156 E5
Moray View Ct 3 AB56 21 C3
Moraypark Gdns IV2 66 F5
Moraypark La 1 IV2 66 F5
Morlich Cres IV12 154 B5
Morlich Ct PH22 169 A7
Morlich Pl PH22 169 A7
Morlich Sq 5 IV36 155 B4
Morriston Rd IV30 158 B5
Mortlach Prim Sch AB55 167 C3
Morven Cres 4 AB56 21 E4
Morven Pl PH33 173 C3
Morven Rd IV2 164 E4
Moss Rd
Fort William PH33 173 C4
Tain IV19 148 B5
Moss St Elgin IV30 158 F4
Keith AB55 161 E3
Mossend Pl IV30 158 E2
Mosset Gr IV36 155 B6
Mosset Pk Football Gd (Forres Mechanics FC) IV36 155 C6
Mosset Rd IV36 155 B6
Mossfield Dr PH33 173 D7
Mossie Rd PH26 168 C7
Mossmill Pk IV32 160 B7
Moss-side Brae IV12 154 A3
Moss-side Broadley Rd IV12 154 A3
Moss-side Dr IV12 49 E6
Moss-side Rd IV12 154 A3
Mosstodloch Prim Sch IV32 160 A7
Mosstowie Prim Sch IV30 35 F3
Mount Cres AB55 167 D2
Mount St AB55 167 D3
Mountrich Pl IV15 152 E8
Moy House Ct IV36 33 B3
Moy Terr IV2 164 F4
Moycroft Ind Est IV30 159 B5
Moycroft Rd IV30 159 B5
Muir of Ord Ind Est IV6 153 D2
Muir of Ord Sta IV6 153 C5
Muircote Rd IV12 154 A4
Muirden Rd 1 IV7 44 B6
Muirfield Cres 1 IV30 158 F1
Muirfield Gdns IV2 165 A7
Muirfield La IV2 165 A7
Muirfield Pk IV2 165 A7
Muirfield Rd Elgin IV30 158 F1
Inverness IV2 165 A7
Muirton PH22 169 B7
Muirton Cres IV31 156 C5
Muirton Ct IV31 156 D1
Muirton Pl IV36 34 B5
Muirtown Prim Sch IV3 162 B2
Muirtown St IV3 162 D2
Muirtown Terr IV3 162 C3
Mulbuie Prim Sch IV6 44 C3
Muldearg Rd IV20 10 E4
Muldearie View AB55 161 D3
Munlochy Prim Sch IV8 46 A4
Munro Cres IV18 9 D1
Munro Ct AB56 157 D4
Munro Pl
2 Conon Bridge IV7 44 C6
Dingwall IV15 152 C7
Elgin IV30 158 F6
Munro St IV18 151 C2
Munro Terr
Alness IV17 149 C4
Fortrose IV10 47 D8
Munro Way AB56 157 D4
Murdoch Wynd 1 IV30 158 E4
Murray Pl 3 Culloden IV2 66 E4
Tain IV19 148 C5
Murray Rd Culloden IV2 66 E4
8 Dornoch IV25 4 B8
Invergordon IV18 151 D3
Murray St Elgin IV30 159 A1
Tain IV19 148 C5
Murray Terr IV2 66 E4
Murrayfield IV32 160 E3
Museum of Childhood★ IV14 25 C1
Myreside Circ IV30 158 E8
Myrtlefield PH22 169 B6
Myrtlefield Ind Est PH22 169 B6
Myrtlefield La 10 IV2 66 E3

N

Nairn Acad IV12 154 B4
Nairn Cres PH33 173 B1
Nairn Fishertown Mus★ IV12 154 D6
Nairn Little Theatre★ IV12 154 D6
Nairn Mus★ IV12 154 D6
Nairn Rd Ardersier IV2 48 C5
Forres IV36 155 A5
Nairn Rd Ind Est IV2 48 C5
Nairn Sports Club IV12 154 D6
Nairn Sta IV12 154 D4
Nairn Swimming Pool IV12 154 C6
Nairn Town & Cty Hospl IV12 154 D4
Nairnside View IV2 66 F2
Natal Pl IV18 151 A2
Neil Gunn Cres IV2 165 C5
Neil Gunn Pl IV15 152 C8
Neil Gunn Rd IV15 152 C8
Neils View 3 IV30 37 E4
Nelson Rd IV36 155 C5
Nelson Sq 4 IV30 158 F7
Nelson St 6 IV3 162 E3
Nelson Terr AB55 161 C3
Ness Bank IV2 164 F8
Ness Gdns IV18 151 A3
Ness Rd IV10 47 D7
Ness Rd E IV10 47 D7
Ness Way IV10 47 D7
Ness Wlk IV3 162 E1
Netherha Rd AB56 157 B4
Netherton Terr AB56 21 D4
Nethybridge Pottery★ PH26 129 E6
Nevis Bank Ind Est PH33 173 D4
Nevis Bank La PH33 173 D4
Nevis Pk IV3 162 A1
Nevis Rd PH33 173 D5
Nevis Terr PH33 173 C4
New Elgin Prim Sch IV30 159 A2
New Elgin Rd IV30 159 A3
New St Balintore IV20 11 A1
Buckie AB56 157 C6
Burghead IV30 17 F6
22 Portknockie AB56 22 A5
Rothes AB38 76 A8
Tain IV20 5 B1
New View Ct 5 AB56 22 D4
Newfield Dr 1 IV30 159 A7
Newfield Pl 2 IV30 159 A7
Newfield Rd IV30 159 A8
Newfield Terr 5 IV30 158 F7
Newhall Prim Sch IV7 28 F8
Newlands IV2 67 D4
Newland's La AB56 157 D6
Newmill Ind Est AB55 161 D6
Newmill Prim Sch AB55 161 F7
Newmill Rd Elgin IV30 159 A5
Keith AB55 161 D5
Newmore Prim Sch IV18 150 F8
Newton Gate IV12 154 C5
Newton Pk IV5 64 A4
Newton Pl Elgin IV30 158 B5
Fochabers IV32 160 B6
Inverness IV5 64 A4
Newton Rd
Dingwall IV16 13 A2
Nairn IV12 49 C2
Newton Rd S IV16 13 B1
Newtonmore Ind Est PH20 171 D5
Newtonmore Prim Sch PH20 171 D6
Newtonmore Rd PH21 170 C3
Newtonmore Sta PH20 171 D4
Nicol St IV30 159 A2
Nicolson Pl 4 IV36 155 C6
Nigg Oil Terminal IV19 16 A4
Normans La IV18 151 B2
North Blantyre St 11 AB56 21 E5
North Castle St 9 AB56 22 D4
North Church Pl 7 IV1 162 E2
North Coll St 3 IV30 158 F4
North Covesea Terr IV31 156 D5
North Deskford St 10 AB56 22 D3
North Guildry St 10 IV30 158 F4
North High St AB56 157 C6
North Kessock Prim Sch IV1 162 B7
North La IV30 158 E4
North Port IV30 158 F4
North Pringle St 6 AB56 157 C6
North Rd Forres IV36 155 C6
Fort William PH33 173 E5
Kinloss IV36 34 B4
North St 10 Dornoch IV25 4 A8
Elgin IV30 158 E4
Forres IV36 155 C6
Rothes AB38 76 A8
Northfield IV30 18 B5
Northfield Pl
12 Elgin IV30 37 D4
1 Fochabers IV32 38 D7
Northfield Terr 8 IV30 158 E4
Novar Cres IV16 13 A1
Novar Rd IV17 149 C3

O

Oak Ave IV2 164 F5
Oak Gr IV36 52 B7
Oakbank Pl 1 IV30 158 E6
Oakdene Ct 5 IV2 66 F5
Oakdene Pl IV12 154 A5
Oakfield Rd IV30 159 B2
Oakleigh Rd IV1 162 C7
Oakwood Ave IV30 158 B5
Obsdale Gdns IV17 149 E4
Obsdale Pk IV17 149 F4
Obsdale Prim Sch IV17 149 F5
Obsdale Rd IV17 149 E4
Ogilvie St 9 AB56 21 C
Ogston La 3 IV31 156
Oich Rd PH32 172 D
Oich Terr IV2 164
Old Bridge Ct IV36 155
Old Church Rd AB56 22 C
Old Craigton Rd IV1 162
Old Distillery Rd PH21 170 C
Old Edinburgh Ct 2 IV2 165 A
Old Edinburgh Rd IV2 164
Old Edinburgh Rd S IV2 165 D
Old Evanton Rd IV15 152 D
Old Glen Rd PH20 171 C
Old Military Rd
Fochabers IV32 160
Grantown-on-Spey PH26 168 C
Old Mill IV1 162 A
Old Mill La IV2 165 E
Old Mill Rd
Invergordon IV18 9 D
Inverness IV13 109 E
Inverness IV2 165 A
Old Mills Rd IV30 158 D
Old Milnafua Rd IV17 149
Old Mint Rd 6 IV36 155 E
Old Perth Rd IV2 163 C
Old River Rd IV15 152 D
Old Sch Pl IV3 162 D
Old Sta The PH26 113 E
Old Steading Rd IV3 164 E
Oldtown Pl IV2 165 A
Oldtown Rd IV2 165 A
Ontario Ct IV30 159 E
Orchard Ct PH21 170 D
Orchard Pk Beauly IV4 63 D
6 Culloden IV2 66 D
Orchard Rd IV36 155 E
Orchard St 4 IV4 63 D
Orchard The
3 Fortrose IV10 47 D
4 Nairn IV12 154 E
Ord House Dr IV6 153 A
Ord Pl IV6 153 C
Ord Rd IV6 153 E
Ord Terr
Invergordon IV18 151 D
Inverness IV3 162 D
Strathpeffer IV14 43 E
Ordiquhill Prim Sch AB45 61 C
Ordiquish Rd IV32 160 D
Ordview Brae IV12 154 A
Ordview Gate IV12 154 A
Ordview La IV12 154 A
Ordview Rd IV12 154 A
Orkney Pl PH33 173 A
Ormond Castle★ IV9 46 F
Ormond Dr 6 IV2 67 A
Ormonde Terr IV9 46 F
Osprey Ctr★ PH25 129 A
Outram St IV18 151 B
Overton Ave IV3 162 A

P

Palace of Spynie★ IV30 19 C
Pansport Ct 7 IV30 159 A
Pansport Pl 3 IV30 159 A
Pansport Rd IV30 159 A
Parade Rd PH33 173 B
Parade Spur N IV30 159 C
Parade Spur S IV30 159 C
Paradise Row IV31 156 D
Park Ave IV14 43 C
Park Gr AB56 157 E
Park Pl IV31 156 F
Park Prim Sch IV18 151 B
Park Rd Inverness IV3 164 D
Lhanbryde IV30 37 D
Strathpeffer IV14 43 C
Park St 3 Avoch IV9 47 A
Balintore IV20 11 A
1 Burghead IV30 17 C
Dingwall IV15 152 E
Nairn IV12 154 E
17 Portknockie AB56 22 A
Park Terr IV14 43 C
Parkland Pl IV20 11 A
Parkland View AB56 157 E
Parkview 1 IV30 159 A
Paterson's La 4 AB56 157 C
Paton St 3 IV2 164 F
Patrol Pl 10 AB56 22 A
Patrol Rd AB56 22 A
Paye The IV11 15 F
Peebles Pl PH33 173 A
Peffery Rd IV15 152 C
Penny La IV12 154 A
Perceval Rd IV3 162 E
Perimeter Rd IV30 159 B
Perimeter Spur IV30 159 B
Perrins Rd IV17 149 D
Perth Pl PH33 173 A
Perth Rd PH20 171 C
Peter St IV12 154 D
Petley Pl 4 IV19 148 D
Petley St 3 IV19 148 D
Petrie Cres IV30 158 D
Pict Ave IV3 162 C
Pike Way IV36 34 A
Pilmuir Pl IV36 155 A
Pilmuir Prim Sch IV36 155 A
Pilmuir Rd IV36 155 A
Pilmuir Rd W IV36 155 A
Pine Dr IV2 164 F

ir IV30 159 C3
a IV32 39 A7
eld Bsns Ctr IV30 159 C3
eld Cres IV30 159 C3
eld Par IV30 159 B3
eld Rd IV30 159 B4
ood Ave IV12 154 B5
ood Rd
ead IV30 17 C5
bers IV32 160 A7
er Pl 3 Elgin IV30 158 F7
gin IV30 158 F7
s Field IV17 149 C4
eny Rd IV30 159 B6
eny Ct 4 IV30 159 B5
eny St 3 IV31 156 F7
field Rd IV3 162 E1
on La IV36 155 C4
ck Wynd IV10 47 C7
arden Pl IV30 158 D4
arden Rd IV30 158 C3
Rd IV1 162 D6
Rd 20 IV25 4 A8
La AB55 161 E4
na PH33 173 E4
Pk Pl IV30 159 A2
t 5 IV20 11 B2
Rd IV36 34 A4
field Bank IV2 164 F8
field Rd 2 IV2 164 F8
ssie Prim Sch AB56 21 C3
ordon Prim Sch
39 E6
nockie Prim Sch
22 A5
nd Pl 3 IV1 162 E2
Office Ave 1 IV1 162 F1
Office La AB55 161 E7
ncts Rd IV10 47 C7
ry Sch IV17 150 A5
e Rd IV30 158 F7
Pl IV30 159 A4
ard Cres 2 IV4 63 D4
St
Bridge IV7 152 C1
all IV7 44 C6
ect Ct 1 IV31 156 F6
ect Terr IV31 156 E6
ect View 1 IV31 156 E6
st Christie Dr 1
76 B8
st Ferguson Rd
148 B5
st Reid Cres AB56 157 D5
st Smith Cres IV2 165 C5
st Smith Way IV2 165 C5
ney St 7 AB56 22 A5
gate Ct IV3 162 D3
gate St 3 IV3 162 E3

y La IV19 148 C5
y Rd Balintore IV20 11 B2
IV30 158 D6
emouth IV31 156 F6
V19 148 A4
yhill AB55 161 D3
ec Ave IV19 148 C4
ec Pl IV30 159 C2
n St Buckie AB56 157 C5
own AB55 167 C3
IV30 159 A4
ness IV3 162 E1
emouth IV31 156 E7
IV12 154 D5
V19 148 C5
n's Dr AB56 22 D3
n's La IV31 156 E5
n's Own Pl 4 IV36 155 B5
n's Rd AB38 166 C3
ns St IV18 150 F2
nsgate 2 IV1 162 F1

ay Rd IV2 165 A7
n Rd AB56 157 E5
eg Prim Sch IV13 109 C4
more Ave IV2 165 C8
more Hospl IV2 165 D8
more Prim Sch IV2 163 C1
ay Terr
more PH22 169 B7
e AB56 157 C5
ness IV1 162 F2
Castle IV12 50 B3
Gdns IV12 154 F5
at Rd IV36 155 A5
ay La IV31 156 E5
emore Rd IV3 162 D1
och Pl 1 IV20 11 B2
burn St AB56 157 E7
St IV2 162 F1
bank Rd 5 IV2 48 C5
ation Pk IV3 164 D5
urn Ave IV2 66 F4
urn Dr AB56 157 B4
raigs Pl IV36 52 B8
ood Ave IV2 165 E2
ood Cres IV2 165 E2
ood Ct IV2 165 E2
Ct 1 PH23 127 F5
ncy Rd AB56 157 E4
nt Ct AB55 161 C5
nt St AB55 161 C4

Reid Rd IV18 151 A3
Reid St IV30 159 A6
Reid Terr 1 AB56 39 D6
Reidhaven Cres 5 AB56 21 E4
Reidhaven Sq AB55 161 E3
Reidhaven St
Buckie AB56 157 F7
Cullen AB56 22 D3
Elgin IV30 158 F4
16 Portknockie AB56 22 A5
Reiket La IV30 159 C2
Renfrew Pl PH33 173 A1
Revack Lodge Gdns
PH26 168 C1
Revoen Dr PH26 168 B6
Reynolds Cres IV30 159 C3
Rhine Dr IV2 163 C1
Rhuarden Ct PH26 168 B6
Rhynie Rd IV20 10 E5
Richmond Pl
Buckie AB56 39 D7
Fochabers IV32 160 D4
Richmond St AB56 157 F7
Richmond Terr AB56 39 D6
Riggs The PH32 172 D5
Rinnes Dr IV31 156 D5
Rinnes Pl AB55 167 C3
River Cl N IV17 149 C3
River Cl S IV17 149 C3
River Dr IV17 149 C3
River La IV17 149 C3
River Pk IV12 154 F5
River St IV25 4 A8
River Wynd IV17 149 A4
Riverbank Rd 4 IV7 44 C6
Riverbank Terr IV12 154 E5
Riverford Cres 11 IV7 44 C6
Riverford Dr 12 IV7 44 C6
Riverside Ct IV2 164 E5
Riverside Dr
Alness IV17 149 C3
Elgin IV30 159 B5
Riverside Field Ind Est
IV15 152 D6
Riverside Medical Ctr
IV3 164 E7
Riverside Pk PH33 173 D7
Riverside Rd IV4 63 D5
Riverside St IV1 162 E2
Robert Ct 3 AB56 157 B5
Robert St AB56 157 B5
Robertson Dr
Alness IV17 149 E3
Elgin IV30 159 B1
Robertson Pl
9 Forres IV36 155 B5
4 Lhanbryde IV30 37 D4
Robertson Rd IV30 37 D4
Rockall Pl IV31 156 D4
Roderick Ct IV25 4 A8
Rodger Cl IV10 47 C8
Rodger Ct IV10 47 C8
Rogie Falls IV14 24 E1
Romach Rd IV36 155 A5
Rose Ave IV30 158 E3
Rose Croft IV6 153 D6
Rose La 2 IV31 156 E5
Rose Pl 2 IV30 158 E3
Rose St 3 Avoch IV9 47 A5
Beauly IV4 63 D5
Fortrose IV10 47 C7
Inverness IV1 162 F2
Nairn IV12 154 D5
Tain IV19 148 C5
Rosebank Prim Sch
IV12 154 D5
Roseberry Ave 7 IV25 4 A8
Rosebery Pl 6 IV2 164 F8
Rosebrae Cres IV30 158 C5
Rosebrae Sch IV30 18 C1
Rosehaugh Cres 3 IV9 46 F6
Rosehaugh Rd IV3 162 D4
Roseisle Dr IV30 158 D7
Rosemarkie Rd IV10 47 C7
Ross Ave IV3 162 D1
Ross Cres Balintore IV20 11 A2
Invergordon IV18 9 D1
Ross Ct IV2 165 A7
Ross House Day Hospl
IV3 164 E8
Ross Meml Hospl IV15 152 F5
Ross Pl Dingwall IV15 152 D7
Fort William PH33 173 A2
Tain IV20 5 B1
Ross St 3 Balintore IV20 11 B2
Tain IV19 148 D4
Ross Wynd IV15 152 B8
Rosshill Dr 2 IV7 44 B6
Rosskeen Dr IV18 151 A3
Rothes Castle AB38 76 A7
Rothes Prim Sch AB38 76 A8
Rothes Visitor Ctr
AB38 76 B7
Rothiemay Prim Sch
AB54 80 E7
Rothiemurchus Visitor Ctr
PH22 169 C2
Rovers Cres 4 IV20 11 B2
Rowan Ave IV25 4 A8
Rowan Cl IV32 38 F6
Rowan Cres
1 Dornoch IV25 4 A8
Forres IV36 52 B7
Rowan Ct 5 IV30 159 B5
Rowan Dr PH33 173 D8
Rowan Lea IV30 159 B2
Rowan Pk PH23 128 A5
Rowan Pl IV12 154 B5

Rowan Rd Forres IV36 52 B7
Inverness IV3 162 C1
Roxburgh Pl PH33 173 A1
Royal Northern Infmy
IV3 164 E7
Royal Oak Dr IV18 151 A2
Royal Wlk 2 IV12 154 D6
Roysvale Pl IV36 155 C4
Russel Pl 2 IV30 158 F7
Russell Pl IV36 155 D6
Ruthven Ct 4 PH21 170 E4
Ruthven Rd
Inverness IV2 164 F4
Kingussie PH21 170 D3
Ryebank IV10 47 D7
Ryvoan Pl IV36 155 A4

S

St Aethans Ave 12 IV30 17 C5
St Aethans Cl 13 IV30 17 C5
St Aethans Rd IV30 17 C5
St Andrew Dr IV3 164 C8
St Andrew's Rd
Lhanbryde IV30 37 D4
Tain IV19 148 C4
St Andrew's Sq 8 AB56 157 B5
St Andrew's Wlk IV10 47 C7
St Andrew's Cath IV3 164 E8
St Andrews Rd
Dingwall IV15 152 E8
Elgin IV30 159 C3
St Brides Ave PH20 171 C6
St Catherines Ct 8
IV36 155 B4
St Catherine's Pl IV30 158 E3
St Catherine's Rd IV36 155 B5
St Clements Sch IV15 152 E5
St Columba Rd PH20 171 C5
St Drostansa IV63 104 B4
St Duthus Pl IV19 148 D5
St Duthus Specl Sch
IV19 148 C5
St Fergus Dr IV3 164 C8
St Gerardine's Prim Sch
IV31 156 E6
St Gerardine's Rd IV31 156 D6
St Gilbert St 18 IV25 4 A8
St Giles Rd 1 IV30 158 F4
St Helena Brae AB56 157 B6
St James' St IV15 152 E5
St John's Ave IV3 164 C8
St Johns Rd PH33 173 D7
St Josephs Cath Prim Sch
IV1 162 E1
St Laurence Ct 10 IV36 155 B5
St Leonard's Ct IV36 155 D4
St Leonard's Dr IV36 155 D4
St Leonard's Rd IV36 155 C5
St Margaret's Rd IV3 164 C8
St Margarets Cres IV31 156 D5
St Margarets Ct 5
IV36 155 C6
St Mary's Ave IV3 164 D8
St Mary's Rd IV5 64 A4
St Mary's Well IV19 148 B6
St Marys RC Sch PH33 173 C3
St Michael's La AB55 167 C2
St Moluag Pl 9 IV30 37 D4
St Mungo Rd IV3 164 C8
St Ninian Dr IV3 164 C8
St Ninian Rd IV12 154 D6
St Paul St AB56 157 B5
St Peter's La IV30 18 B5
St Peter's Rd
Buckie AB56 157 B4
Elgin IV30 18 B5
St Peter's Terr AB56 157 B5
St Peters RC Prim Sch
AB56 157 B5
St Ronan's Rd IV36 155 C6
St Thomas RC Prim Sch
AB55 161 E3
St Valery Ave IV3 164 C8
St Vincent PH21 170 C5
St Vincent Rd IV19 148 B4
Saltburn Rd IV18 151 C2
Salvesen Cres IV17 149 C3
Sampson Pl 6 AB56 22 B5
Samson Ave AB56 157 F7
Samson St AB56 22 B5
Sand Dune Wlk 8 IV20 11 B2
Sand La AB55 161 E7
Sandown Farm La IV12 49 E7
Sandown Rd IV12 154 A4
Sandwood Dr IV12 154 A4
Sandy Rd IV30 158 F1
Sandys Way PH26 113 D3
Sanquahar Rd IV36 155 C4
Sanquhar Dr IV36 155 C4
Sanquhar Terr IV36 155 C4
School Brae 2 Avoch IV9 47 A6
Elgin IV30 159 A2
8 Lhanbryde IV30 37 D4
Lossiemouth IV31 156 E5
School Hill
16 Dornoch IV25 4 A8
10 Findochty AB56 21 E4
School La
2 Buckie AB56 157 D5
1 Inverness IV1 162 F2
Keith AB55 161 E7
School Leisure Ctr
PH23 127 F5
School Pl 1 Ardersier IV2 48 C5
Grantown-on-Spey PH26 129 C7
School Rd 4 Buckie AB56 21 C3

School Rd *continued*
8 Burghead IV30 17 F6
Conon Bridge IV7 44 C5
Grantown-on-Spey PH26 129 C7
Huntly AB54 79 F5
Keith AB55 161 E4
School St IV20 10 E4
School Terr 1 AB38 76 A8
Schoolcroft 1 IV7 27 C2
Schoolhill Terr IV31 156 E6
Scorguie Ave IV3 162 B2
Scorguie Ct IV3 162 B2
Scorguie Dr IV3 162 B2
Scorguie Gdns IV3 162 B2
Scorguie Pl IV3 162 B2
Scorguie Rd IV3 162 B3
Scorguie Terr IV3 162 B2
Scotsburn Ct IV19 148 C4
Scotsburn Rd IV19 148 B2
Scott Terr AB56 157 E5
Scottish Tartans Mus
AB55 161 E3
Sea Pk IV30 17 F6
Sea St 6 AB56 22 D4
Seabank Gdns IV12 154 C5
Seabank Rd
Invergordon IV18 151 C2
Nairn IV12 154 B6
Seafield Ave
Grantown-on-Spey PH26 168 B7
Keith AB55 161 D5
Seafield Cres IV30 159 A4
Seafield Gdns IV12 154 C6
Seafield Hospl AB56 157 A4
Seafield Pl
Aviemore PH22 169 B6
11 Cullen AB56 22 D4
Seafield Prim Sch IV30 158 F6
Seafield Rd Buckie AB56 22 D2
Inverness IV1 163 A3
Seafield Sq 2 AB38 76 A8
Seafield St Elgin IV30 159 A4
Nairn IV12 154 C6
Seafield Terr
Keith AB55 161 E5
Portknockie AB56 22 B5
Seafield Wlk AB55 161 D3
Seaforth Cameron Mus
IV2 48 A7
Seaforth Cres IV18 150 F2
Seaforth Ct IV19 148 D3
Seaforth La IV36 33 E7
Seaforth Pl
2 Conon Bridge IV7 44 C6
Findhorn IV36 33 E7
Forres IV36 155 C6
Seaforth Rd
Muir of Ord IV6 153 C5
Nairn IV12 154 A4
Tain IV19 148 C3
Seaforth St 5 AB56 22 B5
Seanlois IV63 104 A5
Seatown Rd IV31 156 F5
Seaview Pl 9 AB56 157 C6
Seaview Rd
Buckie AB56 157 B5
Burghead IV30 17 E6
3 Findochty AB56 21 E4
Seaview Terr AB56 157 B5
Seld St AB56 157 B5
Selkirk Pl 2 PH33 173 A1
Sellar Ct AB38 166 B2
Sellar Pl Aberlour AB38 166 B2
Conon Bridge IV7 44 C6
Sellar St 1 IV30 17 C5
Seventy Five Straight
IV2 48 C7
Sey Burn Wynd IV30 158 E7
Shackleton Pl IV31 156 D4
Shackleton Way 1 IV36 34 A5
Shandwick St 1 IV19 148 D4
Shankland Ct PH26 168 B6
Shanks La 1 AB56 157 D6
Shaw Pl PH33 173 C3
Shearer Ave AB56 157 E5
Sheriffbrae IV36 155 D5
Sheriffmill Rd IV30 158 B4
Shieldaig Rd IV36 155 A4
Shieling Sta PH22 145 F4
Shop St IV20 5 B1
Shore Rd Dornoch IV25 4 A8
Invergordon IV18 151 B1
Tain IV19 148 C5
Shore St 2 Avoch IV9 47 A5
7 Balintore IV20 11 B2
1 Beauly IV4 63 D5
5 Buckie AB56 39 D7
7 Cromarty IV11 15 F2
Inverness IV1 162 E2
Lossiemouth IV31 156 E7
Nairn IV12 154 F7
Tain IV20 5 B1
Sicily Rd IV2 163 B1
Sidings The IV32 38 D6
Sigurd St 1 IV30 17 D5
Siller St 4 AB56 21 E5
Simpson Pl IV15 152 C6
Simpson St IV12 154 D6
Simpson's La 1 IV3 162 E2
Sinclair Pk 1 IV2 66 E4
Sir Walter Scott Dr IV2 165 C5
Skinner Ct IV3 162 D2
Skinner Pl 5 IV25 4 B8
Skinner Rd IV2 48 A7
Slackbuie Ave IV2 165 A4
Slackbuie Cres IV2 164 F3
Slessor Terr 4 IV36 34 A4
Smiddy Pl 3 IV30 35 B5

Smith Ave IV3 164 D8
Smith Dr IV30 158 D5
Smith St IV30 159 A2
Smithfield Pl 1 IV31 156 C5
Smithton Ind Est IV2 66 E4
Smithton Pk IV2 66 E4
Smithton Prim Sch IV2 66 E4
Smithton Rd IV2 66 E4
Smithton Villas 2 IV2 66 E4
Society St IV12 154 E6
Somme Cres IV2 163 C1
Souter Dr IV2 164 C3
Souters La AB55 161 E8
South Blantyre St 9
AB56 21 E4
South Castle St 1 AB56 22 D3
South Coll St 4 IV30 158 F4
South Covesea Terr
IV31 156 D5
South Ct IV30 158 E3
South Deskford St 2
AB56 22 D3
South Guildry St IV30 158 F3
South La AB38 75 C3
South Land St 7 AB56 157 B5
South Lodge Prim Sch
IV18 151 B3
South March IV32 38 F5
South Pringle St AB56 157 C5
South Rd IV32 38 D7
South St Elgin IV30 158 E4
Fochabers IV32 160 E4
Forres IV36 155 C5
Grantown-on-Spey PH26 168 C6
Keith AB55 161 F7
South View Rd IV30 158 F3
South W St AB56 157 C5
Southpark Ct IV30 158 F3
Southside Pl IV2 165 A8
Southside Rd IV2 163 A1
South-west High St
PH26 168 C6
Spey Ave
Aviemore PH22 169 C8
Boat of Garten PH24 128 D1
Fochabers IV32 160 D3
Grantown-on-Spey PH26 168 C6
Spey Bay Nature Reserve
IV32 38 E8
Spey Cres IV32 160 D3
Spey Ct Elgin IV30 159 B5
Fochabers IV32 160 D3
Spey Dr Aberlour AB38 76 A8
Buckie AB56 157 D4
Fochabers IV32 160 D3
Spey Rd Aberlour AB38 76 C4
Fochabers IV32 160 D3
Spey St Fochabers IV32 160 D4
Kingussie PH21 170 D4
Rothes AB38 76 A8
Spey Valley Smokehouse
PH26 168 C3
Speybank Wlk PH21 143 B4
Speyside Cooperage Visitor
Ctr AB38 76 C4
Speyside Heather Ctr
PH26 129 B5
Speyside High Sch
AB38 166 D3
Spring Bank IV36 52 B7
Springburn Pl IV30 159 B2
Springfield Ct
1 Forres IV36 155 E7
Inverness IV3 164 E7
Springfield Dr IV30 158 F2
Springfield Gdns
Elgin IV30 158 F2
Inverness IV3 164 E7
Tain IV19 148 B5
Springfield Rd IV30 158 E1
Springfield Ret Pk IV30 158 F3
Springfield Terr IV17 149 E4
Spynie Brae IV30 158 E7
Spynie Hospl IV30 158 D6
Spynie Hts IV30 158 E7
Spynie Pl Elgin IV30 158 E7
Lossiemouth IV31 156 E6
Spynie St IV30 158 E6
Square The
Aberlour AB38 75 B3
Ballindalloch AB37 132 C1
Beauly IV4 63 D5
7 Cullen AB56 22 D4
Dufftown AB55 167 C2
Grantown-on-Spey PH26 168 C6
Sraid-na-firrin IV63 103 B5
Stafford Rd IV25 4 B8
Stafford St IV19 148 D4
Stagcroft Pk IV19 148 B5
Station Cres IV10 47 C7
Station Ct
9 Burghead IV30 17 C5
3 Munlochy IV8 46 A4
4 Portknockie AB56 22 A5
Station Dr 8 IV2 48 C5
Station La 5 IV36 155 B5
Station Rd Alness IV17 149 D3
Ardersier IV2 48 C5
Avoch IV9 46 F6
1 Beauly IV4 63 D4
Buckie AB56 39 D7
4 Burghead IV30 17 C5
Carrbridge PH23 127 E5
4 Cullen AB56 22 D4
Dingwall IV15 152 D3